HIPAA

SECOND EDITION

A Practical Guide to the Privacy and Security of Health Data

JUNE M. SULLIVAN
SHANNON B. HARTSFIELD

AMERICAN**BAR**ASSOCIATION

Health Law Section

Cover design by Mary Anne Kulchawik/ABA Design

The materials contained herein represent the opinions of the authors and/or the editors, and should not be construed to be the views or opinions of the law firms or companies with whom such persons are in partnership with, associated with, or employed by, nor of the American Bar Association or the Section of Health Law unless adopted pursuant to the bylaws of the Association.

Nothing contained in this book is to be considered as the rendering of legal advice for specific cases, and readers are responsible for obtaining such advice from their own legal counsel. This book is intended for educational and informational purposes only.

© 2020 American Bar Association. All rights reserved.

No part of this publication may be reproduced, stored in a retrieval system, or transmitted in any form or by any means, electronic, mechanical, photocopying, recording, or otherwise, without the prior written permission of the publisher. For permission contact the ABA Copyrights & Contracts Department, copyright@americanbar.org, or complete the online form at http://www.americanbar.org/utility/reprint.html.

Printed in the United States of America.

24 23 22   5 4 3 2

Library of Congress Cataloging-in-Publication Data
Names: Sullivan, June M., author. | Hartsfield, Shannon B., author. |
 American Bar Association. Health Law Section, sponsoring body.
Title: HIPAA : a practical guide to the privacy and security of health data
 / June M. Sullivan, Shannon B. Hartsfield.
Other titles: Health Insurance Portability and Accountability Act
Description: Second edition. | Chicago, Illinois : American Bar
 Association, [2020] | Includes bibliographical references and index. |
 Summary: "Practical guide to the privacy and security of health data"—
 Provided by publisher.
Identifiers: LCCN 2020000149 (print) | LCCN 2020000150 (ebook) | ISBN
 9781641055727 (paperback) | ISBN 9781641055734 (ebook)
Subjects: LCSH: Medical records—Law and legislation—United States. |
 Medical records—Access control—United States. | Privacy, Right
 of—United States. | United States. Health Insurance Portability and
 Accountability Act of 1996.
Classification: LCC KF3827.R4 S85 2020 (print) | LCC KF3827.R4 (ebook) |
 DDC 344.7304/1—dc23
LC record available at https://lccn.loc.gov/2020000149
LC ebook record available at https://lccn.loc.gov/2020000150

Discounts are available for books ordered in bulk. Special consideration is given to state bars, CLE programs, and other bar-related organizations. Inquire at Book Publishing, ABA Publishing, American Bar Association, 321 N. Clark Street, Chicago, Illinois 60654-7598.

www.ShopABA.org

Contents

Acknowledgments xi
Foreword xiii
Introduction xv

CHAPTER 1
Welcome to HIPAA 1

    I. Title I 2
   II. Title II 3
  III. Title III 6
  IV. Title IV 9
    V. Title V 9
  VI. Overview of Title II 10
        A. Privacy Rule 10
        B. Security Rule 11
        C. Enforcement Rule 13
 VII. Conclusion 14

CHAPTER 2
The Basics 15

   I. Fundamentals 15
       A. Who Needs to Comply? 15
       B. What Information Is Subject to HIPAA? 23
       C. General Rules for Disclosure 27
       D. What If Other Laws Conflict with HIPAA? 29
  II. Conclusion 30

CHAPTER 3
Authorizations for Release of Protected Health Information 33

- I. Consent versus Authorization: What's the Difference? 33
  - A. Consent 34
  - B. Authorization 34
- II. Authorizations 35
  - A. Core Elements 35
  - B. Required Statements in Authorizations 44
  - C. Other Requirements for Authorizations 45
  - D. Other Considerations for Authorizations 46
- III. Federal Trade Commission Act 48
- IV. State Law Requirements 50
  - A. HIPAA Preempts State Laws 50
  - B. Elements of Authorizations under State Law 52
  - C. Psychiatric Records under State Law 52
- V. Conclusion 53

CHAPTER 4
Disclosures without Authorizations 55

- I. Treatment, Payment, or Health Care Operations 56
  - A. Treatment 56
  - B. Payment 57
  - C. Health Care Operations 59
- II. Averting a Serious Threat to Health or Safety 68
- III. Providing Access to Individuals via a Third Party 69
- IV. Law Enforcement 69
- V. Public Health Activities 71
- VI. Victims of Abuse, Neglect, or Domestic Violence 72
- VII. Lawful Oversight Activities 74
- VIII. Judicial and Administrative Proceedings 75
- IX. Informational and Promotional Disclosures 78
  - A. Facility Directories 78
  - B. Friends and Relatives 79

        C. Marketing   80
        D. Fundraising   82
  X. Research   82
  XI. Workers' Compensation   83
  XII. Conclusion   85

CHAPTER 5
Administrative Requirements for Covered Entities and Business Associates   87

  I. Administrative Requirements   88
        A. Notice of Privacy Practices   89
        B. Accounting for Disclosures   95
        C. Disclosures to Public Health Officials   98
  II. Administrative Safeguards   100
        A. Covered Entity Obligations   101
        B. Business Associates   103
  III. Conclusion   104

CHAPTER 6
Summary of the HIPAA Security Rule   107

  I. Purpose and Scope of the Security Rule   107
  II. Who Needs to Comply?   110
  III. Administrative, Physical, and Technical Safeguards   110
        A. Administrative Safeguards   111
        B. Physical Safeguards   119
        C. Technical Safeguards   119
  IV. Organizational Requirements   121
        A. Business Associate Agreements   121
        B. Policies and Procedures   122
  V. Conclusion   122

CHAPTER 7
The HITECH Act 123

    I. Requirements for Business Associates 124
        A. Compliance Requirements for Business Associates 124
        B. Special Business Associate Considerations 128
        C. Business Associate Agreements 131
    II. HIPAA Breaches 133
        A. Risk Assessments 134
        B. Breach Response 135
    III. Other HITECH Act Provisions 135
    IV. Conclusion 136

    Chapter 7 Appendix:
    Sample HIPAA Business Associate Agreement Favorable to Business Associate 137

CHAPTER 8
Responding to a Security Incident or Breach: Mechanics of Incident Response and Breach Notification 151

    I. Definition of a Security Incident under HIPAA 151
    II. Response and Notification Requirements for a Security Incident under HIPAA 152
    III. Definition of a Breach under HIPAA 153
    IV. Analysis of the HIPAA Breach Notification Rule 154
        A. Has a Breach Occurred? 155
        B. Who to Notify? 157
    V. Steps to Take after the Breach 162
    VI. Conclusion 162

APPENDIX A
HIPAA Administrative Requirements and Policies and Procedures for Health Care Providers 163

Table of Contents 166

    I. General Information Applicable to All Privacy and Security Policies 172
       Policy Statement 172
       Scope of These Privacy and Security Policies 172
       Applicability of These Policies 172
       Defined Terms 173
       Definitions 173
    II. When the Provider May Make Disclosures of PHI without Authorization 179
       Purpose of Policy 179
       Policy Detail 179
    III. Notification of Privacy or Security Breaches 188
       Purpose of Policy 188
       Policy Detail 188
    IV. Notice of Privacy Practices Procedures 193
       Purpose of Policy 193
       Policy Detail 193
       Who Is Affected 195
    V. Minimum Necessary Standard 195
       Purpose of Policy 195
       Policy Detail 196
    VI. Individual's Request to Restrict Uses and Disclosures of PHI 201
       Purpose of Policy 201
       Policy Detail 201

- **VII.** Individual's Request for Confidential Communications   203
  Purpose of Policy   203
  Policy Detail   203
- **VIII.** Individual's Right of Access to PHI   204
  Purpose of Policy   204
  Policy Detail   204
- **IX.** Individual's Request to Amend PHI   212
  Purpose of Policy   212
  Policy Detail   212
- **X.** Individual's Request for an Accounting of Disclosures   217
  Purpose of Policy   217
  Policy Detail   217
- **XI.** Refraining from Intimidating or Retaliatory Acts   222
  Purpose of Policy   222
  Policy Detail   222
- **XII.** Waiver of Rights   222
  Purpose of Policy   222
  Policy Detail   222
- **XIII.** Documentation Requirements and Retention of Records   223
  Purpose of Policy   223
  Policy Detail   223
- **XIV.** Training on HIPAA Privacy and Security Policies   225
  Policy Statement   225
  Scope of This Policy   226
  Purpose of Policy   226
  Policy Detail   226
- **XV.** Disciplinary Sanctions for Noncompliance with Provider's Privacy and Security Policies   227
  Purpose of Policy   227
  Policy Detail   227

XVI. Reporting and Mitigating Inadvertent or Improper Disclosures of PHI or Security Incidents 228
  Purpose of Policy 228
  Policy Detail 228
XVII. Administrative, Technical, and Physical Privacy and Security Safeguards 230
  Purpose of Policy 230
  Policy Detail 231
XVIII. Verification of Persons Requesting PHI 241
  Purpose of Policy 241
  Policy Details 241
XIX. Authorizations 244
  Purpose of Policy 244
  Policy Details 244
XX. Requests for Disclosures of an Individual's PHI from Spouses, Other Family Members, and Friends/Facility Directories 246
  Purpose of Policy 246
  Policy Details 246
XXI. Disclosures to Business Associates 248
  Purpose of Policy 248
  Policy Details 248
XXII. De-identified Information, Summary Health Information, and Limited Data Sets 249
  Purpose of Policy 249
  Policy Details 249
XXIII. Complaints 251
  Purpose of Policy 251
  Policy Details 251
XXIV. Designated Record Sets 252
  Purpose of Policy 252
  Policy Details 253

XXV.	Designated Personnel/Access Profiles 254	
	Purpose of Policy 254	
	Policy Detail 254	
XXVI.	State Law Compliance 255	
	Purpose of Policy 255	
	Policy Detail 255	
	Procedural Guidance 256	
XXVII.	Using and Disclosing Psychotherapy Notes 256	
	Background 256	
	Policy 257	
XXVIII.	Workforce Employee Screening 257	
XXIX.	Fundraising 257	
	Purpose of Policy 257	
	Policy Detail 257	
XXX.	Sale of Protected Health Information 259	
	Purpose of Policy 259	
	Policy Detail 259	

APPENDIX B
HIPAA Business Associate Agreement (Favorable to Data Source) 261

Index 281
About the Authors 287

Acknowledgments

The authors wish to express their appreciation to Jeff Salyards, Executive Editor of Book Publishing for the ABA, for his assistance and support throughout this process. They also wish to thank Juliet M. McBride of King & Spalding, Calvin Marshall of Chambliss, Bahner & Stophel, P.C., and Jacklyn DeMar of Taxpayers against Fraud Education Fund for their diligence and insight in editing the manuscript.

From June M. Sullivan:
Ms. Sullivan is grateful for the patience, diligence, and persistence of her coauthor, Shannon Hartsfield, in bringing this manuscript to fruition. Through her contributions, this book has become a reality. It has been a pleasure and honor to work alongside this brilliant health lawyer and experience this wonderful team effort. Ms. Sullivan is also grateful to the leadership, staff, and members of the American Bar Association's Health Law Section for their insight and guidance in shepherding this project to its final days and for recognizing the important contribution this book is for budding HIPAA novices as well as seasoned HIPAA compliance professionals and attorneys.

This author also acknowledges the support and encouragement of her growing family, Cory, Evan, Lauren, Ivy, and Archer Sullivan, without whose understanding and love this book would not have been possible. She is also thankful for the patience and advice of Christopher Brooks, who helped to propel this project forward.

From Shannon Britton Hartsfield:

Ms. Hartsfield expresses her deep appreciation to her coauthor, June Sullivan, for writing such a wonderful first edition and giving her the opportunity to work on this publication. It has been a very rewarding and worthwhile collaboration. She is also thankful for the leaders, staff, and volunteers of the American Bar Association's Health Law Section for providing so many amazing opportunities for attorneys to write and speak about HIPAA and discuss its nuances. Many members of the Section have freely shared their insight and wisdom to contribute to the collective knowledge of health lawyers regarding this important topic.

She is eternally grateful to her daughters, Sabrina and Arienne Hartsfield, whose love and support have enabled her to contribute to this book. God has blessed her immensely through these young women.

Foreword

The American Bar Association Health Law Section is pleased to publish *HIPAA: A Practical Guide to the Privacy and Security of Health Data*, Second Edition, an update to the original practical guide aimed at providing focused, economical resources for the health lawyer.

As noted in the preceding Acknowledgments, many people volunteered their time and talents to provide support for this ambitious book. In particular, the Section expresses special thanks to its Publications Committee and eHealth Privacy & Security Interest Group. Volunteer leaders from each group provided significant editorial assistance for the original publication and this timely update.

Finally, the Section sincerely thanks authors June Sullivan and Shannon Hartsfield, whose dedicated work on this update will undoubtedly benefit healthcare lawyers and their clients. The laws and regulations that set forth a framework to safeguard health information have changed markedly since the original publication of this book in 2005. The willingness of June and Shannon to again share their expertise and insights with their colleagues exemplifies the best of the Section.

The Section is proud to offer this work, which it knows will contribute to the continued advancement of lawyers practicing in this evolving area of healthcare law.

John H. McEniry, IV
Chair (2019–2020)

Introduction

Even before the HIPAA privacy regulations were finalized on December 28, 2000, HIPAA has been the subject of countless hours of study, analysis, and compliance efforts within the health care industry and beyond. Almost two decades later, and more than 15 years after the first edition of this book, the privacy and security requirements of HIPAA are the subject of significant confusion and uncertainty. Some companies have argued that they are not subject to HIPAA's requirements, only to find out that they are now subject to state privacy laws that carve out HIPAA, such as the California Consumer Privacy Act and the Florida Information Protection Act, and those who have complied with HIPAA's requirements have life a bit easier because they are under HIPAA's protective umbrella.

In the coming years, we expect to see the health care industry and Congress focus even more on data privacy and security. Currently, there is discussion at the federal level to strengthen the privacy rules and create a national privacy law similar to the European Union's General Data Protection Rule. As the laws and social pressure evolve and tighten the reigns on health care privacy, patients and providers will continue to become more concerned about maintaining the security and privacy of data while rising to the challenge of balancing privacy while promoting patient access and quality care.

In this book, we have attempted to create a useful guide for those who are new to HIPAA as well as provide updates for seasoned veterans of HIPAA. This book expands on the first edition and includes the Security Rule, the HITECH Act, and the Breach Notification Rule along with extensive discussion about HIPAA's parameters, practical applications, and lessons learned over the past 15 years. To assist you in complying with HIPAA's complex requirements, we have included forms and experiential anecdotes that we hope you will find helpful in your ongoing HIPAA compliance efforts.

Chapter 1

Welcome to HIPAA

If this is your first time exploring health care privacy and security, welcome to this important area of health law. Just about every aspect of health care has been affected by the Privacy and Security Rules of the Health Insurance Portability and Accountability Act of 1996 (HIPAA). In fact, members of the public seem to use the term "HIPAA" as a kind of shorthand for all types of health privacy. HIPAA is intended to make it easier for individuals to obtain copies of their own health records and much more difficult for others to disclose this information. HIPAA imposes many responsibilities on health care providers and their business associates and it casts a wide net. From hospitals to doctors' offices to school health clinics, the HIPAA Privacy and Security Rules have transformed the way health care providers and others handle health records. The Privacy, Security, and Enforcement Rules are the most commonly referenced sections of HIPAA. But there are other portions of HIPAA that are often overlooked. Whether this is your first time examining HIPAA or you are a pro looking for a refresher, this book is intended to provide you with the HIPAA basics as well as updates that have come about since the first edition. This first chapter will provide an overview of the various components of the federal law known as HIPAA. HIPAA is divided into five titles, which are briefly explained in the following subsections.

I. Title I

HIPAA, passed in 1996, also known as the Kennedy-Kassebaum Act, was designed to promote the availability of health care as well as administrative simplification. Title I: Health Care Access, Portability, and Renewability protects workers' health insurance when employees change or lose their jobs and prohibits group health insurers from excluding or discriminating against individuals who have preexisting health conditions. It requires employers and health plans to allow a new employee's medical insurance coverage to continue regardless of whether he or she have had a preexisting condition.

Title I imposes certain restrictions on health insurers when they decide not to renew or to discontinue coverage. A health insurer may discontinue health insurance coverage in the group or individual market only for: (1) nonpayment of premiums; (2) fraud; (3) violation of participation rules; (4) termination of product; (5) enrollee's movement outside of service area; or (6) if the employer's membership stops.[1] As stated above, Title I protects workers and their families from being denied health insurance coverage when the worker changes jobs or loses his or her job, which makes health insurance coverage "portable." But make no mistake, Title I does not require the same health insurance company to provide benefits when the employee changes jobs. Rather, it prevents a worker and his or her family from being denied coverage when the worker is no longer associated with that particular job.[2] For example, if an employee's wife develops cancer and sometime

---

1. Health Insurance Portability and Accountability Act of 1996, Pub. L. No. 104-191, 110 Stat. 1936 (1996), https://www.gpo.gov/fdsys/pkg/PLAW-104publ191/pdf/PLAW-104publ191.pdf [hereinafter HIPAA].
2. U.S. Dep't of Health & Human Servs. (HHS), Protecting Your Health Insurance Coverage (2000), https://www.cms.gov/Regulations-and-Guidance/Health-Insurance-Reform/HealthInsReformforConsume/downloads/protect.pdf.

later the employee leaves that employer to become employed at a different company, the new employer's health insurance company cannot deny coverage to the new employee's family (including the wife), despite the wife's previous existing cancer diagnosis. We take this for granted now and many of us have never known anything different, but there was a time in America when health insurance companies could routinely deny coverage due to a preexisting health condition. Previous to HIPAA, if someone in the family had a chronic or long-lasting health condition such as diabetes or depression, the worker whose job provided health care insurance coverage was obligated to stay at his or her job in order to maintain health insurance coverage for the family.

II. Title II

The next section of HIPAA is Title II, which is the section with which most people are familiar. Title II: Preventing Health Care Fraud and Abuse; Administrative Simplification; Medical Liability Reform is also known as the Administrative Simplification Rule. Title II permits the U.S. Department of Health and Human Services to create standards for electronic health care transactions made by health care providers, health plans, and employers, which includes the security and privacy of health information. This book focuses on the Privacy and Security sections of the Administrative Simplification Rules and are explained in detail throughout the book. Title II contains the HIPAA Privacy, Security, and Enforcement portions as well as the Transactions and Codes Set Standards and the Identifier Standards for Employers and Providers.[3] The intent of Title II is to improve the efficiency and effectiveness of the nation's health care system by encouraging the widespread

---

3. Ctrs. for Medicare & Medicaid Servs., Administrative Simplification Overview, https://www.cms.gov/Regulations-and-Guidance/Administrative-Simplification/HIPAA-ACA (last visited Sept. 15, 2019).

use of electronic data interchange in health care.[4] In creating provisions for the electronic transfer of health information, Congress recognized that safeguards were needed to control the exchange of highly personal and confidential medical information. The standards are meant to improve the efficiency and effectiveness of the nation's health care system by encouraging the widespread use of electronic data interchange in health care.[5]

Title II is also meant to reduce the costs and administrative burdens of health care by standardizing the electronic transmission of certain administrative and financial transactions that had been previously done on paper. In its quest to restrain health care costs, the government determined that a high percentage of every health care dollar spent was on administrative overhead, including processing for enrollment, payment, eligibility, authorizations, filing a claim, supporting a claim, coordinating payments between more than one insurance company, and notifying the provider about payment. In order to rein in costs, the Administrative Simplification Rule was put in place.

This book specifically explains the Privacy, Security, and Enforcement Rules and provides practical information on implementation and compliance. There are three primary types of entities that are covered under HIPAA: health plans, health care clearinghouses, and health care providers who conduct the standard health care transactions electronically. These types of entities that are covered by HIPAA are referred to as "covered entities."[6] As discussed ahead, HIPAA has now been expanded to directly govern business associates of covered entities, as well as their subcontractors.

The final Privacy Rule was published in December of 2000 and later modified in August 2002. As the name implies, the Privacy

---

4. *Id.*
5. Ctrs. for Medicare & Medicaid Servs., Health Insurance Portability and Accountability Act of 1996 (HIPAA), Final Privacy Rule, 65 Fed. Reg. 82,461–510, *available at* https://aspe.hhs.gov/report/standards-privacy-individually-identifiable-health-information-final-privacy-rule-preamble (last visited Sept. 15, 2019).
6. 45 C.F.R. § 160.103.

Rule sets national standards for the protection of individually identifiable health information. Covered entities were required to comply with the Privacy Rule as of April 14, 2003 (April 14, 2004, for small health plans). The Privacy Rule is codified at 45 C.F.R. Part 164, Subparts A & E.

The final Security Rule was published in February of 2003. The Security Rule sets national standards for protecting the confidentiality, integrity, and availability of *electronic* protected health information. Covered entities were required to comply with the Security Rule as of April 20, 2005 (April 20, 2006, for small health plans). The Security Rule is codified at 45 C.F.R. Part 160 and Subparts A and C of Part 164. It requires covered entities to provide appropriate administrative, physical, and technical safeguards to ensure the confidentiality, integrity, and security of electronic protected health information. More details about the Security Rule can be found in Chapter 6.

The Enforcement Rule provides standards for enforcing HIPAA and was published in February of 2006. It contains provisions relating to compliance and investigations, the imposition of civil money penalties for violations of the HIPAA Administrative Simplification Rules, and procedures for hearings. The HIPAA Enforcement Rule is codified at 45 C.F.R. Part 160, Subparts C, D, and E.

Other rules also affect electronic data use in health care and somewhat enhance Title II. For example, as part of the American Recovery and Reinvestment Act of 2009, the Health Information Technology for Economic and Clinical Health (HITECH) Act became effective on February 18, 2009. The HITECH Act, discussed in more detail in Chapter 7, is intended to promote the adoption and meaningful use of health information technology. Subtitle D of the HITECH Act contains several provisions that strengthen the civil and criminal enforcement of the privacy and security rules associated with electronic transmission of health information. The HITECH Act gave individuals the right to be notified of breaches, expanded HIPAA's reach to business associates, and increased penalties.

The interim final rule relating to breach notification for unsecured protected health information, implementing portions of the HITECH Act, was published in August of 2009.[7] A final breach rule, also referred to as the omnibus rule, was published in January of 2013[8] and implements a number of provisions of the HITECH Act.

Another rule that implicates Title II is the Patient Protection and Affordable Care Act (ACA), 42 U.S.C. 18001, Pub. L. No. 111-148, which went into effect on January 7, 2011. The ACA expanded the Administrative Simplification provisions of HIPAA Title II and introduced operating rules to standardize business practices. These operating rules contain certain requirements for transactions under HIPAA that specify the information that must be included when conducting standard transactions.[9] This book includes information about the HITECH Act and the ACA in the discussion about HIPAA Title II.

The official version of all federal regulations is published in the Code of Federal Regulations (C.F.R.). The official versions of the HIPAA rules are available at 45 C.F.R. Part 160, Part 162, and Part 164.

III. Title III

Title III contains the tax-related health provisions of HIPAA. These provisions mostly relate to one of two major topics: medical savings accounts (MSAs) or long-term care. MSAs are the predecessors of health savings accounts (HSAs). MSAs were a federal pilot

---

7. Interim final rule with request for comments, Office for Civil Rights, HHS, Breach Notification for Unsecured Protected Health Information, 74 Fed. Reg. 42,740 (Aug. 24, 2009).
8. Final Rule, Office for Civil Rights, HHS, Modifications to the HIPAA Privacy, Security, Enforcement, and Breach Notification Rules under the Health Information Technology for Economic and Clinical Health Act and the Genetic Information Nondiscrimination Act; Other Modifications to the HIPAA Rules, 78 Fed. Reg. 5566 (Jan. 25, 2013).
9. Ctrs. for Medicare & Medicaid Servs., Administrative Simplification Overview, https://www.cms.gov/Regulations-and-Guidance/Administrative-Simplification/HIPAA-ACA (last visited Sept. 15, 2019).

program within HIPAA in 1996, but were discontinued in the private sector on December 31, 2005. HSAs were established as a permanent feature of the Internal Revenue Code § 223 in 2003 and were developed to replace the MSAs in the private sector. Medicare MSAs were first available to Medicare beneficiaries in 2007. Medicare MSAs and private sector HSAs are similar in that they combine high-deductible health insurance plans with medical savings accounts. The enrollee can initially use his or her pretax health savings account or medical savings account to pay for health care and once the deductible is reached, then the enrollee has health coverage through the high-deductible insurance plan. HSAs and Medicare MSAs provide beneficiaries with more control over health care utilization while still providing coverage against catastrophic health care expenses.[10] For tax year 2018, the individual is limited to contribute to the health savings account no more than $3,450 for an individual or $6,850 for a family high-deductible health plan.[11] The way this works is the employee contributes a certain amount of his or her pretax dollars into a health savings account that is tied to a health plan with a deductible of anywhere between $1,350 to $6,650 for individuals or $2,700 to $13,300 for families (these limits are for 2018 tax year).[12] When the employee (or his or her family) incurs health care-related expenses, the employee can use the money in the health savings account to pay for the health care costs until the deductible is met. Once the deductible is met, the health plan covers the medical expenses.

Funds in the health savings account may be used to cover co-pays, coinsurance, vision, dental care, and other out-of-pocket medical costs. However, any money withdrawn for nonmedical

---

10. CTRS. FOR MEDICARE & MEDICAID SERVS., FACT SHEET ON MEDICARE MEDICAL SAVINGS ACCOUNT (MSA) PLANS, https://www.cms.gov/Medicare/Health-Plans/MSA/Downloads/MSAFactSheet-11-19-10.pdf (last visited Mar. 13, 2018); HSA Connect, Health Insurance Information about HSAs, http://www.hsaconnect.com/hsa-health-savings-accounts/medical-savings-account.php (last visited Mar. 13, 2018).

11. 2018-10 I.R.B. (Mar. 5, 2018), https://www.irs.gov/pub/irs-irbs/irb18-10.pdf.

12. INTERNAL REVENUE SERV. PUBL'N FOR 26 C.F.R. § 601.602: TAX FORMS AND INSTRUCTIONS, https://www.irs.gov/pub/irs-drop/rp-17-37.pdf (last visited Apr. 7, 2018).

expenses before age 65 carries a 20 percent penalty on the withdrawal as well as income tax on the amount.[13] The unused money in the health savings account rolls over year after year and continues to grow tax free in most states (including investment returns or interest). In addition to paying for medical-related expenses, when the employee reaches the age of 65, he or she may withdraw the funds to pay for nonmedical services or items but will pay income tax on any withdrawals used for nonmedical expenses.

The typical health savings account/high-deductible health plan works like this: an individual can elect to contribute $200 per month to a health savings account and have a health insurance plan with a $1,400 deductible. If the individual does not incur any medical expenses after two years, he or she will have $4,800 in the health savings account. If he or she (or qualifying family member) needs health services costing $3,000, the individual may withdraw $1,400 from the health savings account to cover the deductible and the health plan should cover the rest. The remaining $3,400 can be used toward the deductible for the following year, if needed. If it is not needed, the amount and any further contributions simply continue to accrue interest. Additionally, the employee may continue to contribute tax-free dollars to the health savings account.

The long-term care provisions of Title III also create tax incentives for individuals to obtain long-term care insurance. Certain premiums for qualified long-term care insurance are eligible for tax deduction similar to accident and health insurance premiums. Also, proceeds from qualified long-term care policies are generally not treated as income. Employer-provided qualified long-term care insurance costs are also not included in the covered employee's taxable income.[14] Additional provisions of Title III relate to deductions for health insurance costs of self-employed individuals;

---

13. INTERNAL REVENUE SERV. PUBL'N 969, HEALTH SAVINGS ACCOUNTS AND OTHER TAX-FAVORED HEALTH PLANS 8 (2018), https://www.irs.gov/pub/irs-pdf/p969.pdf .

14. Rita DiSimone, *Health Insurance Reform Legislation*, 60 (4) SOC. SEC. ADMIN. BULLETIN (1997), https://www.ssa.gov/policy/docs/ssb/v60n4/v60n4p18.pdf.

the treatment of accelerated death benefits for life insurance; state insurance pools; and other miscellaneous subjects.[15]

IV. Title IV

Title IV: Application and Enforcement of Group Health Plan Requirements added Subtitle K: Group Health Plan Portability, Access, and Renewability Requirements (Sections 9801 through 9806) to the Internal Revenue Code. These provisions impose a tax on group health plans for failure to comply with the portability, nondiscrimination, and guaranteed renewability provisions of HIPAA. Title IV also modified the Consolidated Omnibus Budget Reconciliation Act (COBRA) to require group health plans of 20 or more employees to offer certain employees and their dependents the option of purchasing continued health coverage when there is a "qualified event" (i.e., termination or reduction in hours of employment; death, divorce, legal separation; Medicare entitlement; employer's bankruptcy; or the end of a child's dependency under a parent's health plan). Title IV also modified COBRA to minimize gaps in health coverage for newborns, adopted children, individuals with disabilities, and avoid duplicate coverage for individuals covered under the portability provisions of HIPAA.[16]

V. Title V

Title V: Revenue Offsets amends the Internal Revenue Code and was intended to compensate for government revenue losses under the other HIPAA provisions. There are three subtitles in Title V. Subtitle A: Company-Owned Life Insurance prohibits companies from deducting interest on loans related to company-owned life insurance, including company-owned endowment or annuity

---

15. HIPAA, *supra* note 1.
16. *Id.*

contracts. Subtitle B: Treatment of Individuals Who Lose United States Citizenship revised the income, estate, and gift taxes on individuals who lose citizenship. Subtitle C: Repeal of Financial Institution Transition Rule to Interest Allocation Rules repealed a portion of section 1215(c) of the Tax Reform Act of 1986 (Pub. L. No. 99-514, 100 Stat. 2548).[17]

VI. Overview of Title II

As mentioned previously, this book focuses on the Administrative Simplification provisions of Title II, particularly the Privacy, Security, and Enforcement Rules. The following is an overview of each of these rules and lays the groundwork for introducing the reader to these regulations.

A. Privacy Rule

The HIPAA Privacy Rule protects the confidentiality of individuals' health information while simultaneously allowing health information to be transmitted to intended recipients. This promotes high-quality health care and protects the individual's right to privacy. The HIPAA Privacy Rule attempts to strike a balance between using an individual's health information to advance necessary health care while protecting the individual's privacy when seeking medical care and treatment.[18]

In order to accomplish these goals, the Privacy Rule creates national standards to safeguard the privacy of personal health information. These standards give individuals more control over their health information; set limits on the use and release of health records; require those working with the protected health information to only have access to the minimum amount of information needed; establish safeguards for protection of health information;

---

17. *Id.*
18. HHS, OCR Privacy Brief, Summary of the HIPAA Privacy Rule (revised May 2003), http://www.hhs.gov/ocr/privacysummary.pdf.

and strike a balance between the need for individual's privacy versus the health and safety concerns of others.[19] The Privacy Rule gives individuals the right to control, in certain circumstances, how their health information may be used; to obtain information about disclosures of their health information; and to examine and obtain copies of their own health records and correct inaccuracies.[20] The Privacy Rule contains mandates that prohibit or strictly control disclosures of personal health information. Several exceptions allow the release of health information without the individual's consent.[21] The Privacy Rule can be found at 45 C.F.R. § 160 and § 164, Subparts A and E. This book contains details of the Privacy Rule in Chapter 2.

B. Security Rule

While the Privacy Rule governs all forms of protected health information, whether electronic, written, or oral,[22] the Security Rule creates national standards for the protection of *electronic* health information.[23] The Security Rule contains mandates for certain entities to establish administrative, physical, and technical safeguards for the protection of the confidentiality, integrity, and availability of electronic health information.[24] The need for the Security Rule was evident as the health care industry began to move away from processing paper documents and started embracing new electronic technology. The new technology brought about increased efficiency and financial incentives to electronically transmit claims data, provide health information, and conduct a wide range of other administrative and clinical functions. As the health care industry

---

19. HHS, Frequently Asked Questions (FAQs) 187, https://www.hhs.gov/hipaa/for-individuals/faq/187/what-does-the-hipaa-privacy-rule-do/index.html (last visited Sept. 15, 2019).

20. *Id.*

21. 45 C.F.R. § 164.512, *available at* https://www.ecfr.gov/cgi-bin/text-idx?tpl=/ecfrbrowse/Title45/45cfr164_main_02.tpl (last visited Sept. 15, 2019).

22. 45 C.F.R. § 160.103, definition of "protected health information."

23. 45 C.F.R. § 160 and § 164 subpts. A, C.

24. *Id.*

began to use and rely on the electronic transmission of health data more heavily, the increased use created a higher risk of unauthorized disclosures. The Security Rule was intended to combat this potential threat.

The Security Rule requires that personal health information remain confidential by only allowing electronic health information to be accessible by those who are authorized. It obligates people who access health information to maintain the integrity of the personal health information by making sure that the information is not altered or destroyed in an unauthorized manner. Although the Security Rule puts these restrictions on personal health information, it also mandates that electronic health information be available and accessible as needed by people who are authorized to use it.[25]

In order to accomplish these objectives, the Security Rule sets the standards to ensure that only those who are authorized to access the personal health information actually do. The security standards are separated into three categories: (1) administrative safeguards; (2) physical safeguards; and (3) technical safeguards. Administrative safeguards are managerial functions such as risk analysis, policies and procedures, training, and emergency backup plans.[26] Physical safeguards protect electronic systems, equipment, and data from threats, environmental hazards, and unauthorized use.[27] Physical safeguards include restricting access, facility security, and proper disposal of data.[28] Technical safeguards are automated processes that protect data and control access to data.[29] These consist of mechanisms such as authentication controls that verify users' identity, audits, data encryption, and so on.[30] In addition

---

25. HHS, HIPAA SECURITY SERIES (rev. Mar. 2007), https://www.hhs.gov/sites/default/files/ocr/privacy/hipaa/administrative/securityrule/security101.pdf.
26. 45 C.F.R. § 164.308, Administrative Safeguards.
27. 45 C.F.R. § 164.310, Physical Safeguards.
28. Id.
29. 45 C.F.R. § 164.312, Technical Safeguards.
30. Id.

Chapter 1: *Welcome to HIPAA* 13

to the safeguards, the Security Rule has organizational and documentation requirements.[31] More details about the Security Rule can be found in Chapter 6.

C. Enforcement Rule

The HIPAA Enforcement Rule sets civil monetary penalties and lays out procedures for investigations, imposition of penalties, and hearings for violations of HIPAA.[32] The Enforcement Rule can be found at 45 C.F.R. Part 160, subparts C, D, and E. The U.S. Department of Health and Human Services' Office for Civil Rights (OCR) investigates complaints, conducts compliance reviews, and performs education and outreach to promote compliance with the Privacy and Security Rules' requirements.[33] The OCR also refers appropriate cases to the U.S. Department of Justice for possible criminal violations of HIPAA.[34]

The Enforcement Rule contains provisions for compliance, investigations, penalties, and procedures for hearings.[35] Initially, only covered entities were required to comply with the Privacy and Security Rules.[36] But in 2013 the HITECH Act strengthened the Privacy, Security, and Enforcement Rules by making business associates directly liable for certain violations of the Privacy and Security provisions Rules.[37] HITECH also increased and tiered the civil monetary penalty structure.[38]

---

31. 45 C.F.R. § 164.314 and § 164.316.
32. 45 C.F.R. §§ 160.500–.570.
33. HHS, HIPAA Enforcement, https://www.hhs.gov/hipaa/for-professionals/compliance-enforcement/index.html (last visited Sept. 15, 2019).
34. *Id.*
35. Interim Final Rule, 68 Fed. Reg. 18,895–906 (Apr. 17, 2003) (codified at 45 C.F.R. § 160), *available at* https://www.hhs.gov/sites/default/files/ocr/privacy/hipaa/administrative/privacyrule/moneypenalties.pdf.
36. *Id.* at 18,898, *Basis for Penalty.*
37. 78 Fed. Reg. 5566 (Jan. 25, 2013).
38. *Id.*

VII. Conclusion

HIPAA is more than just health information privacy and security. HIPAA comprises five titles, each having specific functions. The commonly known portions of HIPAA are the portions of Title II better known as the Privacy Rule, Security Rule, and Enforcement Rule. These are the main focus of this book.

Chapter 2

The Basics

I. Fundamentals

Now that you have an overview of HIPAA, particularly the Administrative Simplification portion of HIPAA, let us explore the groundwork that applies to the Privacy, Security, and Enforcement Rules. This chapter provides you with the basic elements of HIPAA that commonly apply to each of those rules. It introduces you to basic concepts and terms used in HIPAA. Some readers may be familiar with much of the material because of its integration into health care delivery, but some may see the material for the first time. Whether it is a refresher or an introduction to these rules, the goal of this chapter is to provide the fundamentals for the in-depth concepts contained in the following chapters.

A. Who Needs to Comply?

All "covered entities" are subject to HIPAA and need to comply.[1] Covered entities have certain obligations under HIPAA and specifics about these obligations can be found in Chapter 5 and

---
1. 45 C.F.R. §§ 160.102 and 103.

Appendix A, which contains sample policies and procedures. But first you should know what a "covered entity" is. A covered entity is a health plan, health care clearinghouse, or health care provider that transmits any health information in electronic form in connection with health care transactions.[2] This chapter examines these entities in more detail.

1. Health Plan

a. What Is a Health Plan?

A "health plan" is an individual or group plan that provides, or pays the cost of, medical care.[3] A health plan includes the following, alone or in combination:[4]

- A **group health plan,** defined as an employee benefit plan including insured and self-insured plans, to the extent that the plan provides medical care including items and services paid for as medical care, to employees or their dependents directly or through insurance, reimbursement, or otherwise that (1) has 50 or more participants or (2) is administered by an entity other than the employer that established and maintains the plan;
- A **health insurance issuer,** defined as an insurance company, insurance service, or insurance organization (including an HMO) that is licensed to engage in the business of insurance in a state and is subject to state law that regulates insurance; it does not include a group health plan;
- A **health maintenance organization** (HMO);
- **Part A or Part B of the Medicare Program** under Title XVIII of the Social Security Act;
- The **Medicaid** program under Title XIX of the Social Security Act, 42 U.S.C. 1396, *et seq.*;

---

2. 45 C.F.R. § 160.103.
3. *Id.*
4. *Id.*

Chapter 2: *The Basics*

- The Voluntary **Prescription Drug Benefit Program** under Part D of Title XVIII of the Social Security Act, 42 U.S.C. 1395w-101 through 1395w-152;
- An issuer of a Medicare supplemental policy as defined in section 1882(g)(1) of the Social Security Act, 42 U.S.C. 1395ss(g)(1) (a health insurance policy or other health benefit plan offered by a private entity to individuals who are entitled to have payment made under the Social Security Act[5]);
- An issuer of a **long-term care policy,** excluding a nursing home fixed-indemnity policy;
- An **employee welfare benefit plan** or any other arrangement that is established or maintained for the purpose of offering or providing health benefits to the employees of two or more employers;
- The **health care program for uniformed services personnel** under Title 10 of the U.S. Code;
- The **veterans health care program** under 38 U.S.C. chapter 17;

---

5. 42 U.S.C. 1395ss(g)(1) defines an "issuer of a Medicare supplemental policy" as a health insurance policy or other health benefit plan offered by a private entity to individuals who are entitled to have payment made under this title, which provides reimbursement for expenses incurred for services and items for which payment may be made under this title but which are not reimbursable by reason of the applicability of deductibles, coinsurance amounts, or other limitations imposed pursuant to this title; but does not include a Medicare+Choice plan or any such policy or plan of one or more employers or labor organizations, or of the trustees of a fund established by one or more employers or labor organizations (or combination thereof), for employees or former employees (or combination thereof) or for members or former members (or combination thereof) of the labor organizations and does not include a policy or plan of an eligible organization (as defined in section 1876(b)) if the policy or plan provides benefits pursuant to a contract under section 1876 or an approved demonstration project described in section 603(c) of the Social Security Amendments of 1983, section 2355 of the Deficit Reduction Act of 1984, or section 9412(b) of the Omnibus Budget Reconciliation Act of 1986, or, during the period beginning on the date specified in subsection (p)(1)(C) and ending on December 31, 1995, a policy or plan of an organization if the policy or plan provides benefits pursuant to an agreement under section 1833(a)(1)(A) For purposes of this section, the term "policy" includes a certificate issued under such policy.

- The **Indian Health Service** program under the Indian Health Care Improvement Act, 25 U.S.C. 1601;
- The **Federal Employees Health Benefits Program** under 5 U.S.C. 8902;
- An approved **state child health plan** under Title XXI of the Social Security Act;
- Part C of the Medicare program (**Medicare Advantage**);
- A **high-risk pool** that is a mechanism established under state law to provide health insurance coverage or comparable coverage to eligible individuals;
- Any other **individual or group plan**, or combination of individual or group plans, that provides or pays for the cost of medical care.[6]

As you can see from this list, there are a variety of programs that are a "health plan." In the employee benefit context, it is important to distinguish the plan from the sponsor. An employer that sponsors a group health plan is not a covered entity merely by virtue of the fact that it sponsors the health plan. "The group health plan is considered to be a separate legal entity from the employer or other parties that sponsor the group health plan. Neither employers nor other group health plan sponsors are defined as covered entities under HIPAA."[7] Employers that sponsor group health plans are not covered entities; however, the group health plan *is* a covered entity and must comply with HIPAA when the plan releases members' information to the employer or plan sponsor.[8] This sharing of information may happen when the information is needed for the plan sponsor to perform certain administrative functions on behalf of the group health plan.[9] The Privacy Rule controls the conditions that the group health plan must meet before releasing such information. "Among these conditions is receipt of

---

6. *Id.*
7. U.S. Dep't of Health & Human Servs. (HHS), Frequently Asked Questions (FAQs) 499, https://www.hhs.gov/hipaa/for-professionals/faq/499/am-i-a-covered-entity-under-hipaa/index.html (last visited Sept. 15, 2019).
8. *Id. See also* 45 C.F.R. § 164.504(f).
9. *Id.*

Chapter 2: *The Basics* 19

a certification from the employer or plan sponsor that the health information will be protected as prescribed by the rule and will not be used for employment-related actions."[10]

b. *What Is Not a Health Plan?*

A number of insurance products use and disclose a great deal of health information, but are not subject to HIPAA.[11] HIPAA excludes from the definition of "health plan" any policy, plan, or program that provides or pays for the cost of:

- Coverage for accident, or disability income insurance (or any combination);
- Coverage issued as a supplement to liability insurance;
- Liability insurance (including general liability insurance and automobile liability insurance);
- Workers' compensation or similar insurance;
- Automobile medical payment insurance;
- Credit-only insurance;
- Coverage for on-site medical clinics;
- Other similar insurance coverage, specified in regulations, under which benefits for medical care are secondary or incidental to other insurance benefits.[12]

HIPAA also excludes any government-funded program other than those listed in section a.[13] The following are examples of insurance policies that are not considered health plans and are not subject to HIPAA:

- long-term or short-term disability;
- workers' compensation; and

---

10. *Id.*
11. They are subject to other privacy laws.
12. 45 C.F.R. § 160.103 and 42 U.S.C. 300 gg-91(c)(1), *available at* https://www.law.cornell.edu/uscode/text/42/300gg-91 (last visited Sept. 15, 2019).
13. 45 C.F.R. § 160.103.

- automobile liability that includes coverage for medical payment.[14]

When in doubt, about a plan's status under HIPAA, the Health and Human Services' Frequently Asked Questions for Professionals[15] provides helpful examples and related information.

2. Health Care Clearinghouse

A "health care clearinghouse" is a public or private entity, including

- a billing service, repricing company, community health management information system, or community health information system, and "value added" networks and switches, that does either of the following functions:
  ○ Processes or facilitates the processing of health information received from another entity in a nonstandard format or containing nonstandard data content into standard data elements or a standard transaction.
  ○ Receives a standard transaction from another entity and processes or facilitates the processing of health information into nonstandard format or nonstandard data content for the receiving entity.[16]

A health care clearinghouse is an entity that receives health care transactions from health care providers or other entities, translates the data from a given format into a format acceptable to the intended payor or payors, and forwards the processed transaction to appropriate payors and clearinghouses.[17] The term "health care

---

14. HHS FAQ 364, https://www.hhs.gov/hipaa/for-professionals/faq/364/which-insurances-are-covered-under-hipaa/index.html (last visited Sept. 15, 2019).

15. *See* https://www.hhs.gov/hipaa/for-professionals/faq/index.html (last visited May 4, 2019).

16. 45 C.F.R. § 160.103.

17. HHS, Office of the Assistant Sec'y for Planning and Evaluation, Standards for Privacy of Individually Identifiable Health Information. Final Rule Preamble, Health Care Clearinghouse (Dec. 28, 2000), *available at* https://aspe.hhs.gov/report/standards-privacy-individually-identifiable-health-information-final-privacy-rule-preamble/health-care-clearinghouse.

clearinghouse" may have different meanings and implications in other situations, but the regulation defines it specifically, and an entity is considered a health care clearinghouse only to the extent that it meets the criteria in this definition.

> Telecommunications entities that provide connectivity or mechanisms to convey information, such as telephone companies and internet service providers, are not health care clearinghouses as defined in the rule unless they actually carry out the functions outlined in our definition. Value added networks and switches are not health care clearinghouses unless they carry out the functions outlined in the definition.[18]

The examples of entities in the definition are health care clearinghouses, as well as any other entities that meet that definition, to the extent that they perform the functions in the definition.

> In order to fall within the definition of clearinghouse, the covered entity must perform the clearinghouse function on health information received from some *other* entity. A department or component of a health plan or health care provider that transforms nonstandard information into standard data elements or standard transactions (or vice versa) is not a clearinghouse for purposes of this rule, unless it also performs these functions for *another* entity.[19]

3. Health Care Provider

A "health care provider" is a provider of services (a hospital, critical access hospital, skilled nursing facility, comprehensive outpatient rehabilitation facility, home health agency, hospice program, etc.), a provider of medical or health services (physicians, pharmacists,

---

18. *Id.*
19. *Id.*

occupational therapists, physical therapists, x-ray technicians, outpatient or partial hospitalization programs, health clinics, health centers, dialysis centers, home dialysis, physician assistants, nurse practitioners, psychologists, clinical social workers, nurse midwives, ambulance companies, etc.) or any other person or organization who furnishes, bills, or is paid for health care in the normal course of business.[20] "Health care" includes care, services, and supplies related to the health of an individual.[21]

It is important to keep in mind that HIPAA does not apply to all health care providers. It applies only to those health care providers, as defined above, that (1) transmit health information electronically in connection with one of the financial or administrative transactions under HIPAA (such as health claims, status of enrollment and eligibility, and authorizations for referral) *and* (2) transmit the health information in a standard electronic format (the national format required under the Administrative Simplification Compliance Act).[22] Therefore, by definition, a health care provider that uses only paper formats and does not submit insurance claims electronically is not subject to HIPAA.[23]

4. What If I Don't Know?

It may be difficult to determine whether an organization is a covered entity. To find out, start the analysis with the question: "Does the organization (or person) deliver health care services and electronically bill for those services?" Let's do the analysis using a blood donor center as an example. The first part of the analysis is: Does the blood donor center deliver health care services? Some readers may say "yes, because health care professionals take the

---

20. 45 C.F.R. § 160.103.
21. *Id.*
22. 45 C.F.R. §§ 164.104 and 164.500 and Final Privacy Rule Preamble, *available at* http://www.cms.hhs.gov/hipaa/hipaa2/regulations/privacy/finalrule.
23. HHS, Health Information Privacy, Covered Entities and Business Associates, https://www.hhs.gov/hipaa/for-professionals/covered-entities/index.html (last visited Jan. 6, 2019).

donor's blood pressure, temperature, and pulse." Depending on the circumstances, the services may be considered delivery of health care. It is be debatable whether these health care professionals deliver "health care services." But for the sake of our analysis with this example, let's presume the answer is "yes" and we will proceed as if they do deliver health care services. The second question in the analysis is: Do these health care professionals electronically bill for the services? If they do not, then the conclusion is that a blood donor center is *not* a covered entity. Keep in mind that blood donor centers that conduct testing of blood samples for the benefit of the blood donor based on a health care provider's orders would be a covered entity under HIPAA if they transmit protected health information electronically in connection with standard transactions (i.e., electronically bill for those services) that are subject to HIPAA.[24]

There are helpful resources that can assist you to determine whether the organization or person is a covered entity and subject to HIPAA. The Centers for Medicare and Medicaid Services (CMS) has a decision tool that helps you determine whether the organization or person is a covered entity.[25]

B. What Information Is Subject to HIPAA?

1. Protected Health Information

HIPAA covers protected health information (PHI).[26] PHI is information that is created or received by a health care provider, health plan, public health authority, employer, life insurer, school or university, or health care clearinghouse that relates to: the past, present, or future physical or mental health of an individual; provision

---

24. HHS FAQ 20111, Are Tissue Repositories Covered Entities?, https://www.hhs.gov/hipaa/for-professionals/faq/20111/are-tissue-repositories-covered-entities/index.html (last visited Jan. 18, 2019).

25. HHS, Ctrs. for Medicare & Medicaid Servs., Covered Entity Guidance (2016), https://www.cms.gov/Regulations-and-Guidance/Administrative-Simplification/HIPAA-ACA/Downloads/CoveredEntitiesChart20160617.pdf.

26. 45 C.F.R. § 160.103.

of health care services; or payment for health care that identifies the individual or can be used to identify the individual.[27] This comprises traditional medical records and billing information that are transmitted or maintained in any form or medium, including electronic media.[28]

2. Not Protected Health Information

a. FERPA

Although "school and university" are mentioned in the definition of health information,[29] you should note that HIPAA specifically *excludes* from PHI individually identifiable health information in education records that are subject to the Family Educational Rights and Privacy Act (FERPA).[30] FERPA defines "education records" as material that contains information directly related to a student and maintained by an educational agency or institution or by a person acting for such agency or institution.[31] For example:

> [I]f a person or entity acting on behalf of a school [that is] subject to *FERPA*, such as a school nurse that provides services to students under contract with or otherwise under the direct control of the school, maintains student health records, these records are education records under *FERPA*, just as they would be if the school maintained the records directly. This is the case regardless of whether the health care is provided to students on school grounds or off-site. As *education records*, the information is protected under *FERPA* and not HIPAA.[32]

---

27. *Id.* See definitions of "protected health information," "individually identifiable health information," and "health information."
28. *Id.*
29. 45 C.F.R. § 160.103, definition of "health information."
30. See definition of "protected health information" in 45 C.F.R. § 160.103; and definition of "education records" in 20 U.S.C. § 1232g(a)(4)(B)(iv).
31. 20 U.S.C. § 1232g(a)(4)(B)(iv).
32. HHS FAQ 514, https://www.hhs.gov/hipaa/for-professionals/faq/514/does-hipaa-apply-to-school-student-health-records/index.html (last visited Jan. 20, 2019).

A complete analysis of HIPAA and FERPA is needed when dealing with these types of records.

b. Employment Records
Additionally, HIPAA excludes employment records held by a covered entity in its role as an employer.[33] Simply because an employer provides health coverage to their employees through a health insurance policy generally does not make the employer subject to HIPAA. However, for employers who sponsor health plans that are "self-insured,"[34] the employer is responsible for the health plan's HIPAA compliance when the plan is not fully insured by an insurance company.

HIPAA affects an employer when the employer needs to obtain an employee's medical records because HIPAA typically applies to the health care entity from which the employer seeks the PHI. For instance, if you work for a covered entity, HIPAA does not apply to your employment records but it does protect your medical records if you are a patient of a covered entity.[35] An employer is not entitled to have access to the employee's PHI just because the employer happens to be a covered entity. A covered entity must obtain an authorization from the employee before the covered entity is allowed to provide a copy of the employee's health information to the employer, even when that employer is a covered entity.[36] This is true even when the PHI is used to satisfy

---

33. 45 C.F.R. § 160.103, definition of "protected health information."
34. A self-insured plan means the employer itself collects premiums from enrollees and takes on the responsibility of paying employees' and dependents' medical claims. These employers may contract for insurance services such as enrollment, claims processing, and provider networks with a third-party administrator, or they can be self-administered by the employer. HealthCare.gov, https://www.healthcare.gov/glossary/self-insured-plan/ (last visited Jan. 27, 2019). An example is when the employer does not enter into a health insurance contract, but instead pays for the health benefits out of the employer's general assets and typically engages a service provider to administer claims.
35. 45 C.F.R. §§ 160.103 and 164.512(b)(1)(v); HHS, Health Information Privacy, Employers and Health Information in the Workplace, https://www.hhs.gov/hipaa/for-individuals/employers-health-information-workplace/index.html (last visited Jan. 20, 2019).
36. 45 C.F.R. § 164.508.

requirements under the Family Medical Leave Act and the American with Disabilities Act.

In the area of workers' compensation, HIPAA allows a covered entity to disclose PHI to the extent necessary to comply with laws relating to workers' compensation or other similar programs that provide benefits for work-related injuries or illnesses without regard to fault.[37] Accordingly, these disclosures are subject to state law regarding workers' compensation.

c. De-identified Records

It is important to remember that in order for the information to be PHI and subject to HIPAA, the information must be "individually identifiable," which means it can be used to identify the individual.[38] "Health information that does not identify an individual and with respect to which there is no reasonable basis to believe that the information can be used to identify an individual is not individually identifiable health information."[39] Health information that is "de-identified" is not subject to scrutiny under HIPAA.

Information can be de-identified if: (1) an expert determines that the risk is very small that the information could be used to identify an individual and the expert documents his or her methods and analysis; or (2) specific identifiers are removed.[40] Some of these identifiers are names; geographic subdivisions smaller than a state (including addresses; full zip codes); all dates except years; telephone and fax numbers; e-mail addresses; social security numbers; medical record numbers; health plan beneficiary numbers; account numbers; license numbers; vehicle identifiers; device identifiers; Internet addresses; biometric identifiers such as finger and voice prints; photographs of the individual's full face; and any

---

37. 45 C.F.R. § 164.512(l).
38. 45 C.F.R. § 160.103, see definition of "individually identifiable health information."
39. 45 C.F.R. § 164.514(a).
40. 45 C.F.R. § 164.514.

Chapter 2: *The Basics* **27**

other unique identifying number, characteristic, and code.[41] Once the PHI is de-identified, it is not individually identifiable and is no longer PHI subject to HIPAA.

*d. Information Disclosed by the Individual
to a Noncovered Entity*

In order for the information to be considered PHI, it must be "created or received" by a covered entity.[42] Information that an individual discloses to his or her doctor becomes PHI because a covered entity (the physician) receives it. But information that is created or received by anyone other than a covered entity is not protected under HIPAA. An example of health information that is not covered under HIPAA is health information that an individual discloses to the staff of a blood donor center that is not a covered entity. Many times, the nurses and medical professionals do not provide health care to the donor nor do they transmit health care information electronically in connection with payment related to the donation of blood. Using that example, the information that an individual discloses to the blood donation center staff is not PHI after the staff receives it. Another example is where a patient discloses his or her own health information to family and friends. HIPAA does not prevent family and friends from disclosing the health information to others. HIPAA does not require these types of recipients to keep the information confidential.

C. General Rules for Disclosure

Under the Privacy Rule, PHI is "disclosed" when it is released, transferred, or otherwise revealed to persons *outside* the covered entity that holds the PHI.[43] Unless one or more of the exclusions apply, HIPAA mandates that the covered entity or business associate obtain a HIPAA-compliant authorization before it discloses

---

41. *Id.*
42. 45 C.F.R. § 160.103.
43. *Id.*

PHI.[44] It is important to note that the authorization must comply with HIPAA's specific core elements.[45] The core elements of a HIPAA-compliant authorization and some optional elements are covered in Chapter 3.

There are several exclusions that allow the covered entity to disclose PHI without the individual's authorization. These are discussed in Chapter 4. As an overview, HIPAA prohibits covered entities from disclosing PHI without a patient's authorization unless the disclosure is made: (1) to the individual; (2) for treatment, payment, or health care operations (see Chapter 4 for further details); (3) for facility directories and to family and friends as long as the individual is notified and does not object; or (4) pursuant to exceptions listed in 45 C.F.R. § 512.[46]

Treatment, payment, or health care operations are covered in detail in Chapter 4, but here is a preview. "Treatment" is the provision, coordination, or management of health care and related services, including consultations, referrals, and coordination of health care with another health care provider.[47] "Payment" includes the activities involved in obtaining health insurance premiums, coverage, benefits, eligibility, billing, collection, preauthorization, appropriateness of care, justification of charges, and reimbursement, among others.[48] "Health care operations" are those activities that a covered entity engages in to conduct quality assessment and improvement; review the competence or qualifications of health care professionals; underwriting or premium rating; conduct or arrange for medical review, legal services, and auditing; engage in business planning and development; and manage business and general administrative activities.[49]

---

44. 45 C.F.R. § 164.502.
45. Id.
46. Id.
47. 45 C.F.R. § 164.501.
48. Id.
49. Id.

The government sought to effectively protect the privacy right of individuals; however, it had the foresight to realize that certain circumstances warranted disclosure. The government recognized the need to balance privacy rights with concerns for safety of the public and the individual. Along those lines, HIPAA allows covered entities to disclose PHI where there is a serious threat to health or safety of either the patient or the public.[50] The disclosure must be necessary to prevent or lessen a serious and imminent threat to the health or safety of a person or the public, and the disclosure must be made to someone who is reasonably able to prevent or lessen the threat, including the person who may be the target of that threat.[51]

Other permitted disclosures include those related to facility directories, next of kin, marketing purposes, fundraising, health oversight activities, judicial and administrative proceedings, law enforcement, public health activities, those required by law, research, workers' compensation, and victims of abuse, neglect, or domestic violence.[52] Certain specific required parameters under each of these types of disclosures must be met prior to disclosure of PHI. The HIPAA rule itself should be reviewed prior to making a disclosure under any of the categories mentioned. These categories will be discussed in detail in Chapter 4.

D. What If Other Laws Conflict with HIPAA?

HIPAA does not preempt state laws that are more stringent in protecting health information.[53] HIPAA is a "floor" for protecting the privacy of health information. HIPAA preempts state laws that are both contrary to HIPAA and less protective. State laws related to the privacy of health information that are *more* stringent than HIPAA remain in effect, even if they are contrary to HIPAA. A state law is more stringent when it provides greater privacy protection

---

50. 45 C.F.R. § 164.512(j).
51. *Id.*
52. *See* 45 C.F.R. §§ 164.501, 164.512, 164.514, and 164.522.
53. *Id.*

for the individual who is the subject of the information or greater access to the individual's own health information. HIPAA does not preempt state laws that govern public health investigations or the reporting of disease or injury, child abuse, birth, or death. State laws that require health plans to report or grant access to information for the purpose of audits, evaluation, or licensure remain in effect, even if they are less protective of individuals' privacy.[54]

II. Conclusion

HIPAA requires covered entities to protect personally identifiable health information. The HITECH Act extended these responsibilities to business associates of covered entities. Covered entities are health plans, health care clearinghouses, or health care providers that transmit any health information in electronic form in connection with health care transactions. Unless the disclosure falls into an exclusion, covered entities and business associates cannot disclose PHI without the individual's valid authorization. For it to be valid, the authorization must contain certain core elements that meet HIPAA requirements.

Not all records that contain health information are subject to HIPAA. Some information, such as student records, are not subject to HIPAA. The entity disclosing the information should be well versed in the rules that cover the type of records and their disclosure of those records.

HIPAA is the first federal law that sets a floor for the protection of the privacy of health information held by a broad range of entities. Prior to HIPAA, the states had a patchwork of laws that varied throughout the nation. For example, a person living in Hawaii had very different protections from someone living in Utah. A person moving from one state to another could not depend on the laws of the former state to protect his or her health information. It was difficult for individuals to understand the different

---

54. *Id.*

laws that varied from state to state. HIPAA provides a more uniform and consistent baseline for protection of health information. However, each state has its own laws that govern the privacy and security of health information. Some state laws are more stringent and protective than HIPAA. But HIPAA does not preempt state laws that are more stringent in protecting health information or those that give individuals greater right to access of their health information.

Chapter 3

Authorizations for Release of Protected Health Information

Unless a particular use or disclosure of protected health information (PHI) is permitted under HIPAA, the regulations require a HIPAA-compliant authorization signed by the individual who is the subject of the information. With a properly executed HIPAA-compliant authorization, there is no need to determine whether the release of PHI is appropriate. HIPAA mandates that the authorization for the release of PHI contain certain information. Beyond the specific HIPAA requirements, the authorization must also contain any information that the particular state mandates. All covered entities must be mindful of the HIPAA requirements as well as the individual state requirements to obtain PHI.

I. Consent versus Authorization: What's the Difference?

There are two types of permission that allow a covered entity to use or disclose PHI: consent and authorization.

A. Consent

HIPAA allows, but does not require, a general "consent" for use or disclosure of PHI for treatment, payment, and health care operations.[1] However, the individual's consent does not permit the covered entity to use or disclose PHI when an authorization is required or when another condition must be met for such use or disclosure. The covered entity may design the consent form as it sees fit. HIPAA does not define "consent" for the purposes of this provision nor does it mandate the substance of the consent form. An individual who refuses to sign the consent form may not realize that HIPAA does not require the covered entity to obtain the consent and subsequently, the refusal to sign a consent is of no consequence to the covered entity. The PHI may be used by the covered entity for treatment, payment, and health care operations even without the consent of the individual,[2] unless state law requires the consent.

B. Authorization

There are uses and disclosures for which an "authorization" is expressly required under HIPAA. The Privacy Rule requires a properly executed authorization for the release of any PHI that is not for treatment, payment, or health care operations;[3] directories at facilities;[4] family and friends;[5] marketing;[6] fundraising;[7] averting a serious threat to health or safety;[8] health oversight activities;[9] judicial and administrative proceedings;[10] law enforcement;[11]

---

1. Health Insurance Portability and Accountability Act of 1996, 45 C.F.R. § 164.506.
2. *Id.*
3. *Id.*
4. 45 C.F.R. § 164.510(a).
5. *Id.* § 164.510(b).
6. *Id.* §§ 164.501 and 164.508(a)(3).
7. *Id.* §§ 164.501, 164.514(f), and 164.522.
8. 45 C.F.R. § 164.512(j).
9. *Id.* § 164.512(d).
10. *Id.* § 164.512(e).
11. *Id.* § 164.512(f).

public health activities;[12] required by law;[13] research;[14] victims of abuse, neglect, or domestic violence;[15] and workers' compensation.[16] Chapter 4 gives a more detailed analysis of these exceptions.

For an authorization to comply with HIPAA, it must contain certain elements. The covered entity is obligated to be sure the authorization contains these elements or it risks disclosing information without the individual's proper permission. Let's examine these requirements.

II. Authorizations

A. Core Elements

HIPAA allows the disclosure of PHI pursuant to a valid authorization.[17] However, the authorization cannot be a generic, blanket authorization. It must comply with the requirements under HIPAA.[18] There are certain core elements that all HIPAA-compliant authorizations must contain. Of course, state laws may have additional requirements for authorizations. Nothing in HIPAA prohibits a state from mandating that an authorization contain more stringent requirements for release of PHI to a third party. A valid HIPAA-compliant authorization is a document that contains the following core elements.

---

12. *Id.* §§ 164.512(b) and 164.514(e).
13. *Id.* § 164.512(a).
14. *Id.* §§ 164.512(i) and 164.514(e).
15. *Id.* § 164.512(c).
16. *Id.* § 164.512(l).
17. *Id.* § 164.502(a)(1)(iv): "A covered entity may not use or disclose protected health information, except . . . pursuant to and in compliance with an authorization that complies with § 164.508."
18. *Id.*

1. Description

The authorization must provide a description of the PHI to be used or disclosed.[19] The description of the information to be used or disclosed must identify the information in a specific and meaningful fashion. The information must be described in such a way as to make known to the individual what information is being disclosed. However, the information does not need to be specifically named.

An authorization is valid if it authorizes the covered entity to use or disclose an "entire medical record" or "complete patient file." However, an authorization to use or disclose "all protected health information" without further clarification may not be specific enough, since protected health information encompasses a wider range of information than that which is generally included in the medical record, and individuals are less likely to understand the breadth of information that may be defined as "protected health information."[20]

2. Person Authorized to Disclose PHI

The authorization must contain the name or other specific identification of the person, persons, or class of person authorized to make the disclosure.[21] The individual may use one authorization form to authorize uses and disclosures by classes or categories of persons or entities, without naming the particular persons or entities.[22] For example, it is satisfactory if an authorization form authorizes disclosures by "any health plan, physician, health care professional, hospital, clinic, laboratory, pharmacy, medical facility, or other health care provider that has provided payment, treatment or services to me or on my behalf" or if an authorization

---

19. 45 C.F.R § 164.508(c)(1).
20. U.S. Dep't of Health & Human Servs. (HHS), Frequently Asked Questions (FAQs) 471 (HIPAA Authorizations), https://www.hhs.gov/hipaa/for-professionals/faq/471/may-a-covered-entity-use-or-disclose-a-patients-entire-medical-record-based-on-the-patients-authorized-signature/index.html (last visited Mar. 23, 2019).
21. 45 C.F.R § 164.508(c)(1)(i).
22. HHS FAQ 471, *supra* note 20.

form authorizes disclosures by "all medical sources."[23] "A separate authorization specifically naming each health care provider from whom protected health information may be sought is not required" by HIPAA.[24]

Generally, the authorization provides the name of the covered entity that controls the PHI. The authorization may, but is not required to, provide specific names of each health care provider that will disclose the PHI. For instance, a proper identification of the health care provider would be "Dr. Christopher Brooks," "Stein and Swartz, P.C.," "Holyoke Medical Center," "Birch Hill Medical Associates," or "Always Ready Health Plan."

An individual may have PHI at more than one location if the individual is being treated by several health care providers simultaneously. Providing the name of the person authorized to release the PHI puts the individual on notice as to which of the health care providers will disclose the PHI. For instance, an individual may have X-rays taken at different radiological and imaging services, but disclosure may be authorized to only one of the entities. It may be important to name the covered entity in the authorization.

3. Person Authorized to Receive PHI

Under HIPAA, the individual has a right to know who will be receiving the individual's PHI. The authorization must specifically list the party to whom the PHI will be disclosed by the covered entity. In lieu of a particular person, the authorization may identify a specific *group* of recipients or class of persons.[25] For instance, in a legal action for personal injury, a disclosure to the "Law Firm of Smith and Associates or its representatives" is valid even though the authorization does not provide a specific attorney or employee of the firm who will actually receive the PHI.

---

23. *Id.*
24. *Id.*
25. 45 C.F.R. § 164.508(c)(1)(iii).

4. Purpose

The authorization must contain a description of each purpose for the use or disclosure.[26] The purpose should have enough detail so as to give notice to the individual of the reason for the disclosure. For example, "for discovery purposes during litigation in the case of *Smith v. Jones*" and "for medical statistical and regulatory purposes related to the research of estrogen receptors" are acceptable descriptions.

An individual may sign an authorization for release of his or her PHI to himself or herself. In such instance, the statement "at the request of the individual" is a sufficient description of the purpose when an individual initiates the authorization and does not or chooses not to provide a statement of the purpose.[27]

5. Expiration Date or Event

HIPAA requires that an authorization contain either an expiration date or an expiration event that relates to the individual or the purpose of the use or disclosure.[28] For example, an authorization may expire "one year from the date the authorization is signed," "upon termination of the litigation, up through and including any time for appeal," "upon the minor's age of majority," or "upon termination of enrollment in the health plan." Unless the individual revokes the authorization in writing before the expiration date or event, the authorization remains valid until its expiration date or event. HIPAA permits the authorization to remain valid even when the expiration date on the authorization exceeds a time period established by state law.[29] The Privacy Rule does not provide a maximum time frame that the authorization is valid but some states

---

26. *Id.* § 164.508(c)(1)(iv).
27. *Id.*
28. *Id.* § 164.508(c)(v).
29. HHS FAQ 476, https://www.hhs.gov/hipaa/for-professionals/faq/476/must-an-authorization-include-an-expiration-date/index.html (last visited Mar. 23, 2019).

have laws that do. In that instance, the more restrictive state law may control how long the authorization is effective.[30]

6. Signature

HIPAA requires that the authorization contain the signature and identity of the individual whose PHI is being requested.[31] The HIPAA Privacy Rule does not require that a document be notarized or witnessed. If the individual has a person appointed to represent the individual for health care decisions, that personal representative may sign in place of the individual.[32] Authorizations may be signed electronically if the signature is valid under applicable law.[33]

a. Personal Representative

If the authorization is signed by the individual's personal representative, a description of the representative's authority to act for the individual must be provided in the authorization.[34] HIPAA does not address *how* a covered entity should confirm the identity of a personal representative. The covered entity should verify and identify the personal representative and must obtain any documentation, statements, or representations, whether oral or written, from the person requesting the PHI when such a documentation, statement, or representation is a condition of disclosure.[35]

The personal representative cannot be someone who has a general power of attorney or a specific power of attorney for other particular reasons, such as a power of attorney to close on real estate. For the purposes of HIPAA, an individual's personal representative is a person with authority under state law to make

---

30. *Id.*
31. 45 C.F.R. § 164.508(c)(1)(vi).
32. *Id.* § 164.502(g).
33. *See* HHS FAQ 554, https://www.hhs.gov/hipaa/for-professionals/faq/554/how-do-hipaa-authorizations-apply-to-electronic-health-information/index.html (last visited May 4, 2019).
34. *Id.*
35. 45 C.F.R. § 164.514(h).

health care decisions for the individual.[36] Except with respect to decedents, a covered entity must treat a personal representative as the individual *only* when that person has authority under law to act on the individual's behalf on matters related to health care.[37] If the power is limited, the covered entity must honor the authority only under those limited circumstances. For example, a person with an individual's limited health care power of attorney regarding only a specific treatment, such as use of artificial life support, is that individual's personal representative only with respect to PHI that relates to health care decisions pertaining to such purpose.[38]

Most importantly, the covered entity does not need to consider the personal representative as the individual if it believes, based on professional judgment and reasonable belief, that doing so would not be in the best interest of the individual because the personal representative is the source of domestic violence, abuse, or neglect toward the individual or because considering the personal representative as the individual would place the individual in danger.[39]

b. Parents and Unemancipated Minors

HIPAA generally allows a parent to have access to the medical records about his or her child, as the minor child's personal representative, when such access is consistent with state or other law.[40] There are three situations in which the parent would *not* be the minor's personal representative under the Privacy Rule:

---

36. HHS, Individuals' Right under HIPAA to Access their Health Information, https://www.hhs.gov/hipaa/for-professionals/privacy/guidance/access/index.html, and HHS, Personal Representatives, https://www.hhs.gov/hipaa/for-professionals/privacy/guidance/personal-representatives/index.html (last visited Mar. 23, 2019).
37. Id.
38. Id.
39. Id.
40. HHS, Individuals' Right under HIPAA to Access their Health Information, https://www.hhs.gov/hipaa/for-professionals/privacy/guidance/access/index.html, and HHS, Personal Representatives, https://www.hhs.gov/hipaa/for-professionals/privacy/guidance/personal-representatives/index.html (last visited Mar. 23, 2019).

(1) when the minor is the one who consents to care and the consent of the parent is not required under State or other applicable law, such as when a State law provides an adolescent the right to obtain mental health treatment without the consent of his or her parent, and the adolescent consents to such treatment without the parent's consent; (2) when someone other than the parent is authorized by law to consent to the provision of a particular health service to a minor, for instance a court may grant authority to make health care decisions for the minor to an adult other than the parent; and (3) when the parent agrees that the minor and the health care provider may have a confidential relationship, for example a physician asks the parent of a 16-year-old if the physician can talk with the child confidentially about a medical condition and the parent agrees. However, even in these exceptional situations, the parent may have access to the medical records of the minor related to this treatment when State or other applicable law requires or permits such parental access. Parental access would be denied when State or other law prohibits such access. If State or other applicable law is silent on a parent's right of access in these cases, the licensed health care provider may exercise his or her professional judgment to the extent allowed by law to grant or deny parental access to the minor's medical information.[41]

As is the case with respect to all personal representatives under the Privacy Rule, a provider may choose not to treat a parent as a personal representative when the provider reasonably believes, in his or her professional judgment, that the child has been or may be subjected to domestic violence, abuse, or neglect, or that treating the parent as the child's personal representative could endanger the child.[42]

---

41. *Id.*
42. *Id.*

c. Decedents

The HIPAA Privacy Rule protects the individually identifiable health information about a decedent for 50 years after the individual's date of death.[43] The individual's personally identifiable health information is no longer PHI after the individual has been deceased for more than 50 years.[44] The Privacy Rule protects the decedent's PHI to the same extent as it protects the PHI of living individuals, but there are special disclosure provisions related to deceased individuals. These allow a covered entity to disclose a decedent's health information: (1) to alert law enforcement to the death of the individual when there is a suspicion that death resulted from criminal conduct;[45] (2) to coroners or medical examiners and funeral directors;[46] (3) for research that is solely on the protected health information of decedents;[47] and (4) to organ procurement organizations or other entities engaged in the procurement, banking, or transplantation of cadaveric organs, eyes, or tissue for the purpose of facilitating organ, eye, or tissue donation and transplantation.[48]

In addition, the Privacy Rule permits a covered entity to disclose PHI about a decedent to a family member, or other person who was involved in the individual's health care or payment for care prior to the individual's death, unless doing so is inconsistent with any prior expressed preference of the deceased individual that is known to the covered entity. This may include disclosures to spouses, parents, children, domestic partners, other relatives, or friends of the decedent, provided the information disclosed is limited to that which is relevant to the person's involvement in the decedent's care or payment for care.[49]

---

43. 45 C.F.R. § 160.103(2)(iv).
44. *Id.*
45. 45 C.F.R. § 164.512(f)(4).
46. 45 C.F.R. § 164.512(g).
47. 45 C.F.R. § 164.512(i)(1)(iii).
48. 45 C.F.R. § 164.512(h).
49. 45 C.F.R. § 164.510(b)(5).

For uses or disclosures of a decedent's health information not otherwise permitted by the Privacy Rule, a covered entity must obtain a written HIPAA authorization from a personal representative of the decedent who can authorize the disclosure. A decedent's personal representative is an executor, administrator, or other person who has authority under applicable state or other law to act on behalf of the decedent or the decedent's estate.[50] It is worth noting that the individual's personal representative during life may be different from the personal representative after the individual is deceased. For example, the individual may choose to name a spouse as the health care proxy but may select someone different to be the executor of his or her estate.

d. Date

The authorization must also contain the date that the individual or personal representative signs the authorization.[51] A covered entity may disclose PHI specified in an authorization even if the information was created after the authorization was signed by the individual, if the authorization encompasses the category of information that was later created and the authorization has not expired or been revoked by the individual.[52] Unless the authorization otherwise expressly limits the disclosure, a covered entity may use or disclose the PHI identified in the authorization regardless of when the information was created.[53]

---

50. 45 C.F.R. § 164.502(g)(4).
51. 45 C.F.R. § 164.508(c)(1)(vi).
52. HHS FAQ 477, https://www.hhs.gov/hipaa/for-professionals/faq/477/may-a-covered-entity-disclose-protected-health-information-specified-in-an-authorization/index.html (last visited Mar. 23, 2019).
53. *Id.*

B. Required Statements in Authorizations

In addition to the core elements of an authorization, HIPAA requires that the authorization contain certain statements in order to put the individual on notice of specific conditions.

1. Right to Revoke

The authorization must contain a statement that notifies the individual of his or her right to revoke the authorization.[54] HIPAA allows an individual to revoke an authorization at any time *provided that* a covered entity did not rely on the authorization to make a use or disclosure of the individual's PHI. The revocation must be in writing and becomes effective when the covered entity receives it, not when a third party receives it.[55] The process for revocation must be clearly stated in the authorization, or if the covered entity creates the authorization and it has the revocation process in its notice of privacy practices, the authorization may refer to the notice of privacy practices.[56] The revocation is not effective if it involves a HIPAA authorization related to obtaining insurance coverage.[57]

2. Treatment, Payment, Enrollment, or Eligibility Not Affected

The authorization must expressly contain statements that notify the individual that the covered entity may not condition the provision of treatment, payment, enrollment in a health plan, or eligibility for benefits on the individual's failure to provide an authorization

---

54. 45 C.F.R. § 164.508(c)(2)(i).
55. HHS FAQ 474, https://www.hhs.gov/hipaa/for-professionals/faq/474/can-an-individual-revoke-his-or-her-authorization/index.html (last visited Mar. 24, 2019).
56. *Id.*
57. *Id.*

for release of PHI.[58] If applicable, the authorization must also list the following exceptions, or the consequences to the exceptions:

- A provider may condition the provision of research-related treatment.[59]
- A health plan may condition enrollment in the health plan or eligibility for benefits.[60]

3. Redisclosure

The authorization must explain that once the PHI is disclosed to the recipient, it may no longer be protected under the HIPAA Privacy Rule and there is a potential for redisclosure by the recipient to another entity.[61] HIPAA applies only to covered entities. The individual must be on notice that if a covered entity discloses PHI to a noncovered entity via a valid authorization, the noncovered entity is not prohibited by federal law from disclosing the health information to others.

C. Other Requirements for Authorizations

1. Plain Language

The authorization must be written in plain language.[62] Plain language is not defined in the regulations, but is sometimes considered to be around an eighth-grade reading level. There should be no complicated concepts, difficult phrases or words, or legal or medical terminology that may confuse the individual. The authorization should be readily understandable by an individual who completed grade school. HIPAA does not specifically require the authorization to be in any foreign language; however, state law may

---

58. 45 C.F.R. § 164.508(c)(2)(ii).
59. 45 C.F.R. § 164.508(b)(4)(i).
60. *Id.*
61. 45 C.F.R. § 164.508(c)(2)(iii).
62. 45 C.F.R. § 164.508(c)(3).

require that the authorization be translated into the individual's native language. Additionally, the Office for Civil Rights, which enforces HIPAA, also enforces Title VI of the Civil Rights Act of 1964, which requires recipients of federal financial assistance to make reasonable efforts to make their services accessible to those with limited English proficiency.[63]

2. Copy to the Individual

If the covered entity requests an authorization from an individual, the covered entity must provide the individual with a copy of the signed authorization.[64] The individual has a right to have a copy of the authorization if the covered entity has presented the authorization.

D. Other Considerations for Authorizations

1. Copy of an Authorization

HIPAA permits a covered entity to use or disclose PHI pursuant to a copy of a valid and signed authorization, including a copy that is received by fax or electronically transmitted.[65]

2. Authorizations Prepared by Third Parties

Under HIPAA, a covered entity is permitted to use or disclose protected health information pursuant to any authorization that meets the Privacy Rule's requirements at 45 C.F.R. § 164.508. As previously stated, HIPAA requires that an authorization contain certain core elements and statements, but it does not specify who may draft an authorization; therefore, it may be drafted by any entity. A valid authorization created by another covered entity

---

63. *See* HHS, Limited English Proficiency, https://www.hhs.gov/civil-rights/for-individuals/special-topics/limited-english-proficiency/index.html (last visited May 4, 2019).
64. 45 C.F.R. § 164.508(c)(4).
65. HHS FAQ 475, https://www.hhs.gov/hipaa/for-professionals/faq/475/is-a-copy-of-a-signed-authorization-valid/index.html (last visited Mar. 24, 2019).

or a third party, such as an attorney, a state bar association, an insurance company, or a researcher, may be used by the covered entity to disclose PHI.[66]

3. No Required Format

HIPAA does not specify or dictate any particular format for an authorization.[67] The authorization may contain any sequence of the core elements and required statements as long as the authorization includes the necessary provisions. Also, the authorization does not need to be notarized or witnessed.[68]

4. Cover Letter Accompanying the Authorization

A transmittal or cover letter cannot be used to expand the scope of the authorization to include PHI not described in the authorization.[69] However, a transmittal or a cover letter can be used to narrow or provide specifics about a request for protected health information as described in an authorization.[70] For example, if an individual authorized the disclosure of "all medical records" to an attorney, the attorney could by cover letter narrow the request to the medical records for the last two years. The cover letter could also specify a particular employee or address for the "class of persons" designated in the authorization to receive the information. But a recipient could not by cover letter extend the time of expiration of an authorization or increase the scope of information set forth in the authorization.

---

66. HHS FAQ 472, https://www.hhs.gov/hipaa/for-professionals/faq/472/does-hipaa-permit-a-covered-entity-to-use-or-disclose-protected-health-information/index.html (last visited Mar. 24, 2019).
67. Id.
68. HHS FAQ 478, https://www.hhs.gov/hipaa/for-professionals/faq/478/does-the-privacy-rule-require-an-authorization-be-notarized/index.html (last visited Mar. 24, 2019).
69. HHS FAQ 479, https://www.hhs.gov/hipaa/for-professionals/faq/479/can-an-authorization-be-used-together-with-other-written-instructions/index.html (last visited Mar. 24, 2019).
70. Id.

5. Exempt from Minimum Necessary Requirement

Generally, when using, disclosing, or responding to a request for PHI, a covered entity must make reasonable efforts to limit the PHI to the minimum necessary to accomplish the intended purpose of the use, disclosure, or request for PHI.[71] However, uses and disclosures that are authorized by the individual are exempt from the minimum necessary requirements.[72] For example, if a covered health care provider receives an individual's authorization to disclose medical information to an attorney for litigation purposes, the provider is permitted to disclose the information requested on the authorization without making any minimum necessary determination. Bear in mind that the authorization must meet the requirements of 45 C.F.R. § 164.508 as stated above.

Once you have drafted an authorization that complies with HIPAA, you must also be sure that the authorization complies with other laws, which we will now consider.

III. Federal Trade Commission Act

If you plan to share consumer health information, the authorization must also comply with the Federal Trade Commission Act (FTC Act).[73] The FTC Act prohibits companies from engaging in deceptive or unfair acts or practices in or affecting commerce. Companies must not mislead consumers about what is happening with their health information.

Your business must consider all of your statements to consumers to make sure that, taken together, they do not create a deceptive or misleading impression. Even if you believe your authorization meets all the elements required by the HIPAA Privacy Rule, if the information surrounding the authorization is deceptive or misleading, it could be a violation of the FTC Act.

---

71. 45 C.F.R. § 164.502(b).
72. *Id.*
73. 15 U.S.C. §§ 41–58, as amended.

To comply with the FTC Act, review your entire user interface. Do not bury key facts in links to a privacy policy, terms of use, or the HIPAA authorization. For example, if you are claiming that a consumer is providing health information only to her doctor, do not require her to click on a "patient authorization" link to learn that it is also going to be viewable by the public. Do not promise to keep information confidential in large, boldface type, but then ask the consumer in a much less prominent manner to sign an authorization that says you will share it. Evaluate the size, color, and graphics of all of your disclosure statements to ensure they are clear and conspicuous.

Take into account the various devices consumers may use to view your disclosure claims. If you share consumer health information in unexpected ways, design your interface so that "scrolling" is not necessary to find that out. For example, you cannot promise prominently on a web page not to share information, only to require consumers to scroll down through several lines of a HIPAA authorization to get the full story.

Tell consumers the full plan before asking them to make a material decision—for example, before they decide to send or post information that may be shared publicly. Review your user interface for contradictions and get rid of them.

The same requirements apply to paper disclosure statements. Do not give consumers a stack of papers where the top page says that their health information is going to their doctor, but another page requests permission to share that health information with a pharmaceutical firm.

For additional guidance on creating effective disclosures, look at the FTC's Disclosures report.[74] If you have a health app, do not forget to consult the mobile health apps interactive tool, the FTC's best practices guidance for mobile health app developers, and the

---

74. FTC's Disclosures Report is available at https://www.ftc.gov/sites/default/files/attachments/press-releases/ftc-staff-revises-online-advertising-disclosure-guidelines/130312dotcomdisclosures.pdf.

Office for Civil Rights developer portal. And when you tell consumers about how you share consumer health information, always remember the FTC Act as well as HIPAA.[75]

IV. State Law Requirements

HIPAA is a federal law that may or may not supersede state laws that provide for the authorization of disclosure of medical information. HIPAA preempts state laws that are contrary to HIPAA and less protective of PHI, providing a "floor" for the minimum requirements for protection of confidentiality and privacy of PHI.[76] HIPAA allows existing or future state laws that are more stringent than the federal rule at protecting PHI to remain in effect, even when the state law is contrary to HIPAA.[77]

A. HIPAA Preempts State Laws

Generally, HIPAA preempts state laws and this general rule applies *unless* there is a condition that falls under one of the following exceptions:

1. Where the Secretary of the U.S. Department of Health and Human Services (HHS) determines that the state law is necessary
   a. To prevent fraud and abuse related to the provision of health care
   b. To ensure appropriate state regulation of insurance and health plans
   c. For state reporting on health care delivery costs
   d. For purposes of a compelling need related to public health, safety, or welfare, and the intrusion into privacy is warranted when balanced against the need.

---

75. HHS, Sharing Consumer Health Information?, https://www.hhs.gov/hipaa/for-professionals/special-topics/hipaa-ftc-act/index.html (last visited Mar. 24, 2019).
76. 45 C.F.R. § 160.203.
77. 45 C.F.R. § 160.203(b).

2. Where the purpose of the state law is to regulate the manufacture, registration, distribution, dispensing, or other control of any controlled substances.
3. Where state law relates to the privacy of PHI and it is more stringent than HIPAA.
4. Where state law provides for the reporting of disease, injury, child abuse, birth, or death or for the conduct of public health surveillance, investigation, or intervention.
5. Where state law requires a health plan to report or provide access to information for the purpose of management audits, financial audits, program monitoring and evaluation, or the licensure or certification of facilities or individuals.[78]

In the circumstances listed above, a covered entity is not required to comply with a contrary provision of the HIPAA Privacy Rule. Additionally, a person, state, or other entity may request that HHS analyze a provision of state law to determine whether a state law provision that is apparently contrary to HIPAA may meet additional criteria that will prevent preemption by HIPAA.[79] In response to a request, preemption of a contrary state law will not occur if the designated HHS official determines that one of the following criteria apply: the state law (1) is necessary to prevent fraud and abuse related to the provision of or payment for health care; (2) is necessary to ensure appropriate state regulation of insurance and health plans to the extent expressly authorized by statute or regulation; (3) is necessary for state reporting on health care delivery or costs; (4) is necessary for purposes of serving a compelling public health, safety, or welfare need, and, if a Privacy Rule provision is at issue, the Secretary determines that the intrusion into privacy is warranted when balanced against the need to be served; or (5) has as its principal purpose the regulation of the manufacture, registration, distribution, dispensing, or other control

---

78. 45 C.F.R. § 160.203.
79. 45 C.F.R. § 160.204.

of any controlled substances (as defined in 21 U.S.C. § 802), or that is deemed a controlled substance by state law.[80]

It is important to recognize that only state laws that are contrary to the federal requirements are eligible for an exemption determination.[81] For these purposes under HIPAA, "contrary" means that it would be impossible for a covered entity to comply with both the state and federal requirements, or that the provision of state law is an obstacle to accomplishing the full purposes and objectives of the Administrative Simplification provisions of HIPAA.[82]

B. Elements of Authorizations under State Law

As previously stated, HIPAA provides a floor by which health information is protected from unauthorized disclosures. Where a state law provision relates to the privacy of PHI and is more stringent than HIPAA, the state law prevails. Thus, where a state requires additional safeguards and clauses in the authorization for release of PHI, the authorization must contain the state law requirements in addition to the HIPAA requirements for authorizations. For instance, where a state law mandates that an individual recipient of the PHI be recorded in the authorization, it is not acceptable to list a general class of recipients, as HIPAA would allow.

C. Psychiatric Records under State Law

Many states treat mental health records more stringently than health information involving physical conditions. In light of the more stringent requirements by some states, it may be necessary for an authorization for release of PHI containing mental health information to contain additional safeguards and privacy protection guarantees. HIPAA does not preempt the more stringent state laws for mental health PHI. Where state law has additional

---

80. 45 C.F.R. § 160.203.
81. *Id.*
82. 45 C.F.R. § 160.202.

provisions for the release of psychiatric or mental health records, the covered entity must ensure that the authorization for release of mental health PHI complies with state laws as well as with the HIPAA Privacy Rule.

V. Conclusion

A HIPAA-compliant authorization for release of protected health information must meet several federal and state law mandatory requirements. It is key for the covered entity to be aware of these requirements. If the authorization lacks these provisions, the covered entity should reject the authorization and refuse to disclose the information until it receives a HIPAA-compliant authorization.

Chapter 4

Disclosures without Authorizations

One of the main goals of the HIPAA Privacy Rule is to protect health information from being disclosed to the wrong person at the wrong time or for the wrong reason. HIPAA provides limited means by which a third party is able to view or obtain protected health information (PHI). There are safeguards that covered entities are required to follow in order to disclose PHI. The most straightforward method for obtaining an individual's medical record is simply to have the individual sign a HIPAA-compliant authorization, as discussed in Chapter 3. However, there are times when it is not possible, practical, or even permissible to obtain the individual's written authorization. HIPAA has exceptions for various circumstances in which it is just not feasible to obtain an authorization for release of PHI.

I. Treatment, Payment, or Health Care Operations

The Privacy Rule allows the health care provider to disclose PHI for its own treatment, payment, or health care operations.[1] The health care provider may disclose PHI for treatment activities of another health care provider.[2] The health care provider may disclose PHI to another covered entity or a health care provider for the payment activities of the entity that receives the information.[3] The Privacy Rule also allows disclosure to another covered entity or health care provider for treatment, payment, or operation activities of the entity that receives the information if that entity had a relationship with the individual who is the subject of the PHI being requested, the information pertains to such relationship, *and* the disclosure is for the purpose of (1) conducting quality assessment and improvement activities; or (2) reviewing the competence or qualifications of health care professionals; evaluating practitioner, provider or health plan performance; or conducting training programs, accreditation, certification, licensing, or credentialing activities.[4] The covered entity may also disclose PHI for the purpose of detecting health care fraud and abuse.[5] Additionally, if the covered entity participates in an organized health care arrangement, it may disclose PHI to another covered entity that also participates in the same organized health care arrangement.[6]

A. Treatment

Treatment is the provision, coordination, or management of health care and related services, including consultations, referrals, and

---

1. Health Insurance Portability and Accountability Act of 1996 (HIPAA), 45 C.F.R. § 164.506 (2003).
2. *Id.*
3. *Id.*
4. 45 C.F.R. § 164.506(c)(4)(i) and 45 C.F.R. § 164.501.
5. 45 C.F.R. § 164.506(c)(4)(ii).
6. 45 C.F.R. § 164.506(5).

coordination of health care between different health care providers.[7] Section 164.506 of HIPAA allows health care providers to discuss the individual's health condition, diagnosis, prognosis, and treatment without violating confidentiality. Consulting with another health care provider about a patient is within the HIPAA Privacy Rule's definition of "treatment" and, therefore, is permissible. In addition, a health care provider (or other covered entity) is expressly permitted to disclose PHI about an individual to a health care provider for that provider's treatment of the individual.[8] For example, a radiologist may discuss the results of a mammogram with the individual's obstetrician or gynecologist without the individual's explicit authorization in order to manage the diagnosis, prognosis, and care of that patient. In the same respect, a physician does not need a patient's written authorization to send a copy of the patient's medical record to a specialist or other health care provider who will treat the patient.

As a practical matter, a pharmacist may use professional judgment and experience with common practice to make reasonable inferences of the patient's best interest in allowing a person other than the patient to pick up a prescription.[9] For example, a relative or friend may go to the pharmacy and ask to pick up a specific prescription for an individual. As long as the individual does not object, the Privacy Rule allows the pharmacist to give the filled prescription to the relative or friend.

B. Payment

The covered entity may use or disclose PHI for its own payment or disclose to another covered entity for the payment activities of the entity that receives the information.[10] Payment includes

---

7. 45 C.F.R. § 164.501.
8. U.S. Dep't of Health & Human Servs. (HHS), Frequently Asked Questions (FAQs), Health Information Privacy, https://www.hhs.gov/hipaa/for-professionals/faq/488/does-hipaa-permit-a-doctor-to-discuss-a-patients-health-status-with-the-patients-family-and-friends/index.html (last visited Mar. 30, 2019).
9. 45 C.F.R. § 164.510(b).
10. 45 C.F.R. § 164.506.

the activities involved in obtaining health insurance premiums, coverage, benefits, eligibility, billing, collection, preauthorization, appropriateness of care, justification of charges, and reimbursement, among others.[11] The Privacy Rule permits a covered entity, or a business associate acting on behalf of a covered entity (e.g., a collection agency), to disclose PHI as necessary to obtain payment for health care, and does not limit to whom such a disclosure may be made. Therefore, a covered entity, or its business associate, may contact persons other than the individual to obtain payment for health care services.[12] However, the Privacy Rule requires a covered entity, or its business associate, to reasonably limit the amount of information disclosed for such purposes to the minimum necessary, as well as to abide by any reasonable requests for confidential communications and any agreed-to restrictions on the use or disclosure of PHI.[13] For example, HIPAA permits the disclosure of PHI in order to bill for services provided by a physician, but only the minimum necessary amount of PHI may be disclosed. HIPAA also allows a provider to disclose PHI to a health plan for the plan's administrative purposes, so long as the period for which information is needed overlaps with the period in which the individual is or was enrolled in the health plan.

The Privacy Rule permits covered entities to continue to use the services of debt collection agencies. Debt collection is recognized as a payment activity within the "payment" definition.[14] Through a business associate arrangement, the covered entity may engage a debt collection agency to perform this function on its behalf. Disclosures to collection agencies are governed by other provisions of the Privacy Rule, such as the business associate and minimum necessary requirements. Where a use or disclosure of PHI is necessary for the covered entity to fulfill a legal duty, the Privacy Rule permits such use or disclosure as required by law.

---

11. *Id.* and 45 C.F.R. § 164.501.
12. 45 C.F.R. § 164.506(c) and the definition of "payment" at § 164.501.
13. 45 C.F.R. §§ 164.502(b), 164.514(d), and 164.522.
14. 45 C.F.R. § 164.501.

The Privacy Rule's definition of "payment" includes disclosures to consumer reporting agencies.[15] These disclosures, however, are limited to the following PHI about the individual: name and address, date of birth, social security number, payment history, and account number. In addition, disclosure of the name and address of the health care provider or health plan making the report is allowed. The covered entity may perform this payment activity directly, or may carry out this function through a third party, such as a collection agency, under a business associate arrangement. The Privacy Rule permits uses and disclosures by the covered entity or its business associate as may be required by the Fair Credit Reporting Act (FCRA) or other law. There is no conflict between the Privacy Rule and legal duties imposed on data furnishers by FCRA.

C. Health Care Operations

The Privacy Rule permits a covered health care provider to disclose PHI for "health care operations" purposes, subject to certain requirements.[16] Health care operations are those activities a covered entity engages in to conduct quality assessment and improvement; review the competence or qualifications of health care professionals; underwrite or rate premiums; conduct or arrange for medical review, legal services, and auditing; plan and develop business; conduct business management; and perform general administrative activities.[17]

Disclosures by a covered health care provider to a professional liability insurer or a similar entity for the purpose of obtaining or maintaining medical liability coverage or for the purpose of obtaining benefits from such insurance, including reporting adverse events, fall within "business management and general administrative activities" under the definition of "health care operations." Therefore, a covered health care provider may disclose individually

---

15. *Id.*
16. 45 C.F.R. § 164.506.
17. *Id.*

identifiable health information to a professional liability insurer to the same extent as the provider is able to disclose such information for other health care operations purposes.[18] For example, when a patient brings a legal action against his or her health care provider, 45 C.F.R. §§ 164.506 and 164.502(a)(1)(ii) allow disclosure of the patient's PHI to the attorney representing the health care provider, without an authorization from the patient. However, the attorney representing the physician must have a business associate agreement in place prior to the disclosure of PHI.[19]

1. Business Associate Agreement

A business associate is a person who, on behalf of a covered entity, performs or assists in the performance of a function or activity involving the use or disclosure of PHI for claims processing, administration, data analysis, processing or administration, utilization review, quality assurance, billing, benefit management, practice management, and repricing; or provides legal, actuarial, accounting, consulting, data aggregation, management, administrative, accreditation, or financial services to or for such covered entity, or to or for an organized health care arrangement in which the covered entity participates, where the provision of the service involves the disclosure of PHI from a covered entity or from another business associate.[20] Members of the covered entity's workforce are not business associates.[21]

When a covered entity discloses PHI to a business associate, it must enter into an agreement with the business associate to ensure that the business associate will handle the PHI confidentially and in the same manner that HIPAA requires the covered entity to handle it. This agreement is a business associate agreement, or it can be a

---

18. *See id.* § 164.502(a)(1)(ii) and the definition of "health care operations" at § 164.501.
19. Business associates and business associate agreements are discussed in Chapter 5 and Appendix B.
20. 45 C.F.R. § 160.103.
21. *Id.*

memorandum of understanding for certain government entities. HIPAA requires a covered entity to have a written business associate agreement prior to the covered entity sharing any PHI with a business associate.[22] In fact, the Office for Civil Rights (OCR) has strongly reinforced the need for business associate agreements and has imposed sanctions on covered entities for failure to obtain business associate agreements.

Prior to 2016, enforcement of the business associate requirement was uncommon. However, in early 2016, the OCR began to ramp up its efforts. Two of those enforcement actions resulted in significant settlements for potentially violating HIPAA Privacy and Security Rules by failing to execute business associate agreements. These included a nonprofit health care system in Minnesota that agreed to settle charges that it failed to obtain a business associate agreement with a major contractor and failed to institute an organization-wide risk analysis to address risks and vulnerabilities to its patient information. The settlement amount was $1,550,000. An orthopedic clinic in North Carolina agreed to settle charges of failing to execute a business associate agreement prior to turning over PHI to a potential business partner. That entity settled for $750,000. In addition to the significant settlement amounts, there were robust corrective action plans.[23]

A business associate agreement is not required with persons or organizations whose functions, activities, or services do not involve the use or disclosure of PHI, and where any access to PHI by such persons would be incidental, if at all.[24] For instance, janitorial services that clean the offices or facilities of a covered entity are not business associates because the work they perform does not involve the use or disclosure of PHI, and any disclosure

---

22. 45 C.F.R. § 164.502(a).
23. *See* North Memorial Health Care Resolution Agreement, *available at* https://www.hhs.gov/sites/default/files/north-memorial-ra-and-cap-march-2016.pdf; Raleigh Orthopaedic Clinic, P.A. Resolution Agreement, *available at* https://www.hhs.gov/sites/default/files/raleigh-orthopaedic-racap.pdf.
24. 45 C.F.R. § 164.506.

of PHI to janitorial personnel that occurs in the performance of their duties (such as may occur while emptying trash cans) is limited in nature, occurs as a by-product of their janitorial duties, and cannot reasonably be prevented.[25] Such disclosures are incidental and permitted by the HIPAA Privacy Rule.[26]

If a service is hired to do work for a covered entity where disclosure of PHI is not limited in nature (such as routine handling of records or shredding of documents containing PHI), it likely would be a business associate.[27] However, when such work is performed under the direct control of the covered entity (e.g., on the covered entity's premises), the Privacy Rule permits the covered entity to treat the service as part of its workforce, and the covered entity need not enter into a business associate contract with the service.[28]

In the same respect, plumbers, electricians, and photocopier repair technicians do not require access to PHI to perform their services, so they do not meet the definition of a "business associate."[29] Under the HIPAA Privacy Rule, "business associates" are contractors or other nonworkforce members hired to do the work of, or for, a covered entity that involves the use or disclosure of PHI.[30] Any disclosure of PHI to such technicians that occurs in the performance of their duties (such as may occur walking through or working in file rooms) is limited in nature, occurs as a by-product of their duties, and cannot reasonably be prevented. Such disclosures are incidental and permitted by the Privacy Rule.[31]

Additionally, the Privacy Rule does not require a covered entity to enter into business associate agreements with organizations that merely act as conduits for PHI, such as the U.S. Postal Service, certain private couriers, and their electronic equivalents.[32] A conduit

---

25. Id.
26. 45 C.F.R. § 164.502(a)(1)(iii).
27. 45 C.F.R. § 164.502(a)(3) and (4).
28. Id.
29. Id.
30. Id.
31. 45 C.F.R. § 164.502(a)(1).
32. 45 C.F.R. § 164.506.

transports information but does not access it other than on a variable or occasional basis as necessary for the performance of the transportation service or as required by law. Since no disclosure is intended by the covered entity, and the probability of exposure of any particular PHI to a conduit is very small, a conduit is not a business associate of the covered entity.[33]

However, the HIPAA Privacy Rule explicitly defines organizations that accredit covered entities as "business associates."[34] Similar to other business associates, accreditation organizations provide a service to the covered entity that requires sharing of PHI. The business associate provisions may be satisfied by standard or model contract forms that require little or no modification for each covered entity. As an alternative to the business associate contract, covered entities may disclose a limited data set of PHI, not including direct identifiers, to an accreditation organization, subject to a data use agreement.[35] If only a limited data set of PHI is disclosed, the satisfactory assurances required of the business associate are satisfied by the data use agreement.[36]

Again, a covered entity may permit a business associate to create, receive, maintain, or transmit PHI on the covered entity's behalf only if the covered entity obtains satisfactory assurances that the business associate will appropriately safeguard the information.[37] To obtain that end, there must be a contract or agreement between the covered entity and the business associate that provides that the business associate will (1) implement administrative, physical, and technical safeguards that reasonably and appropriately protect the confidentiality, integrity, and availability of the PHI that it creates, receives, maintains, or transmits on behalf of the covered entity; (2) ensure that any agent, including a subcontractor to whom it provides PHI, agrees to implement reasonable and appropriate

---

33. *Id.*
34. See the definition of "business associate" at HIPAA, 45 C.F.R. § 160.103.
35. 45 C.F.R. § 164.514(e).
36. 45 C.F.R. § 164.506.
37. 45 C.F.R. § 164.308(b)(1).

safeguards to protect the PHI; (3) report to the covered entity any security incident of which it becomes aware; and (4) authorize the termination of the contract by the covered entity, if the covered entity determines that the business associate violated a material term of the contract.[38]

When in doubt as to whether a business associate agreement is needed, it is best for the covered entity to obtain a business associate agreement.[39]

2. Implementation of Safeguards

The business associate must safeguard the PHI on behalf of the covered entity.[40] The Health Information Technology for Economic and Clinical Health Act[41] (HITECH) requires business associates to comply with the administrative, physical, and technical safeguards for electronic PHI under the HIPAA Security Rule in the same manner as a covered entity. Business associates must develop and establish a written data security program for electronic PHI that complies with the HIPAA Security Rule. There must be certain physical limitations that allow only proper personnel to have access to the PHI. For example, written PHI should be kept in locked storage units. The business associate must also provide technical safeguards. For example, specific pass codes and firewalls should be in place to prevent unauthorized access to electronic PHI.

---

38. 45 C.F.R. § 164.308(b)(1) and § 164.314.

39. Sample business associate agreement terms can be found at HHS, Business Associate Contracts, https://www.hhs.gov/hipaa/for-professionals/covered-entities/sample-business-associate-agreement-provisions/index.html, as well as in Appendix B.

40. *Id.*

41. Pub. L. No. 111-5, 123 Stat. 115, 226 (Feb. 17, 2009); 42 U.S.C. 17931 (Feb. 17, 2009): Application of security provisions and penalties to business associates of covered entities; annual guidance on security provisions, *available at* https://www.hhs.gov/sites/default/files/ocr/privacy/hipaa/understanding/coveredentities/hitechact.pdf. The Health Information Technology for Economic and Clinical Health Act (HITECH) is part of the federal Stimulus Bill signed into law by President Obama on February 17, 2009. HITECH significantly expands the HIPAA Privacy Rule and Security Standards and adds new requirements concerning privacy and security for protected health information that materially and directly affect business associates.

Just as the HIPAA Privacy Rule permits a covered entity to share PHI with another covered entity, the covered entity is permitted to make the disclosure directly to a business associate acting on behalf of that other covered entity.[42]

3. Agents of Business Associates

The business associate must receive reasonable assurances from its agents (i.e., subcontractors) that the agents will implement safeguards to protect the privacy of the PHI.[43] These reasonable assurances should contain information that the business associate can depend on in the event of a breach. HIPAA does not provide the content of the reasonable assurances agreement nor does it mandate that the reasonable assurances be in writing. However, a written agreement to protect PHI that specifically describes the procedures that the agent took is more reliable than an oral agreement between the business associate and its agent. It is important to remember that the business associate works on behalf of the covered entity. A breach of confidentiality of PHI creates an obligation on the part of the covered entity to obtain information from the business associate as to those measures that the business associate took to prevent the breach. A written document for reasonable assurances between the business associate and its agent allows a straightforward approach to providing the covered entity with the information it needs to respond to an inquiry about a breach.

4. Security Incident Reporting

In addition to taking appropriate steps to remedy or mitigate a security incident, the business associate has a duty to report the incident to the covered entity.[44] Also, 45 C.F.R § 164.304 defines

---

42. 45 C.F.R. § 164.506.
43. 45 C.F.R. § 314(a)(2)(i)(B).
44. HITECH, 42 U.S.C. 17932 § 13402, Notification in the Case of a Breach, *available at* https://www.hhs.gov/sites/default/files/ocr/privacy/hipaa/understanding/coveredentities/hitechact.pdf.

a "security incident" as "the attempted or successful unauthorized access, use, disclosure, modification, or destruction of information or interference with system operations in an information system." Section 164.314(a)(2)(i)(C) requires that the contract between the covered entity and business associate obligate the business associate to "report to the covered entity any security incident of which it becomes aware."[45]

However, HIPAA allows a flexible approach to the reporting requirement.[46] HIPAA provides that:

1. Covered entities may use any security measures that allow the covered entity to reasonably and appropriately implement the standards and implementation specifications as specified in 45 C.F.R. § 164.306(b).
2. In deciding which security measures to use, a covered entity must take into account the following factors:
   a. The size, complexity, and capabilities of the covered entity
   b. The covered entity's technical infrastructure, hardware, and software security capabilities
   c. The costs of security measures
   d. The probability and criticality of potential risks to electronic PHI[47]

The cost of reporting every attempted unauthorized access may greatly exceed the anticipated benefit and would be contrary to HIPAA.[48] Therefore, not every attempted access through a firewall needs to be reported by the business associate as a security incident. HIPAA allows for some reasonableness in policies, standards, guidelines, and contract terms. The key is to apply reasonable processes based upon the risks or threats involved. A covered entity may need to have different reporting requirements depending

---

45. 45 C.F.R. § 164.314(a)(2)(i)(C).
46. 45 C.F.R. § 164.306(b).
47. *Id.*
48. 45 C.F.R. § 164.306(b)(2)(iii).

upon the service provided. For example, there should be very strict reporting requirements for the company providing in-home hospice care to the covered entity's HIV patients and less stringent ones for the company performing the covered entity's patient satisfaction surveys.

5. Termination of the Contract by the Covered Entity

HIPAA mandates that the covered entity terminate the business associate agreement if the covered entity determines that the business associate violated a material term of the contract.[49]

6. Reasonable Assurances Agreement

The contract between the covered entity and the business associate may permit the business associate to use the PHI in its capacity for the proper management and administration of the business associate or to carry out the legal responsibilities of the business associate, provided that (1) the disclosure is required by law or (2) the business associate obtains *reasonable assurances* from the person to whom the information is disclosed that the PHI will be held confidentially and used or further disclosed only as required by law or for the purpose for which it was disclosed, and the person notifies the business associate of any breaches in the confidentiality of the PHI of which it is aware.[50]

The business associate must ensure that any agent, including a subcontractor, to whom it provides PHI received from, created by, or received by the business associate on behalf of the covered entity agrees to the same restrictions and conditions that apply to the business associate.[51] In other words, the business associate has a duty to guard the PHI (as discussed earlier) and make certain

---

49. 45 C.F.R. § 164.314(a)(2)(i)(D).
50. 45 C.F.R. § 164.504(e)(4).
51. *See id.* § 164.504(e)(2)(i)(D).

that any agent is aware of and abides by the same restrictions and conditions as the business associate.

II. Averting a Serious Threat to Health or Safety

As long as the use or disclosure is consistent with applicable laws and standards of ethical conduct, a covered entity may use or disclose PHI if the covered entity, in good faith, believes that the use or disclosure is necessary to prevent or lessen a serious and imminent threat to the health or safety of a person or the public. The disclosure must be made to a person reasonably able to prevent or lessen the threat, including someone who is a target of the threat, *or* the disclosure must be necessary for law enforcement authorities to identify or apprehend an individual.[52] For example, if a school bus driver, who is a patient, has a positive drug test result prior to driving his or her route, the physician may disclose PHI to the registry of motor vehicles or the police in order to prevent the patient from endangering the students who ride in the driver's vehicle.

If a disclosure is made to law enforcement authorities to identify or apprehend an individual, it must be made because of a statement by an individual admitting participation in a violent crime that the covered entity reasonably believes may have caused serious physical harm to the victim. However, the covered entity (e.g., physician) may not learn of the statement during the course of treatment to change the propensity of the individual to commit the criminal conduct that is the basis for the disclosure, or during counseling or therapy, or through a request by the individual to initiate or to be referred for the treatment, counseling, or therapy as previously described. For example, the physician may disclose a victim's treatment for a gunshot wound to the police. However,

---

52. 45 C.F.R. § 164.512(j).

the physician cannot disclose a perpetrator's admission of domestic violence if the individual's purpose in seeking treatment from the physician is to obtain counseling to deter his or her acts of domestic violence.

The covered entity may use or disclose PHI when, appearing from all of the circumstances, the covered entity has a good-faith belief that the individual escaped from a correctional institution or from lawful custody. A covered entity is presumed to have acted with a good-faith belief if the belief is based on the covered entity's actual knowledge or in reliance on credible representation by a person with apparent knowledge or authority.[53] For example, if an individual wearing correctional facility clothing seeks treatment for a knife wound, the physician may disclose PHI to law enforcement officials in order to aid in the arrest of the individual.

III. Providing Access to Individuals via a Third Party

Under HIPAA, individuals have a right to access their own PHI.[54] HIPAA allows patients to exercise their access rights by directing covered entities to transmit a copy of PHI to a third party.[55] When exercising access rights in this manner, a full HIPAA authorization form is not required. Instead, the individual just needs to make the request in writing. It must be signed by the individual and must identify who is to receive the PHI and where it should be sent.

IV. Law Enforcement

A covered entity may disclose PHI for a law enforcement purpose only if certain conditions are met.[56] First, the disclosure must be

---

53. *Id.*
54. 45 C.F.R. § 164.524(a)(1).
55. *Id.* at (c)(3)(ii).
56. 45 C.F.R. § 164.512(f).

made to a law enforcement official. Second, the disclosure must be required by law.[57] Such disclosures include disclosures of physical injuries (e.g., gunshot wounds); disclosures in response to a court order, warrant, subpoena, or summons; and disclosures in compliance with an administrative request provided that (1) the material sought is relevant and material to a legitimate law enforcement inquiry, (2) the request is specific and limited in scope to the purpose for which the information is sought, and (3) de-identified information cannot reasonably be used.[58]

Third, a covered entity may disclose PHI in response to a law enforcement official's request in order to identify or locate a suspect, fugitive, material witness, or missing person, provided that the covered entity discloses only the following information of the individual: (1) name and address, (2) date and place of birth, (3) social security number, (4) blood type and Rh factor, (5) type of injury, (6) date and time of treatment, (7) date and time of death (if applicable), and (8) a description of physical characteristics including height, weight, gender, race, hair and eye color, facial hair, scars, and tattoos.[59]

Fourth, a covered entity may disclose PHI in response to a law enforcement official's request for such information about an individual who is or is suspected to be a victim of a crime if the individual agrees to the disclosure or, if the covered entity is unable to obtain permission due to the individual's incapacity or other emergency circumstances, the covered entity determines that the disclosure is in the best interest of the individual where the law enforcement official represents that the information is needed to determine whether a violation of the law by a person other than the individual occurred *and* the law enforcement official represents that it would be adverse to the immediate law enforcement activity to wait for the permission of the individual.[60]

---

57. Id.
58. Id.
59. 45 C.F.R. § 164.512(f)(2)(i).
60. 45 C.F.R. § 164.512(f)(3).

Fifth, a covered entity may disclose PHI to a law enforcement official about an individual who died provided that the purpose of disclosure is to alert the law enforcement official of the death of the individual if the covered entity suspects that the death may have resulted from criminal conduct.[61]

Sixth, a covered entity may disclose PHI to a law enforcement official where the covered entity has a good-faith belief that the PHI constitutes evidence of criminal activity that occurred on the covered entity's premises.[62]

Seventh, a covered entity that provides emergency health care in a medical emergency may disclose PHI to a law enforcement official if the disclosure is necessary to alert the enforcement official to (1) the commission and nature of a crime, (2) the location of a crime, and (3) the identity, description, and location of the perpetrator of such crime.[63] However, if the covered entity believes that the individual in need of emergency health care is the victim of abuse, neglect, or domestic violence, the covered entity may disclose PHI provided that the covered entity meets certain specific criteria as listed in Section VI, "Victims of Abuse, Neglect, or Domestic Violence."[64]

V. Public Health Activities

A covered entity may disclose PHI for "public health purposes" to certain recipients.[65] The PHI may be disclosed to (1) a public health official to prevent or control disease, injury or disability; (2) an official who is authorized to receive reports of child abuse or neglect; (3) the Food and Drug Administration, provided that the covered entity discloses the information for the purpose of activities related to the quality, safety, or effectiveness of a product

---

61. 45 C.F.R. § 164.512(f)(4).
62. 45 C.F.R. § 164.512(f)(5).
63. 45 C.F.R. § 164.512(f)(6).
64. *Id.*
65. 45 C.F.R. §§ 164.512(b) and 164.514(e).

or activity;[66] (4) a person who may have been exposed to a communicable disease or may otherwise be at risk of contracting or spreading a disease or condition;[67] (5) an employer[68] (only under certain strict criteria that protect the workplace); and (6) a public health authority that may use the PHI for public health activities.[69]

VI. Victims of Abuse, Neglect, or Domestic Violence

A covered entity may disclose PHI to a public health authority or other appropriate government authority allowed by law to receive reports of child abuse or neglect.[70]

Additionally, a covered entity may disclose PHI about an individual that the covered entity reasonably believes to be a victim of abuse, neglect, or domestic violence as long as it reports the PHI to a government authority, including a social service or protective services agency, authorized by law to receive reports of abuse, neglect, or domestic violence.[71] The disclosure must be required by law, comply with such law, and be limited to the relevant requirements of such law. Either the individual must agree to the disclosure *or* (1) the disclosure must be expressly authorized by statute or regulation *and* (2) in the covered entity's professional judgment, it believes the disclosure is needed to prevent serious harm to the individual or other potential victims.[72]

If the individual is unable to agree because of incapacity, a public official must indicate that the PHI is not intended to be used against the individual and that an urgent enforcement activity would be adversely affected by waiting until the individual is able

---

66. 45 C.F.R. § 164.512(b)(1)(iii).
67. 45 C.F.R. § 164.512(b)(1)(iv).
68. 45 C.F.R. § 164.512(b)(1)(v).
69. 45 C.F.R. § 164.512(b)(2).
70. 45 C.F.R. § 164.512(b)(1)(ii).
71. 45 C.F.R. § 164.512(c).
72. 45 C.F.R. § 164.512(c)(1).

to agree to the disclosure. The covered entity must promptly inform the individual that such a report has been or will be made. However, if the covered entity believes that informing the individual would place the individual at risk for harm *or* if the covered entity would be informing the individual's personal representative, whom the covered entity believes to be the source of the abuse, neglect, or domestic violence, then HIPAA does not mandate that the covered entity inform the individual or the personal representative.[73]

For example, at a local hospital social workers receive a call from the Department of Social Services, requesting that the hospital staff give them a "heads up" when a particular individual arrives there to deliver her baby. The hospital has no direct knowledge of any abuse. The hospital has no history with either the patient or previous Department of Social Services complaints. The hospital basically knows nothing about the pregnant woman except that the Department of Social Services said it had removed other children from this patient's custody for abuse. The hospital staff has no firsthand knowledge of any concerns for the unborn child and no positive drug or alcohol toxicity screen for the mother. The mother appropriately presents to the hospital for delivery of her child. There may be a state mandatory reporting law that requires disclosure, under which HIPAA permits disclosure of the PHI.[74] Absent a state mandatory reporting law, these circumstances permit the hospital staff to use their professional judgment to determine that there is no choice but to withhold the PHI from the Department of Social Services. There is no good-faith basis to determine that this particular baby is a potential victim of abuse as allowed under 45 C.F.R. § 164.512(c). However, there is nothing in the Privacy Rule that prevents the Department of Social Services from phoning the hospital daily to determine whether the hospital directory lists the woman as being admitted to the facility.

---

73. 45 C.F.R. § 164.512(c)(1)(iii).
74. 45 C.F.R. § 160.203.

In summary, a covered entity may use or disclose PHI to the extent that the law requires such use or disclosure and it complies with and is limited to the relevant requirements of such law.[75] A covered entity must meet the requirements as described above in disclosures for (1) victims of abuse, neglect, or domestic violence;[76] (2) judicial and administrative proceedings;[77] and (3) law enforcement purposes.[78]

VII. Lawful Oversight Activities

Covered entities may become subject to a variety of organizational activities that are necessary for compliance with federal and state regulations. These activities require the disclosure of PHI; however, obtaining an authorization is not feasible. HIPAA allows disclosures of PHI without authorizations when supervision of the health care system, determination of eligibility for government benefits program, determination of compliance with government regulatory programs, and determination of compliance with civil rights laws involves the PHI.

The covered entity may disclose PHI to a health oversight agency for oversight activities authorized by law, including audits; civil, administrative, or criminal investigations; inspection; licensure or disciplinary actions; and civil, administrative, or criminal proceedings or actions.[79] For example, HIPAA allows disclosure of PHI where the public health department seeks medical records during the investigation of a psychiatrist for unscrupulous activities with his or her patients. If it is necessary and relevant, PHI may be used or disclosed for oversight of other activities needed

---

75. 45 C.F.R. § 164.512(a).
76. 45 C.F.R. § 164.512(c).
77. 45 C.F.R. § 164.512(e).
78. 45 C.F.R. § 164.512(f).
79. 45 C.F.R. § 164.512(d).

for appropriate monitoring of the health care system, government benefit programs, government regulatory programs, and civil rights laws.[80]

A health oversight activity does *not* include an investigation or other activity in which the individual is the subject of the investigation and the investigation does *not* arise out of and is *not* directly related to the receipt of health care, a claim for public benefits related to health, or qualification for or receipt of public benefits or services when a patient's health is integral to the claim for public benefits or services. But if there is an investigation or oversight activity that is not associated with a claim for public benefits related to health and that is done in conjunction with an investigation or oversight activity related to health, the joint investigation is considered a health oversight activity that falls within the exception and no authorization is required under HIPAA.[81]

If a covered entity is also a health oversight agency, the covered entity may use PHI for health oversight activities provided it meets the above criteria.[82]

VIII. Judicial and Administrative Proceedings

During the course of any judicial or administrative proceeding, a covered entity may disclose PHI in response to (1) an order of a court or administrative tribunal or (2) a subpoena, discovery request, or other lawful process.[83] The covered entity may disclose PHI in response to an order of a court or administrative tribunal, provided that the covered entity discloses only the PHI expressly authorized by the order.[84]

---

80. Id.
81. 45 C.F.R. § 164.512(d)(4).
82. Id.
83. 45 C.F.R. § 164.512(e).
84. 45 C.F.R. § 164.512(e)(1)(i).

In regards to a subpoena, discovery request, or other lawful process that is not accompanied by an order of the court or administrative tribunal, the covered entity must receive certain "satisfactory assurances" from the party seeking the PHI.[85] If a party to an action sends a request for discovery of PHI to a covered entity without a court order or a duly signed authorization, the covered entity must have satisfactory assurance from the party seeking the PHI that reasonable efforts were made by the party to ensure that the individual who is the subject of the PHI was given notice of the request or that reasonable efforts were made to secure a qualified protective order.[86]

A covered entity receives satisfactory assurance when he or she receives a written statement and accompanying documentation demonstrating that:

1. The party requesting the information made a good-faith attempt to provide written notice to the individual or, if the individual's location is unknown, to mail a notice to the individual's last known address;
2. The notice included sufficient information about the litigation or proceeding in which the PHI is requested to permit the individual to raise an objection to the court or administrative tribunal; and
3. The time for the individual to raise objections to the court or administrative tribunal has elapsed, and
   a. No objections were filed; or
   b. All objections filed by the individual have been resolved by the court or the administrative tribunal and the disclosures being sought are consistent with such resolution.[87]

It is important to note that a written statement, by itself, is inadequate to constitute satisfactory assurances. The statement

---

85. *Id.* at (e)(1)(iii).
86. 45 C.F.R. § 164.512(e)(ii).
87. 45 C.F.R. § 164.512(e)(1)(iii).

also requires documentation that the written notice was actually provided. Alternatively, the covered entity may receive a written statement from the party seeking the PHI that reasonable efforts were made by the party to secure a qualified protective order. The written statement and accompanying documentation must demonstrate that (1) the parties to the dispute giving rise to the request for information agreed to a qualified protective order and presented it to the court or tribunal with jurisdiction over the dispute; or (2) the party seeking the PHI requested a qualified protective order from such court or administrative tribunal.[88]

A "qualified protective order" is an order of a court or an administrative tribunal or a stipulation by the parties to the litigation or administrative proceeding that:

1. Prohibits the parties from using or disclosing the PHI for any purpose other than the litigation or proceeding for which such information was requested; and
2. Requires the return to the covered entity or destruction of the PHI (including all copies made) at the end of the litigation or proceeding.[89]

Notwithstanding the above requirements, a covered entity may disclose PHI in response to a subpoena, discovery request, or other lawful process *without reasonable assurances from the party seeking the PHI if* the covered entity itself makes reasonable efforts to provide written notice to the individual as described above or makes reasonable efforts to seek a qualified protective order as described above.[90]

In light of the duties under HIPAA, many covered entities will not disclose PHI without a court order. Even with a subpoena, discovery request, or other lawful process, covered entities are mindful of the provisions in HIPAA requiring court intervention and are

---

[88]. 45 C.F.R. § 164.512(e)(1)(iv).
[89]. 45 C.F.R. § 164.512(e)(1)(v).
[90]. 45 C.F.R. § 164.512(e)(1)(vi).

reluctant to disclose PHI absent a duly authorized release of medical information. It is common practice in some jurisdictions for the party seeking PHI to request a court-ordered subpoena when a duly signed authorization is not available. In that instance, the medical records are delivered to the court in a sealed envelope. Prior to disclosure to the party seeking the PHI, the court reviews the PHI to determine whether it is pertinent to the litigation or administrative proceeding. Under these circumstances, the covered entity properly responds to the court order under Section 164.512(e).

IX. Informational and Promotional Disclosures

A. Facility Directories

A covered entity may use or disclose PHI for facility directories without the written authorization of the individual provided that (1) the individual is notified *in advance* of the use or disclosure *and* (2) the individual has the opportunity to *agree or object* (opt out) to having his or her name published in the directory. The agreement can be oral. The only information that can be published in the directory is the individual's name, location in the facility, general condition (no specific medical information), and religious affiliation. The information can be released only to people who ask for the individual by name or to members of the clergy. If an emergency exists in which the individual does not have the opportunity to agree or object, the information may be published in the facility's directory *if* (1) it is consistent with prior expressed consent of the individual and (2) the covered entity determines that it is in the best interest of the individual.[91]

For example, when a patient is admitted to the hospital for elective surgery, the hospital admissions staff must ask that patient if he or she would like to be listed in the hospital's patient directory.

---

91. 45 C.F.R. § 164.510(a).

Chapter 4: *Disclosures without Authorizations*

If the patient agrees, the hospital may list only the individual's name, location in the facility, general condition (no specific medical information), and religious affiliation. The hospital may release the information only if an individual asks for it. The hospital may not disclose the information if the patient opts out of having his or her name listed in the directory.

B. Friends and Relatives

A covered entity may disclose relevant PHI to a family member, other relative, or a close personal friend of the individual, or any other person identified by the individual who is involved in the individual's health care and treatment or payment related to the individual's health care, provided that if the individual is present and has the ability to form his or her own health care decisions, the covered entity gives the individual an opportunity to object or agree to the disclosure.[92] If the permission cannot be obtained due to the individual's incapacity or an emergency or if the individual is not present, disclosure to the next of kin is permitted if the covered entity can reasonably infer, based on professional judgment under the circumstances and on its experience with common practice, that the individual does not object. For example, a husband is permitted to pick up prescriptions for his wife at the pharmacy. However, if the individual objects, the covered entity is prohibited from sharing the individual's PHI with the individual's friends or relatives.[93]

Additionally, the individual may restrict the amount or type of information that the covered entity can share.[94] The individual can request that the covered entity release only certain PHI to family or friends. For example, a provider may believe that a

---

92. 45 C.F.R. § 164.510; HHS FAQ 488, https://www.hhs.gov/hipaa/for-professionals/faq/488/does-hipaa-permit-a-doctor-to-discuss-a-patients-health-status-with-the-patients-family-and-friends/index.html.
93. *Id.*
94. 45 C.F.R. § 164.522.

patient's sexually transmitted disease status is directly relevant to providing care for the patient's pregnancy. The patient may agree to release information to her family pertaining to her pregnancy, but may request that the provider not disclose PHI related to her sexually transmitted disease. The covered entity does not have to agree to this restriction. If the provider does not agree to this restriction, the patient retains the right to prohibit the disclosure of *any* PHI to her family and friends. If the covered entity enters into an agreement to disclose only select information, it must abide by the agreement, except for emergency situations.

C. Marketing

HIPAA requires a covered entity to obtain an individual's written authorization to use or disclose PHI for marketing purposes.[95] The rule defines "marketing" as a communication about a product or service that encourages the recipient of the communication to purchase or use the product or service *unless* the communication involves no financial remuneration and is made (1) to describe a health-related product or service (or payment for such service) that is provided by the covered entity making the communication, (2) for treatment of the individual, or (3) for case management or care coordination for the individual or to direct or recommend alternative treatments, therapies, health care providers, or settings of care to the individual.[96] You can generally think about it in this way: the rule requires an individual's authorization for communications that encourage an individual to use or purchase a product or service that is not health related or, if it is health related, that is not provided by the entity making the communication, unless an exception applies.

Communications that promote the sale of products or services that are related to health care and are provided by the covered

---

95. 45 C.F.R. §§ 164.501 and 164.508(a)(3).
96. 45 C.F.R. § 164.501.

entity generally do not qualify as "marketing" under the rule and those communications do not require the individual's authorization. For example, a physician who recommends a brand-name medication does not engage in "marketing" for the purposes of HIPAA, as long as the physician is not being paid to make the communication. A pharmacist who receives financial incentives from a drug manufacturer to recommend that an individual switch to a particular medication manufactured by that particular drug company would need the patient's authorization in order to make the communication. The communication is marketing because, while recommending alternative treatments is not considered marketing in some situations, it is marketing because the covered entity is receiving financial remuneration for making the communication. No authorization is needed only if the communication fits within the refill reminder exception to the definition of marketing. Additionally, any financial relationships between covered entities and third parties for whom they are providing marketing services must comply with state and federal anti-kickback and fee-splitting laws.

The rule also provides that there is no need for an authorization if the communication is made face to face by the covered entity to the individual *or* the communication is in the form of a promotional gift of nominal value provided by the covered entity.[97] For example, a physician does not need your authorization to give you a pen with his or her business address printed on it. On the other hand, a covered entity does need an individual's authorization for any other activity not listed under the rule, such as selling lists of patients to third parties. Additionally, if any marketing activity requiring authorization involves direct or indirect monetary compensation to the covered entity from a third party, the authorization must state that such remuneration exists.[98]

---

97. 45 C.F.R. § 164.508(a)(3).
98. *Id.*

D. Fundraising

A covered entity may use or disclose PHI to a business associate or to an institutionally related foundation without an individual's authorization for the purpose of raising funds for its own benefit provided that the PHI contains only demographic information relating to an individual and dates of health care provided to the individual.[99] In its notice of privacy practices (discussed in Chapter 5), the covered entity must specifically note that it uses information for fundraising purposes. The covered entity must include in any fundraising materials that it sends to an individual a description of how the individual may opt out of (object to) receiving any further fundraising communications. Additionally, the covered entity must make reasonable efforts to ensure that individuals who opt out of receiving future fundraising communications are not sent such communications. "Fundraising" is included in the definition of "health care operations" and an individual has the right to request in advance that the covered entity restrict uses and disclosures for fundraising purposes. Under the rule, the covered entity has no obligation to agree to the restriction.

X. Research

A covered entity may always use or disclose for research purposes health information that has been de-identified in accordance with 45 C.F.R. §§ 164.502(d) and 164.514(a)–(c) of the Privacy Rule. But HIPAA also allows a covered entity to disclose PHI to researchers with an individual's authorization or *without* an individual's authorization if either an institutional review board (IRB) or a privacy board (PB) approves a waiver of the authorization or an alteration of the authorization.[100] The IRB or PB must document

---

99. 45 C.F.R. §§ 164.501, 164.514(f), and 164.522.
100. 45 C.F.R. §§ 164.512(i) and 164.514(e).

the waiver in writing[101] and in accordance with the requirements of 45 C.F.R. § 164.51(i).

The IRB must be established according to federal laws. The PB must have members with varying backgrounds and appropriate professional competency to review the effect of the research protocol on the individual's privacy rights and related interests. The PB must comprise at least one member who is not affiliated with the covered entity or with any entity conducting or sponsoring the research, and not related to any person who is affiliated with any of such entities. No member of the privacy board may have a conflict of interest.

The covered entity may disclose PHI to a researcher for review in preparation for research.[102] However, the covered entity must obtain the following information from the researcher: (1) The use or disclosure is sought solely to review PHI as needed to prepare a research protocol (or similar purposes in preparation for research); (2) no PHI will be removed from the covered entity by the researcher in the course of the review; and (3) the PHI is necessary for the research purposes.[103]

See 45 C.F.R. §§ 164.512(i) and 164.514(e) for other specific restrictions pertaining to research.

XI. Workers' Compensation

Under HIPAA, a covered entity does not need an individual's authorization to disclose PHI in order to comply with workers' compensation laws. A covered entity may disclose PHI without the written authorization of the individual (or the opportunity for the individual to object) to the extent necessary to comply with laws relating to workers' compensation or other similar programs,

---

101. 45 C.F.R. § 164.512(i)(1)(i).
102. 45 C.F.R. § 164.512(i).
103. *Id.*

established by law, that provide benefits for work-related injuries or illness without regard to fault.[104]

Further, individuals do not have a right to request that a covered entity restrict a disclosure of PHI about them for workers' compensation purposes when that disclosure is required by law or authorized by, and necessary to comply with, a workers' compensation or similar law.[105]

The government did not intend for HIPAA to impede the flow of health information to those who need it to process or adjudicate claims, or coordinate care, for injured or ill workers under workers' compensation systems. The minimum necessary standard generally requires covered entities to make reasonable efforts to limit uses and disclosures of, as well as requests for, PHI to the minimum necessary to accomplish the intended purpose. For disclosures of PHI made for workers' compensation purposes under 45 C.F.R. § 164.512(l), the minimum necessary standard permits covered entities to disclose information to the full extent authorized by state or other law. Additionally, where a state workers' compensation board or other public official (for workers' compensation purposes) requests PHI, covered entities are permitted reasonably to rely on the official's representations that the information requested is the minimum necessary for the intended purpose.[106] For disclosures of PHI for payment purposes, covered entities may disclose the type and amount of information necessary to receive payment for any health care provided to an injured or ill worker. The minimum necessary standard does not apply to disclosures required by state or other law or made pursuant to the individual's authorization.[107]

---

104. 45 C.F.R. § 164.512(l).
105. 45 C.F.R. §§ 164.522(a) and 164.512(a) and (l).
106. 45 C.F.R. § 164.514(d)(3)(iii)(A).
107. 45 C.F.R. § 164.502(b), 164.514(d).

XII. Conclusion

HIPAA generally requires a covered entity to have an individual's authorization before it is able to release PHI. However, there are several exceptions to this requirement. An authorization is not needed for a covered entity to release PHI for treatment, payment, or health care operations. An authorization is not needed if the release of PHI comes under an exception in 45 C.F.R. § 164.512, or if an individual is exercising a right to access records. There could be additional elements that must be met prior to release of PHI under these exceptions. It is also very important to remember that state laws could be more stringent, and may require written authorization for disclosures that HIPAA would otherwise permit.

Chapter 5

Administrative Requirements for Covered Entities and Business Associates

As we discovered earlier, covered entities must comply with HIPAA.[1] The HITECH Act expanded those obligations to include business associates, which must now comply with many of HIPAA's requirements.[2] This chapter explores some of the duties and obligations that covered entities and business associates have under HIPAA and HITECH and what they must do to comply.

---

1. 45 C.F.R. §§ 160.102 and 103.
2. Health Information Technology for Economic and Clinical Health (HITECH) Act, Title XIII of Division A and Title IV of Division B of the American Recovery and Reinvestment Act of 2009 (ARRA), Pub. L. No. 111-5, 123 Stat. 226 (Feb. 17, 2009), codified at 42 U.S.C. §§ 300jj *et seq.*; §§ 17901 *et seq.*

I. Administrative Requirements

As we have learned, a covered entity is (1) a health plan; (2) a health care clearinghouse; or (3) a health care provider who transmits any health information in electronic form in connection with a transaction covered under HIPAA.[3] In Chapter 2, we looked at the basic types of covered entities, which include health insurers; HMOs; Medicare; Medicaid; health care clearinghouses; hospitals; pharmacies; and a variety of types of health care providers. In Chapter 4, we learned about business associates and that the HITECH Act requires business associates to comply with the same administrative, physical, and technical safeguards regarding the security of electronic protected health information (PHI) just as the covered entity must. Because covered entities and business associates are entrusted to maintain the confidentiality of individuals' PHI and are required to comply with HIPAA, they have certain responsibilities. This chapter explains the administrative requirements that covered entities and business associates are responsible to fulfill, and also touches on how those compliance obligations differ for the two types of entities.

To comply with HIPAA, covered entities and business associates must adhere to a number of administrative requirements. This chapter does not comprehensively analyze each and every requirement but rather it outlines the requirements and brings these obligations to the reader's attention. Appendix A contains a sample of a suite of policies and templates that address these administrative requirements. The following is information to set the groundwork for the reader to understand these policies.

---

3. 45 C.F.R. § 160.103.

A. Notice of Privacy Practices

The HIPAA Privacy Rule requires that a covered entity (but not a business associate)[4] supply a written notice of the entity's notice of privacy practices (NPP) to each individual it services.[5] An individual has a right to adequate notice of how a covered entity may use and disclose PHI about the individual, as well as his or her rights and the covered entity's obligations with respect to that information. Most covered entities must develop and provide individuals with this notice of their privacy practices. However, the Privacy Rule does not require the following covered entities to develop an NPP:[6]

- Health care clearinghouses, if the only PHI they create or receive is as a business associate of another covered entity.[7]
- A correctional institution that is a covered entity (e.g., that has a covered health care provider component).[8]
- A group health plan that provides benefits only through one or more contracts of insurance with health insurance issuers or HMOs, and that does not create or receive PHI other than summary health information or enrollment or disenrollment information.[9]

The covered entity must give the NPP to the individual at the first patient encounter. As a health care consumer, you have likely gone to a health care provider and received an NPP that lists the activities the health care provider will do and will not do with your

---

4. *See* U.S. Dep't of Health & Human Servs. (HHS), Frequently Asked Questions (FAQs) 390, https://www.hhs.gov/hipaa/for-professionals/faq/390/does-hipaa-require-a-business-associate-to-create-a-notice-of-privacy-practices/index.html) (last visited June 2, 2019).

5. 45 C.F.R. §§ 164.500 and 520.

6. HHS, Notice of Privacy Practices for Protected Health Information, https://www.hhs.gov/hipaa/for-professionals/privacy/guidance/privacy-practices-for-protected-health-information/index.html (last visited May 18, 2019).

7. 45 C.F.R. § 164.500(b)(1).

8. 45 C.F.R. § 164.520(a)(3).

9. 45 C.F.R. § 164.520(a).

PHI. This mandatory document must be written in plain language and must include,[10] among other things,

1. Header with the following statement: "THIS NOTICE DESCRIBES HOW MEDICAL INFORMATION ABOUT YOU MAY BE USED AND DISCLOSED AND HOW YOU CAN GET ACCESS TO THIS INFORMATION. PLEASE REVIEW IT CAREFULLY."
2. Uses and disclosures—This must include:
   - a description and example of the permitted disclosures permitted for treatment, payment, and health care operations;
   - a description of other purposes the covered entity is permitted or required to use or disclose PHI without the individual's written authorization;
   - if there is a use or disclosure for any purpose described above that is prohibited or limited by other law, the use or disclosure must reflect the more stringent law;
   - for each purpose, the description must include enough detail to give notice to the individual of the uses and disclosures that are permitted or required by HIPAA and other law; and
   - a statement that other uses or disclosures will be made only with the individual's written authorization and the individual may revoke such authorization.
3. Separate statements for certain uses or disclosures. The NPP must include the following statements if the covered entity engages in any of the following activities:
   - The covered entity may contact the individual to raise funds for the covered entity;
   - If the covered entity is a group health plan, or a health insurance issuer or HMO with respect to a group health plan, it may disclose PHI to the sponsor of the plan; or

---

10. 45 C.F.R. § 164.520.

- If the covered entity is a health plan (except issuers of certain long-term care policies) and intends to use or disclose PHI for underwriting purposes, it must indicate that the plan is prohibited from using or disclosing genetic information for such purposes.
4. Rights of the individual. The NPP must contain a statement of the individual's rights with respect to PHI and a description of how the individual may exercise those rights. These rights include the right to:
    - Request restrictions on uses and disclosures of PHI;
    - Receive confidential communications of PHI;
    - Inspect and copy his or her own PHI;
    - Request amendment of PHI;
    - Receive an accounting of disclosures of PHI; and
    - Receive a paper copy of the NPP.
5. Covered entity's duties. The NPP must also contain information regarding the duties of the covered entity. Specifically, the notice must contain the following statements:
    - The covered entity is required by law to maintain the privacy of PHI and to provide individuals with notice of tis legal duties and privacy practices with respect to PHI;
    - The covered entity is required to abide by the terms of the notice currently in effect; and
    - The covered entity reserves the right to change the terms of its notice and to make the new notice provisions effective for all PHI that it maintains. The statement must also describe how it will provide individuals with a revised notice.
6. Complaints. The NPP must contain a statement that the individuals may complain to the covered entity and to the Secretary of the U.S. Department of Health and Human Services if they believe their privacy rights have been violated, a description of how the individual may file a complaint with the covered entity, and a statement that the individual will not be retaliated against for filing a complaint.

7. Contact. The NPP must contain the name or title and telephone number of a person or office to contact for further information. The contact person must be responsible for receiving complaints and be able to provide further information about the NPP.
8. Effective date. The NPP must contain the date on which the NPP is first in effect and cannot be earlier than the date on which the NPP is published.

1. Optional Elements of the NPP

There are also optional elements that may be included.[11] For instance, if a covered entity chooses to limit the uses or disclosures it is allowed to make, the covered entity may describe the more limited uses or disclosures in its notice as long as the uses or disclosures do not limit the individual's rights required by law.[12] Whenever there is a material change to the uses or disclosures, the individual's rights, the covered entity's legal duties, or other privacy practices, the covered entity must promptly revise and distribute the NPP.[13]

2. Revisions of the NPP

HIPAA also provides when and how the covered entity may revise its privacy policy and procedures. The covered entity must make its NPP available to individuals. The covered entity must expressly reserve its rights to change the terms of its privacy notice; otherwise the covered entity is bound by the privacy practices in the NPP that was in effect at the time that the PHI was created or received. It must also specify that the changes apply to previously created or

---

11. *Id.*
12. *Id.*
13. *Id.*

received PHI; otherwise any change will apply only to information created or received after the effective date of the revised notice.[14]

3. Availability of the NPP

If a covered entity has a direct treatment relationship with an individual, the covered entity must provide the NPP to the individual on the first day of service to the individual or, in an emergency situation, as soon as reasonably practicable following the emergency treatment situation.[15] The covered entity must make a good-faith effort to obtain a written acknowledgment of receipt of the NPP.[16] If it is not possible to obtain a written receipt, the covered entity must document its good-faith efforts and the reason why it did not obtain the acknowledgment.[17]

If a covered entity is a health plan, it must provide its NPP to individuals covered by the health plan on or before the compliance date deadline and thereafter at the time of enrollment of new enrollees and within 60 days of a material revision to the notice to individuals covered by the health plan at the time of the revision.[18] Every three years or more frequently, the health plan must provide notification to covered individuals of the availability of the NPP and how to obtain it.[19] Providing the NPP to the named insured satisfies the requirement to provide notice to covered individuals.[20]

If a covered entity maintains a website that provides information about the covered entity's customer services or benefits, it must prominently post its NPP on the website and make the NPP available electronically through the website.[21] The covered entity may

---

14. 45 C.F.R. § 164.520.
15. 45 C.F.R. § 164.520(c)(2).
16. *Id.*
17. *Id.*
18. 45 C.F.R. § 164.520(c)(1).
19. *Id.*
20. *Id.* at (c)(1)(iii).
21. 45 C.F.R. § 164.520(c)(3).

provide the NPP via e-mail if the individual agrees to electronic notice and the agreement has not been withdrawn.[22] However, if the covered entity knows that the e-mail transmission failed, a paper copy of the notice must be provided to the individual.[23] Additionally, if the first delivery to an individual is made electronically, the covered health care provider must supply electronic notice automatically and contemporaneously in response to the individual's first request for service from the health care provider and must make a good-faith effort to obtain written acknowledgment of the receipt of the electronic notice.[24] The individual retains the right to obtain a paper copy of the NPP.[25]

4. Joint Notice of Privacy Practices by Separate Covered Entities

A joint NPP may be drafted by covered entities that participate in organized health care arrangements provided that:[26]

- All the covered entities participating in the organized health care arrangement agree to abide by the notice;
- The joint NPP meets all of the required and optional elements of the notice as previously discussed;
- The NPP is altered to reflect that the notice covers more than one covered entity; and
- The NPP describes with reasonable specificity the covered entities and the service delivery sites and (if applicable) states that the covered entities participating in the organized health care arrangement will share PHI with each other to carry out treatment, payment, or health care operations related to the organized health care arrangement.

---

22. *Id.*
23. *Id.*
24. *Id.*
25. 45 C.F.R. § 164.520(c)(3).
26. 45 C.F.R. § 164.520(d).

The provision of the joint NPP to an individual by any one of the covered entities included in the joint notice will satisfy the notice requirement with respect to all other covered entities included in the joint notice.[27]

5. Documentation of Notice

A covered entity must document its compliance with the NPP requirements by retaining copies of the notices issued by the covered entity and any written acknowledgments of receipt of the notice or documentation of good-faith efforts to obtain such written acknowledgment.[28]

B. Accounting for Disclosures

One of the major issues a covered entity faces when disclosing PHI is accounting for the disclosures. Individuals have the right to receive an accounting of disclosures of their PHI made by the covered entity six years prior to the date that the individual requests the accounting, including disclosures to or by business associates. Keep in mind that the right to an accounting pertains only to "disclosures" of PHI, which is the sharing of PHI outside of the covered entity. The covered entity does not need to account for "uses" of PHI, which is the sharing of PHI within the covered entity. Accountings are not required for release of PHI to carry out treatment, payment, and health care operations; to individuals; pursuant to authorizations; in facility directories; for national security purposes; to correctional institutions and law enforcement officials; or incidental to a use and disclosure permitted or required. For example, as of this writing, the individual does not

---

27. *Id.*
28. 45 C.F.R. § 164.520(e).

have a right to receive a listing of all health care providers' employees that have access to his or her PHI.[29]

The HITECH Act of 2009 broadened the accounting requirement. The exception to the accounting requirement for disclosures for treatment, payment, and health care operations would not apply to disclosures of PHI maintained in an electronic health record.[30] As of this writing, regulations implementing that requirement have not been finalized.

1. Contents of the Accounting

The accounting must include the date of each disclosure; the name and, if known, the address of the entity or person who received the information; a description of the information disclosed; and a statement of the purpose of the disclosure. The covered entity must act on the individual's request for an accounting no later than 60 days after it receives a request. If the covered entity cannot provide the requested accounting within the time required under HIPAA, it may extend the time for 30 days provided that it gives the individual a written statement of the reasons for the delay and the date that it will provide the accounting. The covered entity has only one opportunity for an extension of time to act on a request for an accounting. The individual may receive one accounting per year free of charge. Otherwise, the covered entity may impose a reasonable, cost-based fee for each subsequent request.

---

29. In 2011, HHS proposed "to expand the accounting provision to provide individuals with the right to receive an access report indicating who has accessed electronic protected health information in a designated record set." HHS, Office for Civil Rights, Notice of Proposed Rulemaking, HIPAA Privacy Rule Accounting of Disclosures under the Health Information Technology for Economic and Clinical Health Act, 76 Fed. Reg. 31,426 (May 31, 2011). The government later withdrew this notice of proposed rulemaking in its Unified Agenda of Regulatory and Deregulatory Acts (May 9, 2018), *available at* https://www.reginfo.gov/public/do/eAgendaViewRule?pubId=201804&RIN=0945-AA00.

30. 42 U.S.C. § 17935(c).

2. Accounting of Disclosures for Research

If the covered entity made disclosure of PHI for research purposes for 50 or more individuals, the accounting may provide the name of the protocol or other research activity; a description, in plain language, of the research protocol or other research activity, including the purpose of the research and criteria for selecting particular records; a brief description of the type of PHI disclosed; the date or period of time during which such disclosures occurred, or may have occurred, including the date of the last such disclosure during the accounting period; the name, address, and telephone number of the entity that sponsored the research and of the researcher to whom the information was disclosed; and a statement that the PHI of the individual may or may not have been disclosed for a particular protocol or other research activity.[31]

If the individual requests, the covered entity or business associate shall assist in contacting the entity that sponsored the research and the researcher if the accounting provides the above-stated particulars of disclosures for research purposes and if it is reasonably likely that the covered entity disclosed the individual's PHI for research purposes.[32]

3. Time to Respond to Request for Accounting

The covered entity or business associate must provide the individual with the accounting within 60 days after it receives the individual's request for an accounting.[33] If the covered entity or business associate is unable to provide the accounting within 60 days, it may extend the time by no more than 30 days as long as it provides the incidental with a written statement of the reasons for

---

31. 45 C.F.R § 164.528(b)(4)(i).
32. 45 C.F.R. § 164.528(b)(4)(ii).
33. 45 C.F.R. § 164.528(c)(1).

the delay and provide the day by which it will provide the accounting.[34] It is allowed only one such extension of time per request.[35]

4. Fees

The covered entity must provide the first accounting to the individual free of charge in any 12-month period.[36] Thereafter, the covered entity may charge a reasonable, cost-based fee for each subsequent request for an accounting by the same individual within the 12-month period.[37] However, the covered entity must inform the individual in advance of the fee and provide the individual with an opportunity to withdraw or modify the request for the subsequent accounting in order to avoid or reduce the fee.[38]

5. Documentation of the Accounting

A covered entity must document and keep records of the following: (1) the information in the accounting, (2) the written accounting provided to the individual, and (3) the titles of the persons or offices responsible for receiving and processing requests for an accounting by individuals.[39] The records must be kept for six years from the date of its creation or the date when it was last in effect, whichever is later.[40]

C. Disclosures to Public Health Officials

Under the Privacy Rule, making a set of records available for review by a third party constitutes a "disclosure" of the PHI in the entire set of records, regardless of whether the third party actually

---

34. *Id.*
35. *Id.*
36. 45 C.F.R. § 164.528(c)(2).
37. *Id.*
38. *Id.*
39. *Id.*
40. 45 C.F.R. § 164.530(j).

reviews any particular record.[41] By definition, mere access by a third party, such as a public health authority, to PHI is a disclosure and subject to an accounting for disclosures.

Public health departments commonly monitor certain public health concerns using a retrospective review by the public health authority of a collection of patient records to identify reportable events. When the public health authority identifies a reportable case, specific PHI pertinent to the monitoring activity is obtained and reported to the public health authority. For example, a retrospective review of the medical charts for all patients treated by a health care provider or all charts of patients treated in the entity's emergency department may be required to identify cases of new or previously unknown infectious agents, clinical conditions associated with the use or abuse of illicit or prescription drugs, or adverse events or reactions associated with pharmaceuticals or medical devices.

By definition, all records in the above example are deemed to have been disclosed under the Privacy Rule. The covered entity must keep an accounting but because of the universal nature of the access provided, the covered entity need document only the identity (and address if known) of the public health authority to which access was provided, a description of the records and PHI subject to access, the purpose for the disclosure, and when access was provided.[42] The covered entity need not note the disclosure in each record. It is satisfactory for the covered entity to maintain a separate notation of such disclosures that is applicable to all records that were so accessed. If an individual requests an accounting, the covered entity needs to determine whether the individual's records were among the set of records to which the public health authority was granted access. All individuals whose records were

---

41. *Id.* and see definition of "disclosures" in 45 C.F.R. § 164.501.
42. HHS FAQ 465, All Sub-Categories, https://www.hhs.gov/hipaa/for-professionals/faq/465/does-a-covered-entity-have-to-document-each-medical-record-that-may-be-accessed-by-a-public-health-authority/index.html (last visited June 1, 2019).

accessed in this fashion would receive the same accounting for the disclosure.[43]

For example, if on August 1, 2019, a hospital began providing a public health authority ongoing access to the medical charts of all patients treated in its emergency department to identify reportable cases and extract relevant information required for a particular surveillance activity, it would be satisfactory, under 45 C.F.R. § 164.528(b)(2), for the accounting to include the following:

- The identity, and address, if known, of the public health authority
- A statement that the public health authority had access to medical charts for patients treated in the emergency department
- The date (or approximate range of dates) when the individual's record was subject to access (e.g., access provided within a week of treatment in the emergency room on [fill in date of individual visit])
- A statement of the purpose of the access (that is, identify the particular public health surveillance activity)

The same basic statement could then be provided in response to a request for an accounting by any individual who was seen in the emergency department of the hospital on or after August 1, 2019.[44]

II. Administrative Safeguards

HIPAA and HITECH require the covered entity and business associate to have appropriate administrative safeguards to protect electronic PHI.[45] The following are brief summaries:

---

43. *Id.*
44. *Id.*
45. 45 C.F.R. § 164.530.

A. Covered Entity Obligations

1. Personnel Designations

The covered entity must designate a privacy official who is responsible for the development and implementation of the privacy policies and procedures and someone who will receive complaints. This can be the same person. The covered entity must also designate a security official to develop and implement the security policies. The privacy official and security official position could be held by the same person.

2. Training

A covered entity must train all members of its workforce on the policies and procedures regarding PHI as needed for the staff members to carry out their functions for the covered entity. The staff must be trained no later than the compliance date set for the covered entity *and* within a reasonable period of time after a new change becomes effective. A new staff member must be trained within a reasonable time after joining the covered entity. All training must be documented.[46]

3. Safeguards

A covered entity must have in place appropriate administrative, technical, and physical safeguards to protect the privacy of PHI; must safeguard PHI from any intentional or unintentional use or disclosure that violates HIPAA; and must safeguard PHI to limit incidental uses or disclosures.[47]

---

46. 45 C.F.R. § 164.530(b).
47. 45 C.F.R. § 164.530 (c).

4. Complaints

A covered entity must have a process for individuals to make complaints and document all complaints and their disposition.[48]

5. Sanctions

A covered entity must have and apply appropriate sanctions against members of its workforce who fail to comply with the covered entity's privacy policies and procedures. The covered entity must document any sanctions that it applies.[49]

6. Mitigation

A covered entity must mitigate, to the extent practicable, any harmful effect that is known to the covered entity of a use or disclosure of PHI in violation of its policies and procedures or the HIPAA requirements.[50]

7. Retaliation

A covered entity is prohibited from intimidating, threatening, coercing, discriminating against, or taking other retaliatory actions against individuals for exercising their rights or against anyone for filing a complaint, testifying, investigating, or opposing any action made unlawful under HIPAA.[51]

8. Waiver of Rights

A covered entity may not require individuals to waive their rights as a condition of providing treatment, payment, enrollment in a health plan, or eligibility for benefits.[52]

---

48. 45 C.F.R. § 164.530 (d).
49. 45 C.F.R. § 164.530 (e).
50. 45 C.F.R. § 164.530 (f).
51. 45 C.F.R. § 164.530 (g).
52. 45 C.F.R. § 164.530 (h).

9. Policies and Procedures

A covered entity must draft and implement policies and procedures that comply with the HIPAA requirements and update those policies and procedures if the law changes.[53] When the change affects the covered entity's NPP, the covered entity must also change its NPP.[54] The covered entity must keep the policies and procedures in writing or in electronic form and retain any documentation related to the policies and procedures (changes, updates, revisions, communications, etc.) for a period of six years from the date of its creation or effective date, whichever is later.[55]

B. Business Associates

In May of 2019, the Office for Civil Rights (OCR) issued a new fact sheet providing "a clear compilation of all provisions through which a business associate can be held directly liable for compliance with certain requirements of the HIPAA Privacy, Security, Breach Notification, and Enforcement Rules."[56] The U.S. Department of Health and Human Services has indicated that "OCR has authority to take enforcement action against business associates" only for certain requirements that appeared on OCR's list.[57] Those requirements are as follows:

1. Failure to provide the Secretary with records and compliance reports; cooperate with complaint investigations and compliance reviews; and permit access by the Secretary to information, including PHI, pertinent to determining compliance.

---

53. 45 C.F.R. § 164.530 (i).
54. Id.
55. Id.
56. HHS, New HHS Fact Sheet on Direct Liability of Business Associates under HIPAA (May 24, 2019), https://www.hhs.gov/about/news/2019/05/24/new-hhs-fact-sheet-on-direct-liability-of-business-associates-under-hipaa.html.
57. Id.

2. Taking any retaliatory action against any individual or other person for filing a HIPAA complaint, participating in an investigation or other enforcement process, or opposing an act or practice that is unlawful under the HIPAA rules.
3. Failure to comply with the requirements of the Security Rule.
4. Failure to provide breach notification to a covered entity or another business associate.
5. Impermissible uses and disclosures of PHI.
6. Failure to disclose a copy of electronic PHI to either the covered entity, the individual, or the individual's designee (whichever is specified in the business associate agreement) to satisfy a covered entity's obligations regarding the form and format, and the time and manner of access under 45 C.F.R. §§ 164.524(c)(2)(ii) and 3(ii) respectively.
7. Failure to make reasonable efforts to limit PHI to the minimum necessary to accomplish the intended purpose of the use, disclosure, or request.
8. Failure, in certain circumstances, to provide an accounting of disclosures.
9. Failure to enter into business associate agreements with subcontractors that create or receive PHI on their behalf, and the failure to comply with the implementation specifications of such agreements.
10. Failure to take reasonable steps to address a material breach or violation of the subcontractor's business associate agreement.[58]

III. Conclusion

HIPAA requires covered entities and business associates to have administrative, physical, and technical safeguards in place to protect the confidentiality of PHI. This chapter explored some of these

---

58. *Id.*

safeguards but it does not provide a comprehensive compilation of the safeguards that a covered entity or business associate must have in place. HIPAA compliance will require a careful review of all of the regulatory requirements, implementation of those requirements, and regular monitoring and oversight.

Chapter 6

Summary of the HIPAA Security Rule

I. Purpose and Scope of the Security Rule

Compliance with the Security Rule[1] may be the most important aspect of HIPAA compliance, at least with respect to avoiding penalties for the improper disclosure of protected health information (PHI). Loss of electronic data can result in catastrophic breaches, complaints to the Office for Civil Rights (OCR), and subsequent audits. In fact, a number of HIPAA penalties and financial settlements began with a security breach.[2] According to Roger Severino, the director of OCR, breaches that result from hacking or

---

1. 45 C.F.R. pt. 160 and subpts. A and C of pt. 164.
2. *See*, *e.g.*, Office for Civil Rights, Enforcement Highlights, https://www.hhs.gov/hipaa/for-professionals/compliance-enforcement/data/enforcement-highlights/index.html (last visited Sept. 15, 2019) (noting that the "[l]ack of administrative safeguards of electronic protected health information" is one of the compliance issues investigated most); Press Release, Office for Civil Rights, Five Breaches Add Up to Millions in Settlement Costs for Entity That Failed to Heed HIPAA's Risk Analysis and Risk Mitigation Rules (Feb. 1, 2018), https://www.hhs.gov/about/news/2018/02/01/five-breaches-add-millions-settlement-costs-entity-failed-heed-hipaa-s-risk-analysis-and-risk.html).

IT incidents have skyrocketed in recent days. From September of 2009 through December of 2017, only 19 percent of breaches were a result of IT-related incidents or hacking. In the first nine months of 2018, however, those types of incidents accounted for 41 percent of breaches.[3]

Failure to maintain the integrity and availability of electronic protected health information (ePHI) can also have real consequences for patient care. Unlike the HIPAA Privacy Rule, which applies to all PHI, the Security Rule applies only to ePHI. EPHI is PHI that is transmitted by or maintained in electronic media.[4] The Security Rule became enforceable for most covered entities in 2005, and for small health plans in 2006.[5] Under the HITECH Act, business associates and their subcontractors were required to comply with the Security Rule requirements, and regulations extending the HITECH Act to those entities had a compliance deadline of September 23, 2013.[6]

Electronic media is defined[7] to include a wide variety of electronic storage material that allows the storage of data, such as computer hard drives, memory cards, and disks. It also includes transmission media used to exchange electronic information, including the Internet, physical movement of electronic storage media, and dial-up lines. If the information that is transmitted did not start out in electronic form, it is not considered to be a transmission via electronic media. For example, voice transmissions via telephone, or facsimile transactions that started out as paper, would fall into that category. The U.S. Department of Health and Human Services (HHS) OCR has confirmed, in a "frequently asked

---

3. Roger Severino, Dir., Office for Civil Rights, U.S. Dep't of Health & Human Servs., Keynote Address, HIPAA Security Conference (Oct. 18, 2018).

4. 45 C.F.R. § 160.103.

5. Final Rule, Ctrs. for Medicare & Medicaid Servs., U.S. Dep't of Health & Human Servs. (HHS), Health Insurance Reform: Security Standards, 68 Fed. Reg. 8334 (Feb. 20, 2003).

6. Final Rule, Office for Civil Rights, HHS, 78 Fed. Reg. 5566 (Jan. 25, 2013).

7. 45 C.F.R. § 160.103.

question,"[8] that the Security Rule does not apply to oral or written PHI unless it is ePHI. However, ePHI could include "telephone voice response and fax back systems because they can be used as input and output devices for electronic information systems."[9] The Security Rule would not apply to video conferencing, voicemail, or paper-to-paper faxes because the information was not in electronic form prior to transmission.[10]

HIPAA requires covered entities to "ensure the integrity and confidentiality" of ePHI and to protect against reasonably anticipated threats or hazard to security and unauthorized disclosures.[11] In the preamble to the final Security Rule, the Centers for Medicare & Medicaid Services (CMS), which was charged with Security Rule enforcement at the time, opined that Congress's intent, when it used the word "ensure" in the federal statute, "was to set an exceptionally high goal for the security of electronic protected health information."[12] CMS recognized, however, that Congress did not intend to require protection to be provided regardless of how expensive it was.[13] Instead, covered entities must take steps, to the best of their ability, to protect ePHI while balancing identifiable risks and vulnerabilities against the cost of various measures used to protect the data and taking into account the "size, complexity, and capabilities of the covered entity."[14]

---

8. *See* HHS, Frequently Asked Questions (FAQs) 2010, https://www.hhs.gov/hipaa/for-professionals/faq/2010/does-the-security-rule-apply-to-written-and-oral-communications/index.html (last visited Sept.. 15, 2019).
9. *Id.*
10. *Id.*
11. *See* 42 U.S.C. § 1320d-2(d)(2).
12. Final Rule, Ctrs. for Medicare & Medicaid Servs., HHS, Health Insurance Reform: Security Standards, 68 Fed. Reg. 8334, 8346 (Feb. 20, 2003).
13. *Id.* at 8346.
14. *See id.*

II. Who Needs to Comply?

The Security Rule applies to traditional covered entities including health plans, health care clearinghouses, and health care providers engaging in standard transactions. As discussed in more detail in Chapter 7, the HITECH Act of 2009 also expanded the reach of the Security Rule to business associates and their subcontractors.

III. Administrative, Physical, and Technical Safeguards

The Security Rule imposes administrative, physical, and technical safeguards. Administrative safeguards focus on the operational aspects of the entity. Physical safeguards focus on how facilities and devices housing ePHI will be protected. Technical safeguards concentrate on electronic mechanisms to protect data.

The Security Rule is composed of implementation specifications. Some of these specifications are "required" and some are "addressable." The goal of providing both addressable and required specifications was "to provide covered entities additional flexibility with respect to compliance with the security standards."[15] A "required" implementation specification means that it is mandatory.[16] If an implementation specification is "addressable," it means that the covered entity or business associate must determine whether the specification is a reasonable and appropriate safeguard in light of the environment and its likely contribution to protecting ePHI.[17] If the specification is reasonable and appropriate, it must be implemented. If it is not, the entity must document why it is not, and then implement an "equivalent alternative measure if reasonable and appropriate."[18] A matrix listing the required and

---

15. *Id.* at 8336.
16. 45 C.F.R. § 164.306(d)(2).
17. *Id.* at (d)(3).
18. *Id.*

addressable standards can be found in Appendix A to 45 C.F.R. Part 164 Subpart C.[19]

Considering an addressable standard requires careful documentation and analysis. For example, a covered entity may decide that it would like to send out appointment reminders via e-mail. The covered entity may decide that encryption of these messages is not reasonable and appropriate in light of the limited information they contain, and in light of the need for the message to be read by the patient quickly and easily. Additionally, OCR has suggested that appointment reminders could be sent to the patient in a manner that is less than confidential, such as a postcard.[20] Also, OCR has indicated that providers may communicate with patients via unencrypted e-mail in certain situations.[21] The covered entity should document why encryption is not reasonable and appropriate. The analysis does not end there, however. If there is an "equivalent alternative measure," it must be implemented. If there is no such alternative, it would be prudent for the organization to note that in its documentation.

A. Administrative Safeguards

The Security Rule includes requirements relating to documentation, along with requirements to keep that documentation current.[22]

---

19. *Available at* https://www.govinfo.gov/content/pkg/CFR-2007-title45-vol1/pdf/CFR-2007-title45-vol1-part164-subpartC.pdf.

20. *See* HHS FAQ 198, https://www.hhs.gov/hipaa/for-professionals/faq/198/may-health-care-providers-leave-messages/index.html (last visited Nov. 23, 2018).

21. *See* HHS FAQ 570, https://www.hhs.gov/hipaa/for-professionals/faq/570/does-hipaa-permit-health-care-providers-to-use-email-to-discuss-health-issues-with-patients/index.html (last visited Nov. 23, 2018).

22. Final Rule, Ctrs. for Medicare & Medicaid Servs., HHS, Health Insurance Reform: Security Standards, 68 Fed. Reg. 8334, 8346 (Feb. 20, 2003).

1. Security Management Process

The portion of the Security Rule dealing with security management "forms the foundation on which all of the other standards depend."[23]

a. Risk Analysis and Risk Mitigation

One of the most important administrative safeguards in the Security Rule is the requirement for a risk analysis and risk mitigation plan. A risk analysis involves "an accurate and thorough assessment of the potential risks and vulnerabilities to the confidentiality, integrity, and availability of" ePHI.[24] For the risks identified, the entity needs to develop a risk management plan that is sufficient to reduce the identified risks to an appropriate and reasonable level.[25] Failure to have an adequate risk analysis has contributed to a number of OCR settlements related to alleged HIPAA violations.[26]

In a conference in October of 2018, representatives of OCR and the HHS Office of the National Coordinator for Health IT[27] presented the following top ten myths regarding security risk analyses:

1. *"The security risk analysis is optional for small providers."* Although certain small health plans were given extra time to comply with the HIPAA Security Rule,[28] and HIPAA

---

23. *Id.* at 8344.
24. 45 C.F.R. §§ 164.308(a)(1)(ii)(A).
25. *Id.* at (a)(1)(ii)(B).
26. *See, e.g.*, Office for Civil Rights, Press Release, Anthem Pays OCR $16 Million in Record HIPAA Settlement Following Largest U.S. Health Data Breach in History (Oct. 15, 2018), https://www.hhs.gov/about/news/2018/10/15/anthem-pays-ocr-16-million-record-hipaa-settlement-following-largest-health-data-breach-history.html (noting that OCR's investigation revealed that Anthem failed to conduct an enterprise-wide risk analysis).
27. Nick Heesters, Office for Civil Rights, & Rose-Marie O. Nsahlai, Senior Technical Advisor, HHS Office of the Nat'l Coordinator for Health IT, "Safeguarding Health Information: Building Assurance through HIPAA Security—2018," Office for Civil Rights & ONC Security Risk Assessment (SRA) Tool Walk-Through: New Features and New Functionality, HIPAA Security Conference (Oct. 18, 2018), *available at* https://www.healthit.gov/topic/privacy-security-and-hipaa/top-10-myths-security-risk-analysis.
28. Final Rule, Ctrs. for Medicare & Medicaid Servs., HHS, Health Insurance Reform: Security Standards, 68 Fed. Reg. 8334 (Feb. 20, 2003).

is flexible and scalable,[29] it does not give small health care providers the option of avoiding the risk analysis requirement.

2. *"Simply installing a certified EHR fulfills the security risk analysis MU requirement."*
In 2011, CMS established a program to incentivize eligible professionals, eligible hospitals, and critical access hospitals to meaningfully use (MU)[30] certified electronic health record (EHR) technology.[31] Installation of such an EHR system does not allow covered entities to avoid assessing risks to their ePHI.

3. *"My EHR vendor took care of everything I need to do about privacy and security."*
Although some EHR vendors may advertise their systems as being "HIPAA compliant," use of such a system still requires a risk analysis involving ePHI that resides inside and outside the system.

4. *"I have to outsource the security risk analysis."*
"It is possible for small practices to do risk analysis themselves using self-help tools. However, doing a thorough and professional risk analysis that will stand up to a compliance review will require expert knowledge that could be obtained through services of an experienced outside professional."[32]
Rose-Marie O. Nsahlai, a senior technical advisor with the

---

29. *Id.* at 8338 ("[W]e have structured the Security Rule to be scalable and flexible enough to allow different entities to implement the standards in a manner that is appropriate for their circumstances.").

30. The Centers for Medicare & Medicaid Services provides certain incentives to encourage health care entities to use certified electronic health record technology. The MU program was transitioned into a component of the Merit-Based Incentive Payment System (MIPS), which is part of the Medicare Access and CHIP Reauthorization Act (MACRA). *See* HHS, Meaningful Use and MACRA, https://www.healthit.gov/topic/meaningful-use-and-macra/meaningful-use-and-macra (last visited July 7, 2019).

31. *See* Ctrs. for Medicare & Medicaid Servs., Promoting Interoperability, https://www.cms.gov/Regulations-and-Guidance/Legislation/EHRIncentivePrograms/index.html (last visited Sept. 15, 2019).

32. *See* Health IT.gov, Top 10 Myths of Security Risk Analysis, https://www.healthit.gov/topic/privacy-security-and-hipaa/top-10-myths-security-risk-analysis (last visited June 6, 2019).

HHS Office of the National Coordinator for Health IT, has stated, "[T]his is a tricky one. Even if you outsource it, you bear the full responsibility of ensuring" that you are compliant with the Security Rule and the integrity of the information is protected.[33]

5. *"A checklist will suffice for the risk analysis requirement."* Although checklists may be useful tools as part of a risk analysis, this requirement involves a detailed analysis of the risks and vulnerabilities to ePHI. Merely completing a checklist would not likely fulfill the requirement to conduct the "accurate and thorough assessment" required by 45 C.F.R. § 164.308. The government has provided a number of useful tools for the risk analysis. For example, a task group was formed under the authority of Section 405(d) of the Cybersecurity Act of 2015.[34] On December 28, 2018, HHS announced[35] the release of voluntary cybersecurity practice and tools for the health care industry developed by the task group. The tools include analyses of common cybersecurity threats to health care entities, and ways to mitigate those threats.[36]

6. *"There is a specific risk analysis method that I must follow."* A risk analysis can be performed in countless ways. Ms. Nsahlai has noted that "the Security Rule has a lot of flexibility in your approach based on your risk profile, based on your organizational structure, your size, the cost, so there's a lot of flexibility in the HIPAA Security Rule."[37]

7. *"My security risk analysis only needs to look at my EHR."*

---

33. HIPAA Security Conference, Oct. 18, 2018.
34. Pub. L. No. 114-113.
35. Press Release, HHS, in Partnership with Industry, Releases Voluntary Cybersecurity Practices for the Health Industry (Dec. 28, 2018), https://www.hhs.gov/about/news/2018/12/28/hhs-in-partnership-with-industry-releases-voluntary-cybersecurity-practices-for-the-health-industry.html).
36. The task group's cybersecurity reports and tools are available at https://www.phe.gov/Preparedness/planning/405d/Pages/default.aspx (last visited Jan. 3, 2019).
37. HIPAA Security Conference, Oct. 18, 2018.

The risk analysis is not limited to the EHR. "It should be enterprise wide," notes Ms. Nsahlai. "You really need to look at all your assets, your inventory, your devices, your systems, your entire enterprise wide structure needs to be looked at, not just your [electronic health record] . . . your EHR is just but one little system you need to take a look at."[38] It should include all electronic devices that store, capture, or modify ePHI.[39]

The EHR "meaningful use" security requirements differ somewhat from HIPAA. For example, to demonstrate meaningful use, eligible professionals and hospitals must conduct a security risk analysis annually that examines the potential risks and vulnerabilities only to the ePHI created by or maintained in the certified EHR technology, or CEHRT.[40] HIPAA, on the other hand, requires that covered entities and business associates "assess the potential risks and vulnerabilities to the confidentiality, availability, and integrity of all ePHI that an organization creates, receives, maintains, or transmits. This includes ePHI in all forms of electronic media, such as hard drives, floppy disks, CDs, DVDs, smart cards or other storage devices, personal digital assistants, transmission media, or portable electronic media."[41]

8. *"I only need to do a risk analysis once."*
    Ms. Nsahlai notes that "you always have to re-assess, especially if you're implementing new tools or systems. It's an ongoing process . . . it's almost like breathing every day."[42]

---

38. HIPAA Security Conference, Oct. 18, 2018.
39. HealthIT.gov, Top 10 Myths of Security Risk Analysis, https://www.healthit.gov/topic/privacy-security-and-hipaa/top-10-myths-security-risk-analysis (last visited June 6, 2019).
40. *See* Ctrs. for Medicare & Medicaid Servs., HHS, final rules with comment period, Medicare and Medicaid Programs; Electronic Health Record Incentive Program—Stage 3 and Modifications to Meaningful Use in 2015 through 2017, 80 Fed. Reg. 62,762, 62,830 (Oct. 16, 2015).
41. *Id.* at 62,830.
42. HIPAA Security Conference, Oct. 18, 2018.

9. *"Before I attest for an EHR incentive program, I must fully mitigate all risks."*
"You don't have to mitigate all risk . . . you would address all risks that are pertinent to your organization," says Ms. Nsahlai.[43] You need to make sure you address the ones that present the most risk.[44]
10. *"Each year, I'll have to completely re-do my security risk analysis."*
Ms. Nsahlai states, "You do not have to re-do it. It's an ongoing effort. You could have iterations of it. However, you constantly have to improve it."[45]

b. Other Aspects of the Security Management Process

In addition to risk analysis and risk mitigation, a security management process requires a number of other elements. These include workforce sanctions, in which employees are disciplined for failure to comply with the policies that have been put in place. Covered entities must also develop audit logs, access reports, security incident tracking reports, or other procedures to allow regular review of information system activity.[46]

2. Assigned Security Responsibility

The Security Rule contemplates that a specific individual be given the responsibility to oversee security.[47] The security official, often referred to as a "security officer," is the person who is ultimately responsible "for the development and implementation of the policies and procedures" required by the Security Rule.[48] The security

---

43. Rose-Marie O. Nsahlai, Senior Technical Advisor, HHS Office of the Nat'l Coordinator for Health IT, HIPAA Security Conference, Oct. 18, 2018.
44. *Id.*
45. *Id.*
46. 45 C.F.R. § 164.308(a)(1)(ii)(D).
47. 68 Fed. Reg. at 8347.
48. *See* 45 C.F.R. § 164.308(a)(2).

official is sometimes an organization's chief information officer. The same individual could be designated as both the privacy and security official, but this is not required.[49]

3. Information Access Management

HIPAA requires that covered entities address certain information access management functions. For example, organizations must separate their clearinghouse functions from the rest of the organization if a portion of the organization is a clearinghouse.[50] They must address access authorization and access establishment and modification.[51] For a very small entity, like a dentist's office with three employees, it may not be reasonable and appropriate to develop extremely formal security access protocols, but the organization could still document who has access to what PHI.[52]

4. Security Awareness and Training

Employee training is an important step in HIPAA compliance. The Security Rule requires that organizations address special training efforts relating to security. Workforce members must be trained "as reasonable and appropriate to carry out their functions in the facility."[53] Periodic security updates to remind people of their security obligations must also be addressed.[54]

---

49. HHS, HIPAA SECURITY SERIES 2, SECURITY STANDARDS: ADMINISTRATIVE SAFEGUARDS 7 (rev. Mar. 2007), https://www.hhs.gov/sites/default/files/ocr/privacy/hipaa/administrative/securityrule/adminsafeguards.pdf.

50. 45 C.F.R. § 164.308(a)(4)(ii)(A).

51. *Id.* at (a)(4)(B)–(C).

52. *See* 68 Fed. Reg. at 8349 ("A fully automated covered entity spanning multiple locations and involving hundreds of employees may determine it has a need to adopt a formal policy for access authorization, while a small provider may decide that a desktop standard operating procedure will meet the specifications.")

53. *Id.*

54. 45 C.F.R. § 164.308(5)(ii)(A).

5. Security Incident Procedures

Security incident procedures are critical to ensuring that HIPAA breaches are addressed properly. Breach response is discussed in more detail in Chapter 8. The Security Rule requires that organizations be able to detect and mitigate potential or actual security incidents, and they must also document the incidents and their outcomes.[55] HIPAA defines "security incident" broadly. It encompasses more than just actual data breaches. It includes both actual unauthorized access, use, disclosure, modification, and destruction of information or interference with system operations, as well as mere attempts that are not successful.[56]

6. Contingency Plans

HIPAA security involves protecting against more than just computer hackers. The Security Rule requires that organizations develop and implement policies and procedures to deal with emergencies such as fire, vandalism, system failure, and natural disasters that could threaten ePHI.[57] During the rulemaking process for the Security Rule, a number of commenters suggesting deleting the requirement for contingency plans, arguing that the regulation went beyond its intended scope. The government responded that "[a] contingency plan is the only way to protect the availability, integrity, and security of data during unexpected negative events. Data are often most exposed in these events, since the usual security measures may be disabled, ignored, or not observed."[58] Implementation specifications for this requirement include required specifications relating to data backup, disaster recovery, and emergency mode operation. Addressable specifications relate to testing and revision procedures, and applications and data criticality analysis.[59]

---

55. 45 C.F.R. § 164.308(a)(6).
56. 45 C.F.R. § 164.304.
57. *See* 45 C.F.R. § 164.308(a)(7)(i).
58. 68 Fed. Reg. at 8351.
59. 45 C.F.R. § 164.038(a)(7)(ii).

7. Evaluation of How Changes Affect the Security of ePHI

Covered entities and business associates must periodically perform technical and nontechnical evaluations of how changes affect ePHI security. These evaluations must be based on the Security Rule standards initially, and then must be revisited when there are environmental or operational changes.[60]

8. Business Associate Agreements and Similar Arrangements

Business associates may create, receive, maintain, or transmit ePHI on behalf of a covered entity only if the covered entity obtains "satisfactory assurances" that the business associate will handle ePHI properly.[61] Business associate agreements are discussed in more detail in Chapter 7.

B. Physical Safeguards

A number of breaches have resulted from theft of laptops or workstation computers. Control over physical security is a critical element of Security Rule compliance. The regulations require facility access controls, including methods to keep unauthorized individuals out of areas where ePHI may be used or stored. Covered entities and business associates must also have policies regarding workstation use and workstation security, as well as device and media controls.[62]

C. Technical Safeguards

With the rise in breaches that result from computer hacking or IT incidents, technical safeguards are more important than ever. The

---

60. *Id.* at (8).
61. 45 C.F.R. § 164.308(b)(1).
62. 45 C.F.R. § 164.310.

Security Rule contains a number of standards relating to technical measures to protect data, which are as follows:[63]

1. Access Control

Access controls include measures that are probably widely adopted by many organizations, such as requiring unique user identification.[64] Even though unique user identification is required, there must also be procedures for obtaining necessary access to ePHI during an emergency.[65] The regulators believe that organizations should have procedures in place beforehand to provide guidance on potential ways to gain access to ePHI in the event of a power outage or other disaster.[66]

2. Audit Controls

Auditing what happens on a system containing ePHI is an important way to detect potential problems. HIPAA requires organizations to have mechanisms in place that allow activity in information systems to be examined and recorded.[67]

3. Integrity

The integrity provisions of the Security Rule were initially referred to as "data authentication."[68] Organizations must have mechanisms in place to protect ePHI from improper destruction or alteration. They must also address ways to make sure ePHI has not been altered or destroyed in an impermissible manner.[69]

---

63. 45 C.F.R. § 164.312.
64. *Id.* at (a)(2)(i).
65. *Id.* at (a)(2)(ii).
66. 68 Fed. Reg. at 8355.
67. 45 C.F.R. § 164.312(b).
68. 68 Fed. Reg. at 8356.
69. 45 C.F.R. § 164.312(c).

4. Person or Entity Authentication

In a time where phishing is on the rise,[70] making sure that individuals trying to access ePHI are who they say they are is of critical importance. The Security Rule includes a standard requiring organizations to have procedures in place to authenticate individuals or entities that want access to ePHI.[71]

5. Transmission Security and Encryption

Covered entities and business associates must have technical measures in place to make sure that ePHI transmitted over an electronic communications network is protected. This standard has addressable implementation specifications related to integrity controls (making sure ePHI is not improperly modified) and encryption.[72] OCR guidance defines encryption as "a method of converting an original message of regular text into encoded text."[73] The fact that encryption is addressable does not make it optional in most situations, although OCR guidance indicates that encryption is not mandatory.[74]

IV. Organizational Requirements

A. Business Associate Agreements

As discussed in more detail in Chapter 7, HIPAA requires that covered entities and business associates have written contracts in

---

70. *See, e.g.,* Sead Fadilpasic, *Phishing Attacks Are Up, but Awareness Is Also on the Rise,* ITPROPORTAL, Jan. 18, 2018, https://www.itproportal.com/news/phishing-attacks-are-up-but-people-are-more-wary/.
71. 45 C.F.R. § 164.312(d).
72. 45 C.F.R. § 164.312(e).
73. HHS FAQ 2021, https://www.hhs.gov/hipaa/for-professionals/faq/2021/what-is-encryption/index.html (last visited Nov. 23, 2018).
74. HHS FAQ 2001, https://www.hhs.gov/hipaa/for-professionals/faq/2001/is-the-use-of-encryption-mandatory-in-the-security-rule/index.html (last visited Nov. 23, 2018).

place that include certain provisions. The Security Rule requires those agreements to include specific provisions governing ePHI if ePHI is relevant to the arrangement.[75]

B. Policies and Procedures

All of the Security Rule requirements discussed in this chapter must be documented in reasonable and appropriate policies and procedures.[76] Those policies and procedures must be maintained for at least six years, and made available to relevant workforce members. They also must be updated periodically, as needed, in response to changes that could affect ePHI security.

V. Conclusion

The Security Rule is very detailed, and requires both technical know-how and the ability to foresee what could go wrong with data. Compliance requires ongoing, concerted effort, starting with a risk analysis that sufficiently captures where the data is located and how it could go astray. It also requires a reasonable mitigation plan. Careful drafting of policies and procedures, and then training workforce members on those policies, can go a long way in reducing security risks to ePHI.

---

75. 45 C.F.R. § 164.314.
76. 45 C.F.R. § 164.316.

Chapter 7

The HITECH Act

The HITECH Act was passed by Congress as part of the American Recovery and Reinvestment Act of 2009 (ARRA).[1] The full name of Title XIII of the ARRA is the Health Information Technology for Economic and Clinical Health Act.[2] The HITECH Act's goal was "to promote widespread adoption and interoperability of health information technology."[3] It includes amendments, in Subtitle D, aimed at strengthening HIPAA's privacy and security protections.[4] Prior to the HITECH Act, business associates had to enter into written agreements with covered entities requiring the business associates to protect data, but they were not directly subject to HIPAA's requirements.[5] The HITECH Act expanded HIPAA's reach by requiring these service providers to comply with

---

1. Pub. L. No. 111-5.
2. *Id.* at § 13001.
3. Final Rule, Office for Civil Rights, U.S. Dep't of Health & Human Servs., Modifications to the HIPAA Privacy, Security, Enforcement, and Breach Notification Rules under the Health Information Technology for Economic and Clinical Health Act and the Genetic Information Nondiscrimination Act; Other Modifications to the HIPAA Rules, 78 Fed. Reg. 5566, 5568 (Jan. 25, 2013).
4. *Id.* at 5568.
5. *Id.* at 5589.

the HIPAA Security Rule,[6] as well as the provisions of their business associate agreements.[7]

I. Requirements for Business Associates

A. Compliance Requirements for Business Associates

In the so-called "omnibus rule"[8] of 2013, implementing the HITECH Act and making certain other changes,[9] the Office of Civil Rights (OCR) made a number of modifications to the HIPAA Privacy Rule and Security Rule that affected business associates dramatically. Certain types of organizations were included in the definition of "business associate," including persons offering personal health records on behalf of a covered entity, subcontractors, undefined "health information organizations," "e-prescribing gateways," and other persons that provide data transmission services involving protected health information (PHI) that require routine access to the information.[10] Prior to the HITECH Act, business associates focused on compliance needed to implement procedures to make sure they complied with the terms of their business associate agreement, but such procedures, along with workforce training and other compliance tasks, were not mandated by federal law. OCR assumed, however, that at the time of the HITECH Act omnibus rule, business associates and subcontractors would "already have in place security practices that either comply with

---

6. 42 U.S.C. § 17931.
7. 42 U.S.C. § 17934.
8. A number of sources refer to the regulations implementing the HITECH Act as the "omnibus rule." *See, e.g.,* Dianne J. Bourque et al., *Breach Notification Rule Risk Assessments—Applying the New Breach Notification Standard under the HIPAA Omnibus Rule,* ABA HEALTH ESOURCE (Sept. 27, 2018), https://www.americanbar.org/groups/health_law/publications/aba_health_esource/2013-14/july/breach_notification/.
9. *See* 78 Fed. Reg. at 5568–69.
10. 78 Fed. Reg. at 5571, 5573; 45 C.F.R. § 160.103.

the Security Rule, or that require only modest improvements to come into compliance with the Security Rule requirements."[11]

Now that business associates can be held civilly and criminally liable for HIPAA violations,[12] a compliance program is critical. OCR has made it clear that the HIPAA regulations do not dictate particular security measures or technology. Instead, "[c]overed entities and business associates have the flexibility to choose security measures appropriate for their size, resources, and the nature of the security risks they face, enabling them to reasonably implement any given Security Rule standard."[13] The following is a discussion of privacy and security measures that business associates should consider.

1. Privacy Measures for Business Associates

a. Analysis of Entity's Status under HIPAA

Some business associates could also be covered entities or subcontractors. An important question is whether a business associate converts PHI to or from a standard format to be used in connection with a standard transaction, which could make it a clearinghouse and, therefore, a covered entity subject to all of HIPAA's requirements.[14] If a business associate also acts as a health care provider, it should examine carefully whether it transmits PHI in connection with any standard transactions, thus making it a covered entity.[15]

b. Business Associate Agreement

Business associates should also consider developing template business associate agreements (a sample is located in the appendix to this chapter). As discussed ahead, business associate agreements are not all alike, and a business associate may want to include

---

11. 78 Fed. Reg. at 5589.
12. *Id.*
13. *Id.*
14. 45 C.F.R. § 160.103.
15. *Id.*

different provisions in these documents, depending on whether it is contracting with a covered entity or a subcontractor. An important requirement is that subcontractors must agree to the same restrictions and conditions that apply to the business associate with respect to the use and disclosure of PHI.[16] It would be helpful to develop an inventory of business associate agreements, along with notations regarding their term, expiration dates, and provisions that may differ from the business associate's templates.

c. Inventory of PHI
Business associates need to know where PHI is located within the organization, and how it is used and disclosed. Business associates should determine whether there are any uses and disclosures that are not specifically permitted by business associate agreements, or are for purposes unrelated to treatment, payment, or health care operations. If so, patient authorizations may be required.

d. Minimum Necessary Standard
Business associates should also implement procedural "firewalls" to make sure that they are conforming to the minimum necessary rule.[17] The HIPAA minimum necessary rule requires restricting most uses and disclosures of PHI to the minimum amount of information necessary to accomplish the intended purpose. This involves identifying employees who access PHI to determine whether access is restricted to those who need to have the information to do their jobs.

e. Policies and Training
Internal policies and procedures, which must be documented, are an important part of HIPAA compliance. For business associates, these policies and procedures should include systems to ensure that PHI is used and disclosed only as permitted by the entity's business

---

16. 45 C.F.R. § 164.504(e)(2)(ii)(D).
17. 45 C.F.R. § 164.514(d)(1).

associate agreements. It is also critical that workforce members be trained on the policies and procedures relevant to their job duties.

2. Security Measures for Business Associates

Under the HITECH Act, security requirements for covered entities also apply to business associates.[18] Therefore, OCR's extensive guidance pertaining to the Security Rule[19] will be useful for these entities. More details on the Security Rule are found in Chapter 6. In developing a Security Rule compliance plan, business associates should consider the following topics:

- A risk analysis;
- A risk management plan;
- Written policies and procedures, including a sanction policy for workforce members who fail to comply;
- Information system activity review, including audit logs, access reports, and security incident tracking reports;
- Appointment of a security official;
- Procedures for the authorization and supervision of workforce members who access electronic PHI;
- Workforce clearance, access authorization, access modification, and termination procedures;
- Security reminders and security training;
- Protection from malicious software;
- Log-in monitoring;
- Password management;
- Security incident procedures;
- Contingency plans, data backup, disaster recovery, emergency mode operation plans, testing and revisions, and data criticality analysis;

---

18. 42 U.S.C. § 17931.
19. *See, e.g.*, U.S. Dep't of Health & Human Servs. (HHS), Summary of the HIPAA Security Rule, https://www.hhs.gov/hipaa/for-professionals/security/laws-regulations/index.html (last visited Dec. 27, 2018).

- Facility access controls, including a facility security plan, maintenance records, and access control and validation procedures;
- Workstation security;
- Device and media controls;
- Access controls, including unique user identification, emergency access procedures, automatic logoff, encryption, and decryption;
- Audit controls;
- Data integrity mechanisms and integrity controls;
- Person and entity authentication; and
- Transmission security.

B. Special Business Associate Considerations

1. Document Storage

In the preamble to the HITECH Act omnibus rule, OCR provided guidance regarding special issues relating to business associates. For example, OCR declined to define exactly what it means for a business associate providing data transmission services to have "access on a routine basis" to PHI.[20] OCR distinguished these types of data transmission services with "mere conduits," and noted that a "determination will be fact specific based on the nature of the services provided and the extent to which the entity needs access to protected health information to perform the service for the covered entity."[21] OCR noted that "[t]he conduit exception is a narrow one and is intended to exclude only those entities providing mere courier services, such as the U.S. Postal Service or United Parcel Service and their electronic equivalents, such as internet service providers (ISPs) providing mere data transmission services."[22] OCR noted that a conduit could access PHI on a random basis as needed

---

20. 78 Fed. Reg. at 5571.
21. Id.
22. Id.

to make sure the transmitted data is being delivered correctly, and such random access would not turn the conduit into a business associate.[23] On the other hand, a health information organization or other entity that manages PHI exchange on behalf of covered entities through the use or record locator services is considered a business associate.[24] Also, entities that store PHI on behalf of a covered entity are considered business associates, even if they do not view the information.[25]

2. Researchers

OCR also provided guidance regarding whether researchers meet the "business associate" definition. In the omnibus rule preamble, OCR indicated that a person or entity is a business associate only when they are conducting a function or activity governed by the HIPAA rules on behalf of a covered entity, or providing one of the services specifically listed in the "business associate" definition.[26] OCR indicated that a researcher would not be a business associate merely by virtue of performing research activities, even if the research is being conducted for the covered entity.[27] Additionally, an independent institutional review board would not be a business

---

23. 78 Fed. Reg. at 5571–72.
24. *Id.* at 5572.
25. *Id.* ("Thus, document storage companies maintaining protected health information on behalf of covered entities are considered business associates, regardless of whether they actually view the information they hold.") Note that this position OCR took deeming document storage services to be business associates was a reversal of its prior advice to at least one document storage service. *See* Letter from Richard M. Campanelli, J.D., Dir., Office for Civil Rights, U.S. Dep't of Health & Human Servs., to Elizabeth Tindall (May 12, 2003) ("We confirm that a business associate agreement is not required between a covered entity and a document storage company performing functions on behalf of the covered entity, where any protected health information released to the storage company is transferred and maintained in closed and sealed containers, and the document storage company does not otherwise access protected health information. Neither is a business associate agreement needed when, in these circumstances, any access to the information is merely incidental.").
26. 78 Fed. Reg. at 5575.
27. *Id.*

associate by virtue of the research oversight functions it performs.[28] If the researcher does something on behalf of the covered entity other than research, such as creating limited data sets or de-identified data, then the researcher may be a business associate.[29]

3. Financial Institutions

OCR has stated that "[t]he HIPAA Rules, including the business associate provisions, do not apply to banking and financial institutions with respect to" payment processing activities such as cashing a check or transferring funds.[30] The HIPAA statute itself[31] exempts a variety of financial institution activities from HIPAA's requirements, including "authorizing, processing, clearing, settling, billing, transferring, reconciling, or collecting payments for health care or health plan premiums."[32] Banking or financial institutions could be considered business associates, however, "where the institution performs functions above and beyond the payment processing activities identified above on behalf of a covered entity, such as performing accounts receivable functions on behalf of a health care provider."[33]

---

28. *Id.*
29. *Id.*
30. *Id.*
31. *See* 42 U.S.C. 1320d-8 (referring to the definition of "financial institution" in 1101 of the Right to Financial Privacy Act of 1978); *see also* 12 U.S.C. § 3401(1) (defining "financial institution" as including, with certain exceptions, "any office of a bank, savings bank, card issuer as defined in section 1602(n) of title 15, industrial loan company, trust company, savings association, building and loan, or homestead association (including cooperative banks), credit union, or consumer finance institution, located in any State or territory of the United States, the District of Columbia, Puerto Rico, Guam, American Samoa, or the Virgin Islands").
32. 78 Fed. Reg. at 5575.
33. *Id.* (noting that a financial institution that is solely conducting payment activities that are excluded under § 1179 of the HIPAA statute would not have to enter into a HIPAA subcontractor agreement with a business associate).

4. Attorneys

The U.S. Department of Health and Human Services (HHS) has long considered attorneys to be business associates if they are performing a service for a covered entity involving the use or disclosure of PHI.[34] In the preamble to the HITECH Act omnibus rule, OCR noted that, while an insurer is typically not a business associate, it could qualify as one if it performs other services on behalf of the covered entity, including legal services.[35] HHS has rejected arguments that business associate agreements would undermine the attorney/client relationship and interfere with the attorney/client privilege.[36]

C. Business Associate Agreements

All business associate agreements must include the basic elements[37] listed below. The appendix to this chapter includes a template agreement that is somewhat favorable to the business associate.

1. The agreement must establish the permitted and required uses and disclosures of PHI.
2. The document may not allow the business associate to use or further disclose PHI in a way that the covered entity could not, except business associates may be allowed to perform data aggregation services,[38] and may be allowed to use and disclose PHI for their own proper management and administration.[39]

---

34. Final Rule, Office of the Assistant Sec'y for Planning & Evaluation, U.S. Dep't of Health & Human Servs., Standards for Privacy of Individually Identifiable Health Information, 65 Fed. Reg. 82,462, 82,505 (Dec. 28, 2000) (discussing a business associate contract between a covered entity and an attorney).
35. 78 Fed. Reg. at 5575.
36. *See* 65 Fed. Reg. at 82,642 ("[T]he attorney-client privilege covers only a small portion of the information provided to attorneys and so is not a substitute for [a business associate agreement].").
37. *See* 45 C.F.R. § 164.504(e).
38. *See* 45 C.F.R. § 164.504 (e)(2)(i)(B)
39. 45 C.F.R. § 164.504(e)(4).

3. The document must provide that the business associate will:
    a. Not use or further disclose PHI other than as required by law or permitted or required by the business associate agreement;
    b. Comply with the HIPAA Security Rule where applicable and use appropriate safeguards;
    c. Report to the covered entity any breach or other use or disclosure of PHI not permitted by the business associate agreement, as well as security incidents;
    d. Ensure that subcontractors agree to the same restrictions and conditions that apply to the business associate;
    e. Make PHI available to individuals;
    f. Make PHI available for amendment, and incorporate amendments as necessary;
    g. Make information available if required to account for disclosures;
    h. To the extent the business associate is required to carry out the covered entity's obligations under the Privacy Rule, comply with the Privacy Rule with respect to those obligations;[40]
    i. Make available to the Secretary of the Department of Health and Human Services the business associate's internal practices, books, and records relating to how PHI is used and disclosed for the purpose of determining compliance with HIPAA; and
    j. Return or destroy the PHI when the business associate agreement is terminated, if feasible. If the business associate knows that return or destruction will not be feasible, it may be useful to address this in the business associate agreement.
4. The business associate agreement must be terminable by the covered entity if the covered entity determines that the business associate has violated a material term.

---

40. 45 C.F.R. § 164.504(e)(2)(ii)(H).

5. If the business associate commits a "breach," the business associate must report it to the covered entity within 60 days of discovery. Although HIPAA gives the business associate 60 days to report, the parties should consider whether a shorter time frame is appropriate in light of more stringent state laws.
6. If the business associate will be de-identifying or aggregating PHI, or handling substance use disorder information subject to 42 C.F.R. Part 2, the parties should make sure those topics are adequately addressed either in the business associate agreement or the underlying services agreement.

II. HIPAA Breaches

The HITECH Act did more than just expand HIPAA's regulatory reach to business associates. It also gave individuals additional rights, including the right to be notified of a "breach."[41] Under the statute and the omnibus rule,[42] finalized in 2013, a breach is the unauthorized use, disclosure, acquisition, or access of PHI that compromises the security or privacy of the information.[43] An event is not a breach if the unauthorized person who received the PHI would not reasonably have been able to retain it.[44] Certain other situations are deemed not to constitute a breach, including:

- Unintentional acquisition, access, or use of PHI by a workforce member or someone under the authority of a covered entity or business associate, as long as the acquisition, access,

---

41. 42 U.S.C. § 17921.
42. Final Rule, Office for Civil Rights, U.S. Dep't of Health & Human Servs., Modifications to the HIPAA Privacy, Security, Enforcement, and Breach Notification Rules under the Health Information Technology for Economic and Clinical Health Act and the Genetic Information Nondiscrimination Act; Other Modifications to the HIPAA Rules, 78 Fed. Reg. 5566 (Jan. 25, 2013).
43. 42 U.S.C. § 17921; 45 C.F.R. § 164.402.
44. *Id.*

or use was in good faith and within that person's scope of authority. That person must not further use or disclose the PHI in an impermissible manner.
- Inadvertent disclosures by an authorized person to another person authorized to access PHI at the same covered entity, business associate, or organized health care arrangement. As with the exception above, the PHI must not be further used or disclosed inappropriately.[45]

A. Risk Assessments

Unless it falls within an exception, an acquisition, access, use, or disclosure of PHI in a manner that is not permitted under the Privacy Rule is presumed to be a reportable breach. Situations that do not clearly fall within one of the exceptions discussed above could still avoid the breach designation if the covered entity or business associate is able to demonstrate that there is a low probability that PHI has been "compromised." The regulations do not define what "compromised" means, but the assessment requires consideration of at least four factors:

1. The nature and extent of the PHI involved, including the types of identifiers involved in the incident and the likelihood of re-identification;
2. The unauthorized person who received or used the PHI;
3. Whether the PHI was actually acquired or viewed; and
4. The extent to which the risk has been mitigated.[46]

If ransomware was involved, OCR has issued informal guidance[47] suggesting that the risk assessment should examine a number of factors, including the type of variety of the malware, the

---

45. *Id.*
46. 45 C.F.R. § 164.402.
47. HHS, Office for Civil Rights, Fact Sheet: Ransomware and HIPAA (2016) https://www.hhs.gov/sites/default/files/RansomwareFactSheet.pdf.

algorithm it used, whether it moved to other systems, and whether it exfiltrated any PHI. In addition to the four factors above, the covered entity or business associate affected by ransomware should consider whether the situation resulted in a high risk that the integrity of the data was affected, or that PHI would become unavailable.

When a risk assessment is conducted it must be documented. The covered entity or business associate must also maintain sufficient backup documentation sufficient to meet the organization's burden of proof that the incident did not rise to the level of a breach, or that all required notifications were made.[48]

B. Breach Response

Once a business associate has detected a breach or security incident, it has a maximum of 60 days to make a report to the covered entity. Business associates that do not already have a plan in place to detect and report incidents may have significant difficulty complying with breach notification requirements in the regulations and their agreements. Business associates should make sure there are policies in place to deal with breaches and that workforce members have been trained on those policies. Workforce members should know the right person to contact immediately if they suspect an incident or breach. Procedures should already be established to make sure that incidents are escalated quickly to the security official. The organization should make sure it is following its own policies and procedures with respect to incident response. Chapter 8 discusses incident response and breach notification in detail.

III. Other HITECH Act Provisions

The HITECH Act contains a number of other provisions that affect covered entities and business associates. For example, it increased

---

48. 45 C.F.R. § 164.414.

penalties for HIPAA violations.[49] It also made it clear that individuals could be held criminally liable for HIPAA violations.[50] The law also gave individuals new rights. In addition to the right to be notified of a breach, as discussed above, the law gave individuals the right to receive an accounting of all disclosures from an electronic health record.[51] The HITECH Act was confirmation that Congress believes that HIPAA and data privacy and security are important; therefore, covered entities and business associates must continue to implement and monitor their compliance programs.

IV. Conclusion

Although the initial HIPAA law held covered entities liable for privacy and security violations, the HITECH Act extended certain responsibilities and expanded liability to the business associate, making them clearly subject to fines and criminal penalties. Business associates are wise to implement measures that comply with these mandates.

---

49. ARRA § 13410 (codified at 42 U.S.C. § 1320d-5(a)(1)).
50. ARRA § 13409 (codified at 42 U.S.C. § 1320d-6(a)).
51. ARRA § 13405 (codified at 42 U.S.C. § 17935). The statute gives individuals the right to receive an accounting of disclosures through an electronic health record during the prior three years. Regulations implementing this requirement have not yet been finalized.

Chapter 7 Appendix

Sample HIPAA Business Associate Agreement Favorable to Business Associate

Note: This document is for a hypothetical business associate or subcontractor, and it may not be appropriate for certain situations. It is designed to be somewhat favorable to the data recipient. Note that if the business associate re-distributes PHI to subcontractors, the subcontractors must agree to the same restrictions and conditions that apply to the business associate. The data recipient should consider whether limitations of liability, insurance or other provisions should be addressed. Individuals drafting a business associate agreement should also review OCR's sample provisions.[52]

HIPAA Business Associate Agreement

To the extent that _____ ("Covered Entity") discloses Protected Health Information to _____ ("Business Associate"), or Business Associate handles Protected Health Information on Covered Entity's behalf, in connection with services or products provided to Covered Entity, or as otherwise required or allowed by the Administrative Simplification provisions of the Health Insurance Portability and Accountability Act of 1996, Public Law 104-191, codified at 42 U.S.C. §1320d through d-9, as amended ("HIPAA"), Covered Entity and Business Associate agree to the following terms and conditions, which are intended to comply with HIPAA, the Health Information Technology for Economic and Clinical Health Act ("HITECH Act"), and their

---

52. Office for Civil Rights, Business Associate Contracts (Jan. 25, 2013), https://www.hhs.gov/hipaa/for-professionals/covered-entities/sample-business-associate-agreement-provisions/index.html.

implementing regulations. The privacy and security provisions of this BA Agreement shall be applicable to Business Associate only in the event and to the extent Business Associate meets, with respect to Covered Entity, the definition of a Business Associate set forth at 45 C.F.R. §160.103, or applicable successor provisions. Now, therefore, in consideration of the foregoing and other good and valuable consideration, the sufficiency and receipt of which are hereby acknowledged, the parties agree as follows:

1. **General Terms, Conditions, and Definitions**
    (a) "BA Agreement" shall mean this HIPAA Business Associate Agreement.
    (b) "Business Associate" shall generally have the same meaning as the term "business associate" at 45 C.F.R. §160.103, and in reference to the party to this BA Agreement, shall mean [insert name of Business Associate]. *[Note: If this document is being used for a Subcontractor arrangement with a Business Associate, the terms will need to be adjusted accordingly.]*
    (c) "Covered Entity" shall generally have the same meaning as the term "covered entity" at 45 C.F.R. §160.103, and in reference to the party to this BA Agreement, shall mean [insert name of Covered Entity].
    (d) "HIPAA Rules" shall mean the Privacy, Security, Breach Notification, Administrative, and Enforcement Rules at 45 C.F.R. Parts 160, 162, and 164, as amended from time to time.
    (e) "Service Agreement" shall mean the separate agreement(s) between the parties in which Business Associate performs functions or activities on behalf of Covered Entity.
    (f) Other Definitions: The following terms used in this BA Agreement shall have the same meaning as those in the HIPAA Rules: Breach, Data Aggregation, Designated Record Set, Disclosure, Health Care Operations,

Individual, Minimum Necessary, Notice of Privacy Practices, Protected Health Information (to the extent such Protected Health Information is created, transmitted, received, used, disclosed, accessed or maintained by Business Associate), Required by Law, Secretary, Security Incident, Subcontractor, Unsecured Protected Health Information, and Use. Other terms shall have the definitions set forth in this BA Agreement.

2. **Obligations and Activities of Business Associate**
   (a) Business Associate agrees to not Use or Disclose Protected Health Information other than as permitted or required by this BA Agreement, as Required by Law, or as contemplated by the Service Agreement.
   (b) Business Associate agrees to use appropriate safeguards, including compliance with Subpart C of 45 C.F.R. Part 164 with respect to electronic Protected Health Information, to prevent Use or Disclosure of the electronic Protected Health Information other than as permitted by this BA Agreement.
   (c) Business Associate agrees to report to Covered Entity's Privacy Official any Use or Disclosure of Protected Health Information not provided for by this BA Agreement of which it becomes aware, including Breaches of Unsecured Protected Health Information as required by 45 C.F.R. §164.410, and any Security Incident of which it becomes aware. For reports of incidents constituting a Breach, the report shall include, to the extent available, the identification of each Individual whose Unsecured Protected Health Information has been, or is reasonably believed by Business Associate to have been, accessed, acquired, or Disclosed during such Breach. Security Incidents that do not result in any unauthorized access, use, disclosure, modification, destruction of information or interference with system operations will be reported in the aggregate upon written request of Covered Entity

in a manner and frequency mutually acceptable to the parties. Business Associate hereby reports to Covered Entity that incidents including, but not limited to, ping sweeps or other common network reconnaissance techniques, attempts to log on to a system with an invalid password or username, and denial of service attacks that do not result in a server being taken off line, may occur from time to time.

(d) In accordance with 45 C.F.R. §§164.502(e)(1)(ii) and 164.308(b)(2), if applicable, Business Associate agrees to ensure that subcontractors that create, receive, maintain, or transmit Protected Health Information on behalf of Business Associate agree to the same restrictions and conditions that apply through this BA Agreement to Business Associate with respect to such information.

(e) To the extent Business Associate has Protected Health Information in a Designated Record Set, and only to the extent required by HIPAA, Business Associate agrees to make available Protected Health Information in a Designated Record Set, to Covered Entity as necessary to satisfy Covered Entity's obligations under 45 C.F.R. §164.524. The parties agree and acknowledge that it is Covered Entity's responsibility to respond to all such requests.

(f) Business Associate agrees to make Protected Health Information available for purposes of any amendments to Protected Health Information in its possession contained in a Designated Record Set as agreed to by Covered Entity pursuant to 45 C.F.R. §164.526 or take other measures as necessary to satisfy Covered Entity's obligations under 45 C.F.R. §164.526. The parties agree and acknowledge that it is Covered Entity's responsibility to respond to all such requests.

(g) Business Associate agrees to maintain and make available to Covered Entity the information required to

provide an accounting of disclosures by Business Associate as necessary to satisfy Covered Entity's obligations under 45 C.F.R. §164.528. The parties agree and acknowledge that it is Covered Entity's responsibility to respond to all such requests.
  (h) To the extent, under the terms of the Service Agreement, Business Associate is to carry out one or more of Covered Entity's obligations under Subpart E of 45 C.F.R. Part 164 of the HIPAA Rules, Business Associate agrees to comply with the requirements of Subpart E that apply to Covered Entity in the performance of such obligations.
  (i) Business Associate agrees to make its internal practices, books, and records related to Business Associate's Use and Disclosure of Protected Health Information received from Covered Entity available to the Secretary for purposes of determining compliance with the HIPAA Rules.
3. **Permitted Uses and Disclosures of Protected Health Information by Business Associate**
  (a) Business Associate may Use or Disclose Protected Health Information as necessary to perform the services set forth in the Service Agreement, as permitted in this BA Agreement or the Service Agreement, and as otherwise permitted by the HIPAA Rules.
  (b) Business Associate may Use or Disclose Protected Health Information as Required by Law or as permitted by 45 C.F.R. §164.512.
  (c) Business Associate agrees to make Uses and Disclosures and requests for Protected Health Information consistent with the requirements in the HIPAA Rules regarding Minimum Necessary uses and disclosures. Covered Entity represents and warrants that its Minimum Necessary policies and procedures and the Notice of Privacy Practices are consistent with, and not more stringent than, the HIPAA Rules or, to the extent that

Covered Entity's Notice of Privacy Practices or policies and procedures regarding the Minimum Necessary requirements of the HIPAA Rules impose additional particular restrictions on Business Associate, Covered Entity agrees to provide such policies to Business Associate in writing prior to requesting that Business Associate perform a particular function or activity on behalf of Covered Entity that would be affected by such policies and procedures.

(d) Business Associate may Use Protected Health Information to create de-identified information that may be Used and Disclosed by Business Associate as Business Associate deems appropriate, provided that the information is de-identified in accordance with the HIPAA Rules.

(e) Business Associate may Use Protected Health Information to provide Data Aggregation services. Business Associate may also use Protected Health Information to create, Use, and Disclose a Limited Data Set consistent with the HIPAA Rules.

(f) Business Associate may Use and Disclose Protected Health Information to report violations of law to appropriate Federal and State authorities, in a manner consistent with the HIPAA Rules.

(g) Business Associate may not Use or Disclose Protected Health Information in a manner that would violate Subpart E of 45 C.F.R. Part 164 if done by Covered Entity, except for the specific uses and disclosures set forth below.

(h) Business Associate may Use Protected Health Information for the proper management and administration of Business Associate or to carry out the legal responsibilities of Business Associate.

(i) Business Associate may Disclose Protected Health Information for the proper management and administration of Business Associate or to carry out the legal responsibilities of Business Associate, provided that the Disclosures are Required by Law or Business Associate obtains reasonable assurances from the person to whom the information is disclosed that the information will remain confidential and Used or further Disclosed only as Required by Law or for the purposes for which it was disclosed to the person, and the person notifies Business Associate of any instances of which it is aware in which the confidentiality of the information has been breached.

4. **Obligations of Covered Entity** *[Note: Inclusion of this Section 4 may require the Business Associate to terminate this agreement if it becomes aware of a material violation. This section is optional, but it could be important, particularly if state law requires special authorizations to Disclose PHI to the Business Associate.]*

(a) Covered Entity shall notify Business Associate, in writing and in a timely manner, of any limitations in the Notice of Privacy Practices of Covered Entity under 45 C.F.R. §164.520, and its policies regarding the "Minimum Necessary" requirements in 45 C.F.R. §164.502(b), to the extent that such limitations may affect Business Associate's Use or Disclosure of Protected Health Information, and shall notify Business Associate in writing of any material changes thereof.

(b) Covered Entity shall notify Business Associate, in writing and in a timely manner, of any changes in, or revocation of, permission by Individual to Use or Disclose Protected Health Information, if such changes may affect Business Associate's Use or Disclosure of Protected Health Information.

(c) Covered Entity shall notify Business Associate, in writing and in a timely manner, of any restriction on the Use and/or Disclosure of Protected Health Information to which Covered Entity has agreed or is required to abide by, to the extent that such restriction may affect Business Associate's Use or Disclosure of Protected Health Information.

(d) Covered Entity agrees to comply with all applicable state and federal privacy and security laws and regulations, including the HIPAA Rules. Covered Entity agrees to obtain any patient authorizations or consents that may be required under state or federal law or regulation in order to transmit Protected Health Information to Business Associate and to enable Business Associate and its subcontractors and agents to Use and Disclose Protected Health Information as contemplated by this BA Agreement and the Service Agreement, including consents and authorizations relating to mental health, HIV, substance use disorders, and other particularly sensitive conditions.

(e) Covered Entity may not ask Business Associate to Use or Disclose Protected Health Information in any manner that would not be permissible under applicable laws and rules, including the HIPAA Rules, if done by Covered Entity, except that Business Associate may Use and Disclose Protected Health Information for its proper management and administration, data aggregation, and other activities permitted by this BA Agreement.

5. **Term and Termination**
   (a) <u>Term</u>

   Except as otherwise provided herein, the term of this BA Agreement shall coincide with the Service Agreement and shall be terminable in accordance with the termination provisions of the Service Agreement, or the date either party terminates for cause, as authorized in paragraph (b) of this Section, whichever is sooner.

   (b) <u>Termination for Cause</u>

   Upon a party's reasonable determination of a material breach of this BA Agreement by the other party, the

non-breaching party shall provide written notice to the breaching party and may terminate this BA Agreement if the breaching party does not cure the breach or end the violation within 30 days of receipt of such notice.

(c) <u>Effect of Termination</u>
   (i) Except as provided below in Subsection 5(c)(ii) of this BA Agreement, upon termination of this BA Agreement, for any reason, Business Associate shall return or destroy, at Covered Entity's expense, all Protected Health Information received from Covered Entity, or created or received by Business Associate on behalf of Covered Entity, that Business Associate still maintains in any form. Business Associate shall retain no copies of the Protected Health Information.
   (ii) In the event that Business Associate determines that it, or a Subcontractor or agent, needs to retain Protected Health Information in order to maintain, Use, or Disclose Protected Health Information for its own management and administration or to carry out its legal responsibilities, Business Associate, or the Subcontractor or agent, may retain such Protected Health Information. Upon termination of this BA Agreement for any reason, Business Associate, or the subcontractor or agent, with respect to Protected Health Information received from Covered Entity, or created, maintained, or received by Business Associate, subcontractor, or agent, on behalf of Covered Entity, shall:
   1. Retain only that Protected Health Information which is necessary for Business Associate, Subcontractor, or agent to continue its proper management and administration or to carry out its legal responsibilities;
   2. Return or destroy the remaining Protected Health Information that Business Associate, Subcontractor, or agent still maintains in any form;

3. Continue to use appropriate safeguards to comply with Subpart C of 45 C.F.R. Part 164 with respect to electronic Protected Health Information to prevent Use or Disclosure of the Protected Health Information, other than as provided for in this Section, for as long as Business Associate, subcontractor, or agent retains the Protected Health Information;
4. Not Use or Disclose the Protected Health Information retained by Business Associate, subcontractor, or agent other than for the purposes for which such Protected Health Information was retained and subject to the same conditions set out at Subsections 3(h)–(i) above which applied prior to termination; and
5. Return to Covered Entity or destroy the Protected Health Information retained by Business Associate, subcontractor, or agent when it is no longer needed by Business Associate, Subcontractor, or agent for its proper management and administration or to carry out its legal responsibilities.

(d) Business Associate's rights and obligations under this Section 5 shall survive the termination of this BA Agreement and shall end when all of the Protected Health Information provided by Covered Entity to Business Associate, or created or received by Business Associate on behalf of Covered Entity, is destroyed or returned to Covered Entity.

6. **Interpretation and Amendment of this BA Agreement**

   A regulatory reference in this BA Agreement to a section of the HIPAA Rules means such section as in effect or as amended. Any ambiguity or inconsistency in this BA Agreement shall be interpreted to permit compliance with the HIPAA Rules. This BA Agreement supersedes any and all prior representations, understandings, or agreements, written or oral, concerning the subject matter herein, including conflicting provisions of the Service Agreement. In the event of a conflict between this BA Agreement and the Service Agreement, the BA Agreement shall control. The parties hereto agree to negotiate in good faith to amend this BA Agreement from time to time as is necessary for compliance with the requirements of HIPAA or any other applicable law and for Business Associate to provide services to Covered Entity. However, no change, amendment, or modification of this BA Agreement shall be valid unless it is set forth in writing and signed by both parties. When provisions of this BA Agreement are different than those in the HIPAA Rules, but are nonetheless permitted by the HIPAA Rules, the provisions of this BA Agreement shall control.

7. **No Third-Party Rights/Independent Contractors**
   The terms and conditions of this BA Agreement are intended for the sole benefit of Business Associate and Covered Entity and do not create any third-party rights. The parties declare that they are independent contractors and not agents of each other.

8. **Notices**
   Any notice required or permitted by this BA Agreement to be given or delivered shall be in writing and shall be deemed given or delivered if delivered in person, or delivered by courier or expedited delivery service, or delivered by registered or certified mail, postage prepaid, return receipt requested to the address set forth below. Each party may change its address for purposes of this BA Agreement by written notice to the other party.

9. **Governing Law**
   To the extent not preempted by federal law, the BA Agreement shall be governed and construed in accordance with the state laws governing the Service Agreement, without regard to conflicts of law provisions that would require application of the law of another state.

10. **Binding Nature and Benefits**
    This BA Agreement binds and benefits the parties, and their respective successors, and their permitted assigns.

11. **Severability**

    Whenever possible, each provision of this BA Agreement shall be interpreted so as to be effective and valid under applicable law. If any provision of this BA Agreement should be prohibited or found invalid under applicable law, such provision shall be ineffective to the extent of such prohibition or invalidity without invalidating the other of such provision or the remaining provisions of this BA Agreement; provided, however, that if any such invalid provision is material to an extent that a party would not have entered into the BA Agreement absent such provision, then that party may terminate the BA Agreement upon ninety (90) calendar days' prior written notice to the other party.

12. **Liability** *[Note: These provisions may not be appropriate for all arrangements. HIPAA does not require these provisions.]*

    (a) NOTWITHSTANDING ANY PROVISION IN THE SERVICE AGREEMENT TO THE CONTRARY, IN NO EVENT WILL EITHER PARTY BE LIABLE OR RESPONSIBLE TO THE OTHER FOR ANY TYPE OF INCIDENTAL, SPECIAL, EXEMPLARY, PUNITIVE, INDIRECT, OR CONSEQUENTIAL DAMAGES, INCLUDING, BUT NOT LIMITED TO, LOST REVENUE, LOST PROFITS, LOSS OF DATA, OR CIVIL OR CRIMINAL PENALTIES, EVEN IF ADVISED OF THE POSSIBILITY OF SUCH DAMAGES. THIS LIMITATION OF LIABILITY IS INTENDED TO APPLY TO ANY CLAIM, INCLUDING WITHOUT LIMITATION CLAIMS BASED IN STATUTE, COMMON LAW, CONTRACT, WARRANTY, FIDUCIARY DUTY, NEGLIGENCE OR OTHER TORT, OR STRICT LIABILITY. THIS LIMITATION OF LIABILITY SHALL ALSO APPLY AFTER TERMINATION OF THIS BA AGREEMENT AND THE SERVICE AGREEMENT.

(b) NOTWITHSTANDING ANY PROVISION IN THE SERVICE AGREEMENT TO THE CONTRARY, BUSINESS ASSOCIATE'S AGGREGATE LIABILITY TO COVERED ENTITY UNDER THIS ADDENDUM SHALL NOT EXCEED THE AMOUNT ACTUALLY PAID TO BUSINESS ASSOCIATE FOR THE PORTION OF THE WORK GIVING RISE TO SUCH LIABILITY, AND A RETURN OF SUCH AMOUNTS PAID SHALL BE COVERED ENTITY'S EXCLUSIVE REMEDY FOR ANY DAMAGES. THIS LIMITATION OF LIABILITY IS INTENDED TO APPLY TO ANY CLAIM, INCLUDING WITHOUT LIMITATION CLAIMS BASED IN STATUTE, COMMON LAW, CONTRACT, WARRANTY, FIDUCIARY DUTY, NEGLIGENCE OR OTHER TORT, OR STRICT LIABILITY. THIS LIMITATION OF LIABILITY SHALL ALSO APPLY AFTER TERMINATION OF THIS BA AGREEMENT AND THE SERVICE AGREEMENT.

13. **Counterparts**

    This BA Agreement may be executed in multiple counterparts, which shall constitute a single agreement, and by facsimile or pdf signatures, which shall be treated as originals.

IN WITNESS WHEREOF, the parties have executed this BA Agreement, effective _____, 20___.

Covered Entity:

By: _____

Title:_____

Address:_____

_____

Business Associate:

By:_____

Title: _____

Address:_____

_____

Chapter 8

Responding to a Security Incident or Breach: Mechanics of Incident Response and Breach Notification

HIPAA imposes specific requirements regarding data breaches. As discussed in Chapter 7, the HITECH Act gives individuals the right to be notified if there is a "breach" of their protected health information (PHI). The Security Rule requires covered entities and business associates to take action to address both "security incidents" and breaches. These two terms are distinct, although some security incidents could result in a reportable breach.

I. Definition of a Security Incident under HIPAA

HIPAA defines a "security incident" broadly. Security incidents include unauthorized access, uses, disclosures, modifications, or destruction of information. They also include interference with system operations in an information system. Importantly, a security incident includes *unsuccessful* incidents as well.[1]

Organizations should have documented policies in place outlining what would constitute a "security incident" in that particular organization. In the preamble to the final Security Rule, the Centers for Medicare & Medicaid Services, which, at the time, enforced the HIPAA security standards, noted that the information involved and an entity's environment will inform whether a specific action would constitute a security incident.[2]

II. Response and Notification Requirements for a Security Incident under HIPAA

Once an organization's policies and procedures are in place that define a security incident, a critical component of planning for such an incident or breach is training workforce members regarding those policies. The Office for Civil Rights (OCR) has stated that "covered entities should ensure their workforce members and other agents are adequately trained and aware of the importance of timely reporting of privacy and security incidents and the consequences of failing to do so."[3] Security awareness training should ensure that workforce members know exactly how to identify a security incident and, once they do, how to report it quickly.

There must be procedures and a definitive plan in place to respond adequately and promptly to reported security incidents. Depending on the size and complexity of the organization, it may be useful to appoint an incident response team that can work

---

1. 45 C.F.R. § 164.304.

2. *See* Final Rule, Ctrs. for Medicare & Medicaid Servs., U.S. Dep't of Health & Human Servs. (HHS), Health Insurance Reform: Security Standards, 68 Fed. Reg. 8334, 8350 (Feb. 20, 2003).

3. Interim final rule with request for comments, Office for Civil Rights, Dep't of Health & Human Servs., Breach Notification for Unsecured Protected Health Information, 74 Fed. Reg. 42,740, 42,749 (Aug. 24, 2009).

with the security official to investigate the security incident and manage the response. This team ideally would include legal counsel. It should include technical and nontechnical individuals who can help with various facets of the analysis. Covered entities and business associates are required to regularly review security incident tracking reports,[4] and this team could play an integral role in ensuring that requirement is met.

Depending on the scope of the incident, it may need to include team members who can handle media and public relations. The team should collaborate to determine whether the occurrence was actually a security incident or breach. The team should develop a containment and mitigation process to respond to the security incident[5] and try to contain any breach and prevent further disclosures. Depending on the advice of legal counsel, the organization may need to disseminate document retention and litigation hold instructions. If the entity is a publicly traded company, employees may need to be prohibited from stock trades, and the board of directors may need to be notified.

III. Definition of a Breach under HIPAA

The HITECH Act defines a "breach" as "the unauthorized acquisition, access, use, or disclosure of protected health information which compromises the security or privacy of such information, except where an unauthorized person to whom such information is disclosed would not reasonably have been able to retain such information."[6] The breach definition exempts certain unintentional access, use, or acquisition of PHI by employees, workforce members, or business associates.[7] The acquisition, access, or use must be made in good faith and within the scope of the employee's

---

4. 45 C.F.R. § 164.308(a)(1)(D).
5. 45 C.F.R. § 164.308(a)(6).
6. 42 U.S.C. § 17921(1)(A).
7. *Id.* at (1)(B).

or individual's professional relationship with the covered entity or business associate, and the PHI may not be further acquired, accessed, or used by anyone.[8] A breach also does not include inadvertent disclosures from individuals who are authorized to access PHI at the facility to another similarly situated individual at the same facility, as long as the PHI disclosed is not further acquired, accessed, used, or disclosed without authorization.[9]

The HITECH Act rules have exceptions to the "breach" definition that contain similar wording.[10] The regulations also except circumstances where the covered entity or business associate has a good-faith belief that the person who received the PHI would not reasonably have been able to retain the information.[11] This exception could apply if, for example, a health care provider gives the patient the wrong discharge papers by mistake, but is then able to recover the PHI quickly.[12]

IV. Analysis of the HIPAA Breach Notification Rule

The HITECH Act regulations provide useful guidance regarding whether an incident is a reportable breach. Acquiring, accessing, using, or disclosing PHI in a manner not permitted by the HIPAA Privacy Rule is presumably a breach unless a risk assessment shows that there is a low probability of compromise, as discussed below.[13]

An incident is a reportable breach, requiring notification to individuals, the U.S. Department of Health and Human Services

---

8. *Id.*
9. *Id.*
10. 45 C.F.R. § 164.402.
11. *Id.*
12. *See* Final Rule, Office for Civil Rights, U.S. Dep't of Health & Human Servs., Modifications to the HIPAA Privacy, Security, Enforcement, and Breach Notification Rules under the Health Information Technology for Economic and Clinical Health Act and the Genetic Information Nondiscrimination Act; Other Modifications to the HIPAA Rules, 78 Fed. Reg. 5566, 5640 (Jan. 25, 2013).
13. 45 C.F.R. § 164.402.

(HHS), and possibly the media, only if it involves "unsecured" PHI.[14] PHI is unsecured if it "is not rendered unusable, unreadable, or indecipherable to unauthorized persons through the use of a technology or methodology specified by the Secretary in the guidance issued under section 13402(h)(2) of Public Law 111-5."[15] PHI is secured if one or both of the following apply:

- Electronic PHI has been encrypted in accordance with valid encryption protocols, such as those that are consistent with the standards of the National Institute of Standards and Technology (NIST).
- The media used to store the PHI has been destroyed by shredding or similar destruction of paper records, or electronic media have been cleared, purged, or destroyed in accordance with NIST standards, so that the PHI cannot be recovered.[16]

If encrypted PHI was involved, this critical fact should be documented carefully. If the information was encrypted, the response team should confirm that the encryption key could not have been compromised.

A. Has a Breach Occurred?

Before an incident involving unsecured PHI is deemed to be a breach that is reportable under HIPAA or state law, it will need to be analyzed carefully. The response team should analyze the incident, based on the definition of a "breach," to determine whether the incident is exempted from the breach definition; whether it should be presumed to be a breach; or whether a risk assessment is warranted.

---

14. 45 C.F.R. § 164.404.
15. 45 C.F.R. § 164.402.
16. *See* HHS, Office for Civil Rights, Guidance to Render Unsecured Protected Health Information Unusable, Unreadable, or Indecipherable to Unauthorized Individuals (July 26, 2013), https://www.hhs.gov/hipaa/for-professionals/breach-notification/guidance/index.html.

A risk assessment may show that there is a low probability that PHI has been compromised, in which case the incident would not constitute a breach.[17] A risk assessment should consider at least the following factors:

1. The nature and extent of the PHI involved, including the types of identifiers and the likelihood of re-identification;
2. The unauthorized person who used the PHI or to whom the disclosure was made;
3. Whether the PHI was actually acquired or viewed; and
4. The extent to which the risk to PHI has been mitigated.[18]

Special precautions may be necessary if the incident involves ransomware. A ransomware incident will require careful analysis of whether PHI was exfiltrated or made unavailable. The organization should determine whether backup data was also infected, or if there are other factors creating a high risk to the data's availability or integrity.[19] The risk assessment should be documented in writing. The covered entity or business associate will have the burden to prove that an incident did not constitute a breach, or that all required disclosures were made.[20]

If a breach is identified, the incident response team will need to consider issues regarding sharing of risk. Insurers may need to be notified in accordance with insurance contracts. Those contracts should be examined (preferably well before an incident happens) to confirm whether coverage is available. The incident response team should also consider whether contribution from or indemnification by third parties could be available, and whether those parties should be put on notice.

---

17. *See* 45 C.F.R. § 164.402.
18. *Id.*
19. *See* HHS, Office for Civil Rights, Fact Sheet: Ransomware and HIPAA 6–7 (2016), https://www.hhs.gov/sites/default/files/RansomwareFactSheet.pdf.
20. 45 C.F.R. § 164.414.

B. Who to Notify?

1. Law Enforcement Notification

It may be important to notify local law enforcement, the Department of Homeland Security, the FBI, and/or the state attorney general, depending on the facts and circumstances. If a law enforcement agency requests a delay in breach notification, that must be documented carefully, in writing, in accordance with the HIPAA rules.[21] If the scope of the breach is significant, the organization should consider whether to alert lawmakers who may receive angry calls from constituents.

2. Notification by Business Associates to Covered Entities

If an organization experiences a breach as a business associate, the business associate will have reporting obligations to the covered entity or business associate it serves. HIPAA requires business associates to report any security incident or breach.[22] Business associates must also report any use or disclosure not permitted by the business associate agreement.[23]

If a security incident or impermissible use or disclosure rises to the level of an actual breach, HIPAA mandates that the business associate make a report to the covered entity without unreasonable delay but, in any event, within 60 calendar days of discovery.[24] Business associates faced with a notification obligation should also examine state law and the provisions of the relevant business associate agreements to determine whether a shorter reporting deadline applies. These reports should include, to the extent possible, the identification of each individual whose unsecured PHI

---

21. 45 C.F.R. § 164.412.
22. *See* 45 C.F.R. § 164.314(a)(2)(C).
23. *See* 45 C.F.R. § 164.504(e)(2)(C).
24. *See* 45 C.F.R. § 164.410(b).

was involved, as well as other information that the covered entity will need to provide the required notices.[25]

3. Notification to Individuals

The HITECH Act of 2009 gave individuals the right to be told about situations where their unsecured PHI was or was reasonably believed to have been accessed, acquired, or disclosed improperly.[26] These notices must be provided "without unreasonable delay and in no case later than 60 calendar days after discovery of a breach."[27] Breaches are treated as discovered on the first day the covered entity knows of the breach or would have known of it through exercising reasonable diligence.[28] The notices must be drafted carefully to comply with regulatory requirements, and the organization must be prepared to receive and answer questions regarding the incident.

As a practical matter, these notices are likely to trigger concern from patients. It will be important to write the notices in plain language, and provide credit monitoring or identity theft protection if the nature of the breach was such that it could create particular risks to individuals. The entity providing the notice should also be prepared to receive and adequately handle calls and other communications from concerned individuals. Specifically, the notices to individuals must include the following:

1. A brief description of what happened, including the date of the breach and the date of the discovery of the breach, if known;
2. A description of the types of unsecured PHI that were involved in the breach (such as whether full name, social security number, date of birth, home address, account

---

25. *Id.* at (c).
26. *See* 42 U.S.C. § 17932.
27. 45 C.F.R. § 164.404(b).
28. 45 C.F.R. § 164.404(a)(2).

number, diagnosis, disability code, or other types of information were involved);
3. Any steps individuals should take to protect themselves from potential harm resulting from the breach;
4. A brief description of what the covered entity is doing to investigate the breach, to mitigate harm to individuals, and to protect against any further breaches; and
5. Contact procedures for individuals to ask questions or learn additional information, which should include a toll-free number, an e-mail address, website, or postal address.[29]

4. Notification to OCR

Covered entities are also required to notify the Secretary of HHS when there is a breach. This is done through a link on the OCR website.[30] If the breach involves 500 or more individuals, the Secretary must receive notice contemporaneously with the notice provided to individuals. If the breach involves fewer than 500 individuals, covered entities must maintain a log or other documentation of the breach, and make sure it is reported to the Secretary no later than 60 days after the end of the calendar year in which the breach was discovered.[31]

Once notice is provided to OCR, or if someone files a complaint with OCR regarding the incident, the organization should be prepared to respond to governmental inquiries. Typical OCR data requests ask for a substantial amount of information. For example, such requests could include:

---

29. 45 C.F.R. § 164.404(c).
30. HHS, Office for Civil Rights, Submitting Notice of a Breach to the Secretary, https://www.hhs.gov/hipaa/for-professionals/breach-notification/breach-reporting/index.html (last visited May 4, 2019).
31. 45 C.F.R. § 164.408.

- Documentation of employee training and the content of such training;
- Policies and procedures that were in place on the date of the breach;
- The risk analyses that were done prior to the breach, and any risk management plans;
- Documentation that notice was provided to HHS, individuals, and to the media if required;
- Evidence that any appropriate sanctions were imposed on workforce members who were involved;
- Documentation regarding any required substitute notice; and
- Documentation of complaints regarding the breach.

Notice must be sent by first class mail to the individual's last known address, unless the individual has agreed to receive electronic notice and such agreement has not been withdrawn. If the covered entity knows an individual has died and knows how to contact the next of kin, the next of kin or personal representative must receive notice.[32] Once required breach notifications have been distributed, an organization that has experienced a breach should gather and maintain relevant documentation and keep it for at least six years.

5. Substitute Notice

A frequent complication that arises in breach notifications is insufficient contact information for certain individuals. If a covered entity has insufficient contact information for a particular person who must receive notice, unless the covered entity knows the individual has died, the covered entity needs to come up with a "substitute form of notice reasonable calculated to reach the individual."[33] If there is insufficient contact information for fewer than ten individuals, substitute notice may be provided by an alterna-

---

32. 45 C.F.R. § 164.404(d).
33. 45 C.F.R. § 164.404(d)(2).

tive form of written notice, telephone, or other means.³⁴ If there are more than ten individuals lacking contact information, then the substitute notice must either be in the form of a conspicuous posting on the home page of the covered entity's website for 90 days, or conspicuous notice in major broadcast or print media in geographic areas where the affected individuals likely live. The notice must include a toll-free phone number that remains active for at least 90 days where individuals may learn whether their information was involved.³⁵ In emergency situations where the breach may cause "imminent misuse" of unsecured PHI, covered entities may provide telephone or other notice in addition to the required written notice.³⁶

6. Media Notice

Some breaches require press releases or similar notice to the media. Specifically, if a breach involves more than 500 individuals in a particular state or jurisdiction, the covered entity must notify "prominent media outlets" serving the area.³⁷ Unless there is a law enforcement delay, the notice must go out no later than 60 calendar days after discovery of the breach, and must contain the same information that would be included in a notice to individuals.³⁸

7. Other Potential Notifications

When working on breach notices, it is important to determine whether other entities must be notified as well. For example, state laws may require notification to the state attorney general. State laws may also require notification to credit bureaus, depending on the type of information involved.

---

34. *Id.* at (d)(2)(i).
35. *Id.* at (d)(2)(ii).
36. *Id.* at (d)(3).
37. 45 C.F.R. § 164.406(a).
38. *Id.*

V. Steps to Take after the Breach

Once a breach has been identified, contained, and properly addressed, what next? Covered entities and business associates should update their risk analyses to make sure that the factors and circumstances leading to the breach have been addressed adequately. Changes to the policies and procedures and additional workforce training may be necessary. It is important to take reasonable measures to try to reduce the chance of future breaches.

VI. Conclusion

Although no one expects to experience a breach, it is important to analyze and understand the steps an entity should take to respond to a breach. By carefully considering its obligations, anticipating its role and planning the actions to take, the entity is well positioned to appropriately respond to a breach. Investment of resources, time, and planning today goes a long way to maintain the entity's reputation and weather the impact of a breach if it happens tomorrow.

Appendix A

HIPAA Administrative Requirements and Policies and Procedures for Health Care Providers[1]

The HIPAA regulations require Covered Entities and Business Associates to document and implement "reasonable and appropriate policies and procedures" to comply with the Security Rule. The policies should take into account the organization's capabilities, size, and complexity; the technical infrastructure; costs; and relative risk. Similarly, Covered Entities must develop policies and procedures designed to comply with the Privacy Rule. Because they

---

1. The authors would like to acknowledge Nicole D. Bogard, a partner with Seyfarth Shaw in Atlanta, Georgia, for her substantial contribution to an early draft of the policy and procedure templates, as well as Eddie Williams III, a partner with Holland & Knight LLP in Tallahassee, Florida, and the members of the ABA Health Law Section's eHealth, Privacy & Security Interest Group for their input on subsequent revisions.

must enter into Business Associate agreements dealing with both the privacy and security of data, HIPAA Business Associates and Subcontractors should also implement policies and procedures to ensure compliance with their privacy obligations. A Covered Entity's privacy official is responsible for developing and implementing the policies and procedures. For both Business Associates and Covered Entities, a security official must also be identified who is responsible for developing and implementing security-related policies and procedures. Workforce Members must be trained on the policies.

This sample document is for a hypothetical health care provider that is a Covered Entity under HIPAA and it will not be appropriate for every entity or situation. This is a sample framework and, standing alone, does not constitute a set of HIPAA-compliant policies. By themselves, they will not make an entity HIPAA compliant. Instead, these templates should be used merely as a starting point and must be tailored to the entity's actual risks, as identified in its risk analysis, and its actual policies and procedures. Providers must also comply with state laws, which may be more stringent than HIPAA.

HIPAA PRIVACY AND SECURITY POLICIES AND PROCEDURES OF

THE [*Insert Name of Health Care Provider*]

Effective [*Insert effective date*]

[*Insert name of Health Care Provider*]

[*Insert address*]

[*Insert phone number*]

Table of Contents

I. **General Information Applicable to All Privacy and Security Policies**
   Policy Statement
   Scope of These Privacy and Security Policies
   Applicability of These Policies
   Defined Terms
   Definitions

II. **When the Provider May Make Disclosures of PHI without Authorization**
   Purpose of Policy
   Policy Detail
   Required Disclosures.
   Payment, Treatment, and Health Care Operations.
   Other Permitted Disclosures.
   Uses and Disclosures Requiring an Opportunity for the Individual to Agree or Object.

III. **Notification of Privacy or Security Breaches**
   Purpose of Policy
   Policy Detail

IV. **Notice of Privacy Practices Procedures**
   Purpose of Policy
   Policy Detail
   Step 1: Provision of Notice.
   Step 2: Acknowledgment of Receipt.
   Step 3: Availability on Request.
   Step 4: Posting of Notice.
   Step 5: Website.

Step 6: Revisions to Notice.
Step 7: Documentation.
Who Is Affected

V.   Minimum Necessary Standard
Purpose of Policy
Policy Detail
Provider's Workforce Use of Relevant Records Offsite.
Monitoring of the Policies and Procedures Governing Access to PHI.
Access to Relevant Records.
Return of Relevant Records.
Provider's Workforce Obligations.
Routine/Recurring Disclosures.
Disclosures to Which the Minimum Necessary Standard Applies.
Disclosures to Which the Minimum Necessary Standard Does Not Apply.
Provider's Workforce.

VI.   Individual's Request to Restrict Uses and Disclosures of PHI
Purpose of Policy
Policy Detail
Denial of Individual's Request.
Approval of Individual's Request.
Terminating the Restriction.

VII. Individual's Request for Confidential Communications
Purpose of Policy
Policy Detail

VIII. Individual's Right of Access to PHI
Purpose of Policy
Policy Detail
No Right to Access.
Denial of Access.
Time Limits.
Approval of Access.

Reasonable Fees.
Retaining Documentation.

Request for Access to Protected Health Information

IX. **Individual's Request to Amend PHI**
Purpose of Policy
Policy Detail
Denial of Request.
Time Limits.
Approval of Request.

Request to Amend or Correct Protected Health Information

X. **Individual's Request for an Accounting of Disclosures**
Purpose of Policy
Policy Detail
Content of the Accounting.
Multiple Disclosures to Same Person or Entity.
Timing of Provider's Response.
Imposing Fees for Accounting.
Temporary Suspension of Right to an Accounting.
Retaining Documentation.

Form: Request for an Accounting or Disclosures of Medical Information

XI. **Refraining from Intimidating or Retaliatory Acts**
Purpose of Policy
Policy Detail

XII. **Waiver of Rights**
Purpose of Policy
Policy Detail

XIII. **Documentation Requirements and Retention of Records**
Purpose of Policy
Policy Detail
Policies and Procedures.
Communications.
Written or Electronic Record.

Documents Provider Must Retain.
How Long Provider Must Retain Documents.
Document Destruction.

XIV. **Training on HIPAA Privacy and Security Policies**
Policy Statement
Scope of this Policy
Purpose of Policy
Policy Detail
Content of Training.
Documentation.
Retaining Documentation.

XV. **Disciplinary Sanctions for Noncompliance with Provider's Privacy and Security Policies**
Purpose of Policy
Policy Detail

XVI. **Reporting and Mitigating Inadvertent or Improper Disclosures of PHI or Security Incidents**
Purpose of Policy
Policy Detail

XVII. **Administrative, Technical, and Physical Privacy and Security Safeguards**
Purpose of Policy
Policy Detail
Risk Analysis, Evaluation of Security, and Ongoing Risk Management.
Activity Review of ePHI System Security.
Safeguards.

XVIII. **Verification of Persons Requesting PHI**
Purpose of Policy
Policy Details
Requests Made by an Individual.
Requests Made by a Parent Seeking the PHI of a Minor Child.
Request Made by a Personal Representative.
Requests Made by a Public Official.

XIX. **Authorizations**
Purpose of Policy
Policy Details

XX. **Requests for Disclosures of an Individual's PHI from Spouses, Other Family Members, and Friends/Facility Directories**
Purpose of Policy
Policy Details
Objections to Disclosures.
Verification.

XXI. **Disclosures to Business Associates**
Purpose of Policy
Policy Details

XXII. **De-identified Information, Summary Health Information, and Limited Data Sets**
Purpose of Policy
Policy Details
Remove Identifiers.
Retain Expert.
Limited Data Sets.
Approval from Privacy Official Required.

XXIII. **Complaints**
Purpose of Policy
Policy Details
Written Acknowledgment.
Privacy Official's Investigation.
Retaining Documents.

XXIV. **Designated Record Sets**
Purpose of Policy
Policy Details

XXV. **Designated Personnel/Access Profiles**
Purpose of Policy
Policy Detail
Privacy Official.

Security Official.
Contact Office for Questions and Complaints.
Access Profiles for Workforce.

XXVI. State Law Compliance
Purpose of Policy
Policy Detail
Procedural Guidance

XXVII. Using and Disclosing Psychotherapy Notes
Background
Policy

XXVIII. Workforce Employee Screening

XXIX. Fundraising
Purpose of Policy
Policy Detail

XXX. Sale of Protected Health Information
Purpose of Policy
Policy Detail

I. General Information Applicable to All Privacy and Security Policies

Policy Statement

It is the policy of _____ (**Provider**) to Use and Disclose Protected Health Information (**PHI**) only for the purpose of Provider's Treatment, Payment, or Health Care Operations purposes or as otherwise allowed by law.

Provider will comply with applicable state laws except to the extent that it is not possible to comply with both state law and HIPAA, and will consult with legal counsel when questions arise regarding the applicability of state law. *[Note: Organizations should implement specific policies and procedures to deal with particular provisions of state law that are different than or more stringent than HIPAA.]*

These policies are designed to comply with HIPAA and the Health Information Technology for Economic and Clinical Health Act of 2009 (**HITECH Act**). These policies are not a contract and do not create any legal rights.

Scope of These Privacy and Security Policies

These policies apply to the Provider with respect to the PHI of Individuals obtained in the course of administering and providing health care items or services.

Applicability of These Policies

These policies are intended to guide the Provider's workforce members about how they are to protect the PHI of Individuals in carrying out their functions. *[If applicable: Provider is a Hybrid Entity. Its health care components subject to these policies are as follows: _____.]*

Appendix A: *HIPAA Administrative Requirements and Policies* 173

Defined Terms

Certain words in these policies are defined terms and have a specific meaning. The defined terms and their definitions are generally set forth below, and may be more specifically addressed in the Privacy Rule and Security Rule.

Definitions

"**Breach**" is the acquisition, access, Use, or Disclosure of PHI in a manner not permitted under the Privacy Rule which compromises the security or privacy of the PHI.

"**Business Associate**" is a person or entity who has been retained to carry out various functions on behalf of Provider that require that it receive PHI from Provider, or create and/or maintain PHI on behalf of Provider. Business Associates are required to sign a contract that obligates them to protect Individuals' PHI in the same way as does Provider.

"**Covered Entity**" means a health care provider who transmits any health information in electronic form in connection with a transaction subject to HIPAA electronic standards; a health plan; or a health care clearinghouse.

"**Designated Record Set**" means a group of records maintained by or for Provider that are medical and billing records about Individuals; enrollment, payment, claims adjudication records; or records used, in whole or in part, by or on behalf of Provider to make decisions about Individuals. For purposes of this definition, the term "record" means any item, collection, or grouping of information that includes PHI and is maintained, collected, Used, or disseminated by or for Provider in written or electronic format. See also policy "XXIV. Designated Record Sets."

"**DHHS**" means the United States Department of Health and Human Services.

"**Disclosure**" means the release, transfer, provision of access to, or divulging in any other manner information outside the entity holding the information.

"**ePHI**" means PHI stored or maintained electronically.
"**Health Care Operations**" generally include:

- quality assessment activities;
- reviewing the qualifications of health care professionals;
- underwriting, premium writing and other activities relating to creating, obtaining, or renewing health insurance or health benefits, including a contract of reinsurance or stop-loss insurance obtained in connection with the provision of health plan benefits, either directly or indirectly;
- conducting or arranging for medical review, legal services, and auditing functions including fraud and abuse detection and any required compliance programs;
- business planning and development, such as conducting cost-management and planning-related analyses related to managing and operating provider;
- creating deidentified information or Limited Data Sets, if needed; and
- business management and general administrative activities of Provider.

"**Health Oversight Agency**" means an agency or authority of the United States, a State, a territory, a political subdivision of a State or territory, or an Indian tribe, or a person or entity acting under a grant of authority from or contract with such public agency, including the employees or agents of such public agency or its contractors or persons or entities to whom it has granted authority, that is authorized by law to oversee the health care system (whether public or private) or government programs in which health information is necessary to determine eligibility or compliance, or to enforce civil rights laws for which health information is relevant.
"**HIPAA**" means the Administrative Simplification provisions of the Health Insurance Portability and Accountability Act of 1996, Public Law 104-191, codified at 42 U.S.C. § 1320d through d-9, as amended.

"**HIPAA Rules**" means the Privacy, Security, Breach Notification, and Enforcement Rules at 45 CFR Part 160 and Part 164.

"**Hybrid Entity**" means a single legal entity that is a Covered Entity; whose business activities include both covered and non-covered functions; and that designates health care components of the Covered Entity. For example, a health care provider that has a research laboratory may choose to designate itself as a hybrid entity and exclude the laboratory from its health care component. A component must be included in the covered portion of the Hybrid Entity if it would meet the definition of a Covered Entity or Business Associate if it were a separate legal entity. Health care components also may include a component only to the extent it performs covered functions.

"**Individual**" means the person who is the subject of the protected health information. The term also includes personal representatives who are entitled to act on behalf of an Individual as provided in the HIPAA Privacy Rule.

"**Law Enforcement Official**" means an officer or employee of any agency or authority of the United States, a State, a territory, a political subdivision of a State or territory, or an Indian tribe, who is empowered by law to investigate or conduct an official inquiry into a potential violation of law, or to prosecute or otherwise conduct a criminal, civil, or administrative proceeding arising from an alleged violation of law.

"**Limited Data Set**" is Protected Health Information that excludes the following direct identifiers of the Individual or of relatives, employers, or household members of the Individual:

- Names.
- Postal address information, other than town or city, state, and zip code.
- Telephone numbers.
- Fax numbers.
- Electronic mail addresses.
- Social security numbers.

- Medical record numbers.
- Health plan beneficiary numbers.
- Account numbers.
- Certificate/license numbers.
- Vehicle identifiers and serial numbers, including license plate numbers.
- Device identifiers and serial numbers.
- Web Universal Resource Locators (URLs).
- Internet Protocol (IP) address numbers.
- Biometric identifiers, including finger and voice prints.
- Full face photographic images and any comparable images.

"Notice of Privacy Practices" is a document that must be maintained by most Covered Entities that explains to Individuals how the Covered Entity may Use and Disclose their PHI.

"Organized Health Care Arrangement" has the definition set forth in 45 C.F.R. § 160.103 and includes, among other things, a clinically integrated care setting, such as a hospital, in which Individuals typically receive health care from more than one health care provider.

"Payment" includes a broad range of activities undertaken by Provider to obtain reimbursement for the provision of health care, including:

- determinations of eligibility or coverage;
- adjudication or subrogation of health benefit claims;
- billing, claims management and collection activities;
- obtaining payment under a contract of reinsurance, including stop-loss or excess loss insurance;
- review of health care services with respect to medical necessity, coverage under a health plan, appropriateness of care and justification of charges;
- utilization review activities, including pre-certification and pre-authorization, concurrent and retrospective review;

- disclosure to consumer reporting agencies of only the following individually identifiable information that is related to the collection of reimbursements:
  - Name and address.
  - Date of birth.
  - Social security number.
  - Payment history.
  - Account number (if any).
  - The name and address of the Individual's health care provider and/or his or her health plan.

"Privacy Official" means the Individual with the authority to make or amend policies and procedures, delegate functions, execute Business Associate Agreements, and to perform other duties necessary to comply with the Privacy Rule. The term "Privacy Official" shall refer to the Privacy Official's designee when the Privacy Official has delegated a particular task or function to the designee.

"Privacy Rule" means the Standards for Privacy of individually Identifiable Health Information, as published in 45 C.F.R. Parts 160 and 164.

"Protected Health Information" or **"PHI"** means any information, whether oral or recorded, in any form or medium that is created by a health plan, a health care provider, a health care clearinghouse, or the employer that relates to the past, present, or future physical or mental health of an Individual, including the provision of and payment for health care, that either identifies the Individual or provides a reasonable basis for such identification, except for health information in certain educational records. PHI does not include de-identified health information. PHI specifically includes protected health information stored or maintained electronically ("ePHI"). PHI does not include employment records held by a Covered Entity in its role as employer, or information regarding a person who has been deceased for more than 50 years.

"**Required by Law**" means a mandate contained in law that compels an entity to make a Use or Disclosure of protected health information and that is enforceable in a court of law.

"**Provider**" means _____ *[Insert legal name of Provider]*.

"**Secretary**" means the Secretary of the United States Department of Health and Human Services.

"**Security Incident**" means the attempted or successful unauthorized access, Use, Disclosure, modification, or destruction of information or interference with system operations in an information system.

"**Security Official**" means the individual with the authority to make or amend policies and procedures, delegate functions, and perform other duties necessary to comply with the Security Rule. The term "Security Official" shall refer to the Security Official's designee when the Security Official has delegated a particular task or function to the designee.

"**Security Rule**" means the Health Insurance Reform: Security Standards, as published in 45 C.F.R. Parts 160 and 164.

"**Standard Transactions**" means the electronic transmission of information between two parties to carry out financial or administrative activities related to health care in the standardized format (including code sets and data elements) set forth under the HIPAA Standards for Electronic Health Care Transactions.

"**Treatment**" means the provision, coordination, or management of health care and related services by one or more health care providers, including the coordination or management of health care by a health care provider with a third party; consultation between health care providers relating to a patient; or the referral of a patient for health care from one health care provider to another.

"**Use**" means, with respect to individually identifiable health information, the sharing, employment, application, utilization, examination, or analysis of such information within an entity maintaining such information.

"**Workforce**" or "**Workforce Member**" means and includes current employees, and other persons whose conduct, in the performance of work at the Provider are under the direct control of the Provider, whether or not they are paid by the Provider. Provider's workforce includes those Provider employees who are responsible for the administration of Provider and listed under policy "V. Minimum Necessary Standard."

II. When the Provider May Make Disclosures of PHI without Authorization

Purpose of Policy

To describe generally the ways in which the Provider and its workforce members may appropriately Use and Disclose PHI.

Policy Detail

Required Disclosures. The Provider is required to Disclose PHI:
<u>To Individuals.</u> To an Individual, when the Individual requests access to his or her records maintained by the Provider in the Provider's Designated Record Set, or requests an accounting of Disclosures of PHI maintained in the Provider's Designated Record Set. PHI of deceased Individuals will be protected as if the Individual were alive. Under the HIPAA Rules, an Individual's information is no longer considered PHI beyond 50 years after the Individual's death. State law may be more stringent, however.
<u>To The Secretary of the DHHS.</u> When required by the Secretary of the DHHS to investigate or determine the Provider's compliance with HIPAA and the Privacy Rule.
Payment, Treatment, and Health Care Operations. Provider may Use and Disclose PHI for Payment, Treatment, and Health Care Operations.

Payment. Provider may Use or Disclose PHI to carry out the Provider's Payment obligations and functions without an express authorization from the Individual. Provider may disclose PHI to another Covered Entity or health care provider for the Payment activities of the entity that receives the information.

Treatment. Provider may Use and Disclose PHI as needed for Treatment purposes, without an express authorization from the Individual. Provider may exchange an Individual's PHI electronically for Treatment and other permissible purposes.

Healthcare Operations. Provider may Use or Disclose PHI to carry out Provider's Health Care Operations without an express authorization from the Individual. Provider may also disclose PHI to another Covered Entity for the Health Care Operations of the entity that receives the information, if each entity either has or had a relationship with the Individual who is the subject of the PHI being requested, the PHI pertains to such relationship, and the Disclosure is for any of the following purposes:

- For the purpose of health care fraud and abuse detection or compliance.
- For the purpose of the following Health Care Operations:
- Conducting quality assessment and improvement activities, including outcomes, evaluation and development of clinical guidelines, provided that the obtaining of generalized knowledge is not the primary purpose of any studies resulting from such activities; population-based activities relating to improving health or reducing health care costs, protocol development, case management and care coordination, contacting of health care providers and patients with information about treatment alternatives; and related functions that do not include treatment.
- Reviewing the competence or qualification of health care professionals, evaluating practitioner and provider performance, health plan performance, conducting training programs in which students, trainees, or practitioners in areas

of health care learn under supervision to practice or improve their skills as health care providers, training non-health care professionals, accreditation, certification, licensing, or credential activities.

Other Permitted Disclosures. Provider may Use or Disclose PHI for purposes other than Treatment, Payment, or Health Care Operations to the extent otherwise permitted by the Privacy Rule. The Minimum Necessary Standard applies to most permitted Disclosures, except for disclosures for treatment, to the Individual patient, made pursuant to an authorization, to the Secretary of the Department of Health and Human Services, as required by law, or Uses and Disclosures required for HIPAA compliance. These Disclosures include the following:

Incidental Disclosures. Provider may Use or Disclose PHI if such Use or Disclosure is merely incidental to an otherwise permitted or required Use or Disclosure, and complies with the Minimum Necessary Standards (*see* policy on "Minimum Necessary Standard").

Organized Health Care Arrangement. Provider participates in an Organized Health Care Arrangement (**OHCA**) consisting of the following entities or individuals: *[Note: Only applies if Provider is part of an OHCA. Define and list components of the OHCA here]*, and is permitted to disclose PHI about an individual to another Covered Entity that participates in the OHCA for the Health Care Operations of that OHCA member.

Abuse, Neglect, Domestic Violence. Provider may make disclosures about victims of abuse, neglect, or domestic violence if any of the following apply:

- The Individual agrees with the disclosure.
- A statute or regulation expressly authorizes the disclosure and the disclosure prevents harm to the Individual (or other victim).
- The Individual is incapacitated and unable to agree and the information will not be Used against the Individual. The disclosure must be necessary for an imminent enforcement

activity. The Individual must be promptly informed of the disclosure, unless this would place the Individual at risk, or if informing would involve a personal representative who is believed to be responsible for the abuse, neglect, or violence.

<u>Court Order, Subpoenas, Discovery Requests.</u> Provider may make disclosures for judicial and administrative proceedings, in response to:
- an order of a court or administrative tribunal if the Disclosure is limited to the PHI expressly authorized by the order;
- a subpoena, discovery request, or other lawful process that is not accompanied by an order from a court or administrative tribunal, if:
- Provider receives satisfactory assurance from the party seeking the information that reasonable efforts have been made by such party to ensure that the Individual who is the subject of the PHI that has been requested has been given notice of the request. Provider must receive from the requesting party a written statement and accompanying documentation demonstrating that:
  o The party requesting such information has made a good-faith attempt to provide written notice to the Individual (or, if the Individual's location is unknown, to mail a notice to the Individual at the Individual's last known address);
  o The notice included sufficient information about the litigation or proceeding in which the PHI is requested to permit the Individual to raise an objection to the court or administrative tribunal; and
  o The time for the Individual to raise objections to the court or administrative tribunal has elapsed and no objections were filed, or all objections filed by the Individual have been resolved by the court or the administrative tribunal and the disclosures being sought are consistent with such resolution.

While HIPAA allows disclosures pursuant to a protective order, state law may restrict the ability to rely on such an order, unless it is also a court order requiring disclosure. Protective orders should be reviewed by qualified legal counsel.

Workforce Members receiving a request pursuant to a subpoena, discovery request, or other lawful process or a judicial or administrative order should not make any disclosure without first contacting the Privacy Official or his or her designee for guidance. Subpoenas that request sensitive information that may be protected under other laws including, but not limited to, information relating to mental health, HIV, and substance abuse, may require a patient authorization, or filing a motion to quash.

<u>Law Enforcement.</u> Provider may make disclosures to a Law Enforcement Official for law enforcement purposes under the following conditions:

- The PHI sought is relevant, material, and limited to amounts reasonably necessary, and it is not possible to satisfy the request by using de-identified information.
- The PHI requested is limited to information needed to identify a suspect, fugitive, material witness, or missing person.
- For information about a suspected victim of a crime (a) if the Individual agrees to the disclosure, or (b) without the Individual's agreement, if the PHI is not to be used against the victim, if the need for information is urgent, and if disclosure is in the best interest of the Individual.
- For information about a deceased Individual upon suspicion that the Individual's death resulted from criminal conduct.
- For information that constitutes evidence of criminal conduct that occurred on Provider's premises.

<u>Required by Law.</u> Provider may make disclosures that are required by law. For example, workforce members may be required to Use and Disclose PHI in connection with reports to the Centers for Medicare and Medicaid Services for audits and

other purposes. Provider will Use and Disclose PHI when compelled to do so by applicable law. Such disclosures must meet the following criteria:

1. Provider will disclose only the PHI mandated by the applicable law.
2. Provider will ensure that the individuals or entities that receive the PHI are authorized to receive it under applicable law.
3. The disclosure will be recorded in accordance with the policy regarding accounting.

If a disclosure of PHI is Required by Law, and is made in accordance with applicable law, the Individual's authorization is not required. However, any such disclosure must comply with any other policies that may apply to the Disclosure.

In order to ensure they meet HIPAA's requirements, personnel should consult the Privacy Official before making disclosures of PHI pursuant to the following exceptions:

Public Health Activities. Provider may make disclosures to appropriate Public Health Authorities for public health activities.

Health Oversight Activities. Provider may make disclosures to a Health Oversight Agency for health oversight activities, as authorized by law.

Coroner or Medical Examiner. Provider may make disclosures to a coroner or medical examiner about decedents for purposes of identifying a deceased person, determining the cause of death or other duties as authorized by law.

Organ Donations. Provider may make disclosures for cadaveric organ, eye, or tissue donation purposes to organ procurement organizations or other entities engaged in the procurement, banking, or transplantation of organs, eyes, or tissues for the purposes of facilitating transplantation.

Research Purposes. Provider may make disclosures for certain limited research purposes provided that a waiver of the authorization required by the Privacy Rule has been approved by an appropriate privacy board or institutional review board, or an appropriate patient authorization has been obtained. An authorization form for research-related treatment can be combined with other authorizations that also condition treatment, payment, or enrollment in a health plan upon the patient signing the authorization form. Any compound authorization created under this paragraph must clearly differentiate between the conditioned and unconditioned components and provide the Individual with an opportunity to opt in to the research activities described in the unconditioned authorization.

Serious Threat to Health or Safety. Provider may make disclosures to avert a serious threat to health or safety based upon a good-faith belief that the Use or Disclosure is necessary to prevent a serious and imminent threat to the health or safety of the Individual or the general public.

National Security/Correctional Institutions. Provider may make disclosures for specialized governmental functions including disclosures to federal authorities for the conduct of national security activities and disclosures of an inmate's PHI to a correctional institution or Law Enforcement Official having lawful custody of the inmate if the correctional institution or Law Enforcement Official represents that such PHI is necessary for the provision of health care to the inmate, the health and safety of the inmate or other persons, or safety, security and good order of the correctional institution.

Armed Forces Personnel. Provider may Use or Disclose PHI of Armed Forces personnel for activities deemed necessary for an appropriate military mission. Provider may make Disclosures to authorized federal officials for the provision of protective services under 18 U.S.C. § 3056 and 22 U.S.C. § 2709(a)(3), and to conduct investigations authorized by 18 U.S.C. §§ 871 and 879.

Workers' Compensation. Provider may make Disclosures for workers' compensation programs to the extent necessary to comply with laws relating to workers' compensation or other similar programs.

Whistleblowers. A workforce member may disclose PHI if the workforce member believes in good faith that the Provider or a Business Associate has engaged in conduct that is unlawful or otherwise violates professional or clinical standards, or that the care, services, or conditions provided potentially endanger one or more patients, workers, or the public. These disclosures may be made only to: (1) a health oversight agency or public health authority authorized by law to investigate or otherwise oversee the relevant conduct or conditions; (2) an appropriate health care accreditation organization for the purpose of reporting the allegation of failure to meet professional standards or misconduct; or (3) an attorney retained by or on behalf of the disclosing person or Provider for the purpose of determining the legal options of the person or Provider with regard to the relevant conduct.

Disclosures by Workforce Member Crime Victims. A workforce member who is the victim of a criminal act may disclose PHI to a Law Enforcement Official provided that the PHI disclosed is about the suspected perpetrator of the criminal act and the PHI is limited to: (1) name and address; (2) date and place of birth; (3) social security number; (4) ABO blood type and rh factor; (5) type of injury; (6) date and time of treatment; (7) date and time of death; and (8) a description of distinguishing physical characteristics, including height, weight, gender, race, hair and eye color, presence or absence of facial hair, scars and tattoos.

Uses and Disclosures Requiring an Opportunity for the Individual to Agree or Object. Provider may, in accordance with HIPAA and any Business Associate Agreements that may be applicable, make the following disclosures:

Friends and Family. Provider may disclose to a family member, other relative, or close personal friend of the Individual, or any other person identified by the Individual, the PHI directly relevant to such person's involvement in the Individuals' health care or payment related to the Individual's health care.

Identification or Location. Provider may Use or Disclose PHI to notify, or assist in the notification of (including identifying or locating) a family member, a personal representative of the Individual, or another person responsible for the care of the Individual of the Individual's location, general condition, or death.

<u>Use and Disclosure with the Individual present.</u> If the Individual is present for, or otherwise available prior to, a Use or Disclosure that is allowed, then the Individual must be given an opportunity to agree or object to disclosures to friends and family or for identification or location purposes, if the Individual has the capacity to make their health care decisions. Provider may Use or Disclose the PHI if it obtains the Individual's agreement; provides the Individual with the opportunity to object to the disclosure, and the Individual does not express an objection; or Provider reasonably infers from the circumstances, based on the exercise of professional judgment, that the Individual does not object to the disclosure.

<u>Limited Uses and Disclosures when the Individual is not present.</u> If the Individual is not present, or the opportunity to agree or object to the Use or Disclosure cannot practicably be provided because of the Individual's incapacity or an emergency circumstance, the Covered Entity may, in the exercise of professional judgment, determine whether the disclosure is in the best interest of the Individual and, if so, disclose only the PHI that is directly relevant to the person's involvement with the Individual's care or payment related to the Individual's health care or need for notification purposes. A Covered Entity may use professional judgment and its experience with common practice to make reasonable inferences of the Individual's best interest in allowing a person to act on behalf of the Individual to pick up filled prescriptions, medical supplies, X-rays, or other similar forms of PHI.

<u>Disaster Relief.</u> Provider may Use or Disclose PHI to a public or private entity authorized by law or by its charter to assist in disaster relief efforts, for the purposes of coordinating with such entities the notification of a family member, a personal representative, or another person responsible for the Individual's care of the Individual's location, general condition, or death.

Uses and Disclosures when the Individual is deceased. Provider will protect the PHI of a deceased individual (up to 50 years following death) as if the Individual were alive. Once the Individual is deceased, Provider may disclose to a family member, or other relatives, close personal friends, or any other person identified by the Individual, PHI of the Individual that is relevant to such person's involvement, unless doing so is inconsistent with any prior expressed preference of the Individual that is known to the Provider.

III. Notification of Privacy or Security Breaches

Purpose of Policy

To describe how Provider will comply with the HIPAA Rule and HITECH Act requirements regarding notifying Individuals of Breaches.

Policy Detail

(Also see Section XVI). To guard against and to detect potential Security Incidents and Breaches, Provider trains its workforce regarding proper Uses and Disclosures of PHI, and how to report suspected Security Incidents. Provider will provide written notification to affected Individuals in those instances where Provider has determined based upon a risk assessment that there is more than a low probability that affected Individuals' unsecured PHI has been compromised, thereby constituting a Breach under the HIPAA Rules and HITECH Act. A Breach is defined as the acquisition, access, Use, or Disclosure of PHI in a manner not permitted under the HIPAA Privacy Rule which compromises the security or privacy of the PHI.

If a Security Incident or Breach occurs, the Privacy Official, and if the PHI is electronic, the Security Official, must be notified immediately so they can initiate and coordinate an investigation. Law enforcement may need to be notified, depending on the facts and circumstances. Law enforcement may request that a Breach notice be delayed. A law enforcement request for a delay in notification shall be documented. If the statement is in writing and specifies the time for which a delay is required, delay the notification for the time period specified by the official. If the statement is made orally, document the statement, including the identity of the official making the statement, and delay the notification no longer than 30 days from the date of the oral statement, unless a written statement is submitted during that time.

There are certain exceptions to the notification requirement. A incident, including a Security Incident, will not be considered a Breach and notification will not be required for:

1. Any unintentional acquisition, access, or Use of PHI by a workforce member or person acting under the authority of Provider, if such acquisition, access, or Use was made in good faith and within the scope of authority and does not result in further Use or Disclosure in a manner not permitted under the HIPAA Privacy Rule;
2. Any inadvertent Disclosure by a person who is authorized to access PHI at Provider or a Business Associate to another person authorized to access PHI at the same Covered Entity or Business Associate, or Organized Health Care Arrangement in which the Covered Entity participates, and the information received as a result of such disclosure is not further Used or Disclosed in a manner not permitted under the Privacy Rule; or
3. A Disclosure of PHI where the Provider or Business Associate has a good-faith belief that an unauthorized person to whom the disclosure was made would not reasonably have been able to retain such information.

A Breach is presumed to have occurred unless the Provider or Business Associate demonstrates that there is a low probability that the unsecured PHI has been compromised based on a risk assessment of at least the following factors:

 a. The nature and extent of the PHI involved, including the types of identifiers and the likelihood of re-identification;
 b. The unauthorized person who Used the PHI or to whom the Disclosure was made;
 c. Whether the PHI was actually acquired or viewed; and
 d. The extent to which the risk to the PHI has been mitigated.

If ransomware is involved, the risk assessment should also consider the following additional factors:

 e. Whether there is a high risk of unavailability of PHI; and
 f. Whether there is a high risk to the integrity of the PHI.

Breaches of unsecured PHI require notification to the Individuals whose information was subject to the Breach, as well as to the Department of Health and Human Services, and possibly to the media. The HIPAA Rules define "unsecured protected health information" as PHI "that is not rendered unusable, unreadable, or indecipherable to unauthorized persons through the use of a technology or methodology specified by the Secretary in the guidance issued under section 13402(h)(2) of Public Law 111-5." If the PHI involved in the incident was encrypted in accordance with industry standards, and the decryption key was maintained in a secure manner, it is unlikely that the PHI would be considered "unsecured protected health information" and, therefore, a reportable Breach is unlikely.

Within 60 days of a Breach of unsecured PHI, or within a shorter time that may be required by state law, notices should be sent to the affected Individuals (or next of kin) via first class mail when address information is available. If the person has expressed a preference to accept communications electronically, an e-mail notification is allowed. If the Breach involves PHI of more than 500 people in one state or jurisdiction, a notice must be provided to prominent media outlets serving that state or jurisdiction. If the Breach involves PHI of ten or more Individuals for whom there is no current address, a website notice must be posted as a substitute notice, or a notice must be placed in major print or broadcast media, including major media in geographic areas where the Individuals affected by the Breach likely reside In the case where there is insufficient contact information for fewer than ten Individuals, substitute notice may be provided by other written notice, telephone, or through other means.

If urgent notice is required because of possible imminent misuse of unsecured PHI, notice may be provided by telephone in addition to other notices required under this policy. If a Breach involves social security numbers, bank account numbers, or similar information, there may be applicable state laws which must also be followed.

If the Breach involves unsecured PHI of 500 or more Individuals, notice must be provided to the federal Department of Health and Human Services (HHS) immediately. This should be done online through the HHS Office for Civil Rights web portal. If fewer than 500 Individuals are involved, the Breach must be maintained in a log and reported to HHS no later than 60 days after the close of the calendar year in which the Breach was discovered.

Notices governed under both state law and HIPAA must comply with both sets of laws, unless it is impossible to comply with both, in which case the more stringent law governs. Documentation related to the Breach and subsequent notice must be maintained for six years or longer as required by applicable law.

When notification is required, it should advise the affected Individuals of information similar to the following, depending on the facts and state law requirements:

[Company letterhead]
[Date]

VIA FIRST CLASS MAIL *[Note: May be sent via e-mail if Individual has indicated a preference for that and has agreed to it in writing.]*
[Last known address of Individual]

Dear:

On behalf of _____ ("Company"), I am writing to you because a recent incident may have involved your protected health information. We have learned that there is a possibility that an unauthorized person accessed a _____ containing medical records and other information. On _____, 20__, *[include a brief description of what happened, including the date of the Breach and the date of discovery, if known]*. We believe that the individual(s) responsible may have had access to a database containing *[describe the types of unsecured protected health information that were involved in the Breach (full name, social security number, date of birth, etc.)]*.

[Include a discussion of the steps Individuals should take to protect themselves from potential harm resulting from the Breach, such as contacting credit bureaus and placing a fraud alert on the Individual's credit file.]

[Include a brief description of what the Covered Entity involved is doing to investigate the Breach, to mitigate loss, and to protect against any further Breaches. An example is below.]

Provider has filed a law enforcement report with the *[insert agency]*. The incident report number is _____. Management immediately launched an internal investigation into this matter, and began taking steps to reduce the risk of future unauthorized access to information. Once we have compiled all relevant facts, we will consider additional action as necessary to prevent the theft of personally identifiable information. While we are uncertain whether your personal information was actually obtained during

Appendix A: *HIPAA Administrative Requirements and Policies*   **193**

the unauthorized access, we want to bring this situation to your attention, and urge you to take actions to minimize your potential risk of identity theft.

We want to assure you that we take our responsibility to safeguard personal information very seriously. As a result of this incident, we are also undertaking further steps to increase this security, such as _____.

If there is anything Company can do to assist you, of if you have any questions or require additional information, please contact us at _____ *[must include a toll-free telephone number, an e-mail address, Website, or postal address].*

We apologize for any inconvenience or concern this incident may cause you. *[Note whether additional information will be provided in a later mailing.]*

Sincerely,

_____

IV. Notice of Privacy Practices Procedures

Purpose of Policy

This policy outlines how Provider will provide the Notice of Privacy Practices ("Notice") to patients. Provider will provide each patient with adequate notice of the Uses and Disclosures of PHI that may be made by the Provider, and of the patient's right and the Provider's legal duties with respect to PHI. Provider shall update the Notice from time to time.

Policy Detail

The Provider and Workforce Members will follow the steps set forth below to provide each patient with adequate notice of the Uses and Disclosures of PHI that may be made by the Provider, and of the patient's rights and the Provider's legal duties with respect to PHI.

Step 1: Provision of Notice.

Except in an emergency, the Provider will provide a copy of the Notice of Privacy Practices to patients no later than the date of the first service delivery (including service delivered electronically). In emergency treatment situations, the Provider shall provide a copy of the Notice to patients as soon as reasonably practicable after the emergency treatment.

Step 2: Acknowledgment of Receipt.

Except in an emergency, the Provider will make a good-faith effort to obtain a written acknowledgment of receipt of the Notice. If a Provider is unable to obtain the acknowledgment, the Provider shall document its attempt to obtain the acknowledgment and the reason for not obtaining it.

Step 3: Availability on Request.

The Provider will make the Notice available upon request.

Step 4: Posting of Notice.

In addition to providing a copy of the Notice in accordance with Step 1, the Provider will post a copy of the Notice in a clear and prominent location where it is reasonable to expect the Provider's patients to be able to read the Notice.

Step 5: Website.

The Provider will prominently post the Notice on the entity's website and make the Notice available electronically through that website. If the first service delivery to a patient is delivered electronically, the Provider will provide electronic Notice automatically and contemporaneously in response to the patient's first request for service. The Provider will maintain a record of the Individual's acknowledgment that they received the electronic Notice. The patient who is the recipient of electronic Notice retains the right to obtain a paper copy of the Notice upon request.

Step 6: Revisions to Notice.

The Provider will revise the Notice, and implement the revised Notice, within 60 days of a material change to the Uses or Disclosures, the patient's rights, the Provider's legal duties, or other privacy practices stated in the Notice. Whenever the Notice is revised, the Provider will make the Notice available upon request on or after the effective date of the revision.

Step 7: Documentation.

- The Provider will retain a representative copy of each Notice it distributes for 6 years from the date when it last was in effect.
- The Provider will retain the written acknowledgments (or documentation of good-faith efforts to obtain written acknowledgment) for 6 years.

Who Is Affected

Provider and Workforce Members must follow this Policy.

V. Minimum Necessary Standard

Purpose of Policy

To ensure compliance with the HIPAA Privacy Rule regarding the minimum necessary requirements for requests for the Uses or Disclosures of PHI.

Policy Detail

Provider will:

- identify those persons or classes of persons in its workforce who need access to PHI to carry out their duties with respect to Treatment, Payment, or Health Care Operations;
- determine the access needed and any conditions appropriate to such access by those persons or classes of persons; and
- make reasonable efforts to limit the access of such persons or classes to PHI consistent with this Policy.

Provider's Workforce Use of Relevant Records Offsite. Provider employees are restricted from keeping, accessing, and transporting records containing PHI outside of the Provider's premises, except as expressly permitted herein. *[Insert provisions regarding whether and how records may be transported offsite.]*

Monitoring of the Policies and Procedures Governing Access to PHI. The Security Official and/or Privacy Official will regularly monitor the Provider's policies and procedures designed to protect PHI to ensure that it is operating in a manner reasonably calculated to prevent unauthorized access to, or Use of PHI The Security Official and/or Privacy Official will identify appropriate revisions or upgrades to the Provider's policies and procedures to reduce and mitigate the risk of unauthorized access to or Use of PHI.

Access to Relevant Records. The Security Official and/or Privacy Official is responsible for the management of exiting employees including, but not limited to, terminated employees, retiring employees, and employees who have voluntarily resigned from their employment at the Provider (collectively, the "Exiting Employees") The Security Official and/or Privacy Official will take steps to ensure that Exiting Employees are prevented from having access to records containing PHI prior to their leaving the premises after being terminated. Access removal includes both physical and electronic access. Steps taken to ensure that access is removed include, at a minimum: (i) deactivating applicable user accounts and passwords, (ii) confiscating keys to file cabinets and other storage areas containing PHI in the Exiting Employee's control, (iii) confiscating keys or ID badges that would allow the Exiting Employee to access Provider physical premises, and (iv) notifying building security that a particular Exiting Employee has been terminated.

Return of Relevant Records. The Security Official and/or Privacy Official will collect from the Exiting Employee (i) all records containing PHI, in any form or medium, currently in the Exiting Employee's possession or control, and (ii) all copies of records containing PHI, in any form or medium, currently in the Exiting Employee's possession or control.

Provider's Workforce Obligations. In addition to the other responsibilities set out in these policies, each Provider workforce member shall be responsible for:

- Regularly reviewing these policies, including all revisions and updates that are made to these policies and procedures to the extent they are relevant to the workforce member's job duties;
- Complying with all relevant policies and procedures that have been developed and implemented;
- Executing such workforce member's revised confidentiality agreement (if applicable), and returning an executed copy to the Security Official and/or Privacy Official;
- Understanding and complying with any responsibilities given to such employee pursuant to these policies, including all related development, implementation, monitoring, and maintenance obligations;
- Knowing and complying with all policies and procedures related to the access, use, and treatment of all records containing PHI;
- To the extent they are relevant to the workforce member's job duties, reviewing all internal and external risks identified in annual audits in accordance with these policies in

order to be more aware of potential threats to the integrity and security of records containing PHI;
- Providing feedback and suggestions to the Security Official and /or Privacy Official relating to the policies and procedures implemented to protect PHI;
- Reporting to the Security Official and/or Privacy Official all suspicious activity relating to records containing PHI such as unauthorized use of such records by other employees, or unauthorized attempts to access such records by other parties;
- Immediately reporting any discovered Security Incidents or potential Breaches to the Security Official and or Privacy Official;
- Understanding and complying with all physical and electronic security measures adopted to protect the integrity and confidentiality of PHI;
- Protecting all assigned passwords so that they are not accessible or used by other parties; and
- Complying with all exit requirements when the workforce member leaves employment (including returning keys and any PHI or other confidential materials in the workforce member's possession).

Routine/Recurring Disclosures. Any type of Disclosure that Provider makes on a routine and/or a recurring basis will be made in accordance with standard protocols developed by Provider with respect to each type of routine or recurring Disclosure so as to limit the PHI disclosed to the amount reasonably necessary to achieve the purpose of the Disclosure. *[List routine and recurring Disclosures and protocols.]*

Disclosures to Which the Minimum Necessary Standard Applies. For all other Disclosures to which the Minimum Necessary Standard applies, Provider will:

- utilize a Limited Data Set whenever possible;
- utilize criteria designed to limit the PHI disclosed to the information reasonably necessary to accomplish the purpose for which Disclosure is sought; and
- review requests for Disclosure on an individual basis in accordance with such criteria.

Provider may rely, if such reliance is reasonable under the circumstances, on a requested Disclosure as the minimum necessary for the stated purpose when:

- making Disclosures to public officials that are permitted under the HIPAA Privacy Rule, if the public official represents that the information requested is the minimum necessary for the stated purpose(s);
- the information is requested by another Covered Entity;
- the information is requested by a professional who is a member of Provider's workforce or is a Business Associate of Provider for the purpose of providing professional services to Provider, if the professional represents that the information requested is the minimum necessary for the stated purpose(s); or
- a person who is requesting the information for research purposes and who has provided documentation or representations that comply with the applicable Privacy Rule.

Provider will limit any request for PHI to that which is reasonably necessary to accomplish the purpose for which the request is made, when requesting such information from other Covered Entities.

Provider may not use, disclose, or request an entire medical record, except when the entire record is specifically justified as the amount that is reasonably necessary to accomplish the purpose of the use, disclosure, or request.

Disclosures to Which the Minimum Necessary Standard Does Not Apply. The Minimum Necessary Standard does not apply to the following kinds of Disclosures or requests:

- Disclosures to or requests by a health care provider for Treatment.
- Disclosures to the Individual whose PHI is being disclosed pursuant to their request.
- Disclosures made pursuant to a HIPAA-compliant authorization.
- Disclosures made to the Secretary.
- Disclosures that are Required by Law.
- Disclosures that are necessary to comply with applicable requirements of the Privacy Rule.

Provider's Workforce. Provider's workforce and their appropriate access profiles are described below. Access privileges for individual Workforce Members will be terminated or changed in conjunction with the termination of employment, contract, or change of level of access required. The IT Group will audit the access privileges *[insert frequency]* and shall report to Security Official and/or Privacy Official if any changes are needed.

- *[Insert titles or brief job description (for example, "Receptionist whose duties include scheduling appointments") of employees that will create or receive protected health information. Also insert description of the kinds of PHI this person must access. Providers should think carefully about who with the Provider may need access to PHI other than those involved with Treatment, Payment, or Health Care Operations on a daily basis (for example, CFO, accounting, IT department). This policy should also describe the entity's workforce clearance and termination procedures.]*

Appendix A: *HIPAA Administrative Requirements and Policies* **201**

Job Class	Categories of PHI to Which Workforce Member Needs Access	Access Profile (physical and electronic)
Privacy Official Security Official		Unlimited Access: Unlimited access to PHI, including demographic information, medical information, and enrollment data, is necessary for the operation of Provider and verification of compliance with HIPAA. Complete access to individual files, copy machines, fax machines, data screens.
Legal Counsel		Limited Access: Limited access required as needed to provide legal advice to Provider. The Privacy Official will determine necessary access on a case-by-case basis.
IT Group		
Risk Manager		
[Insert other workforce members]		

VI. Individual's Request to Restrict Uses and Disclosures of PHI

Purpose of Policy

To ensure compliance with applicable laws regarding requests from Individuals to restrict the Uses and Disclosures of their PHI.

Policy Detail

Provider will permit an Individual to request restrictions on the Uses or Disclosures of the Individual's PHI to carry out Provider's Payment or Health Care Operations and other Uses and Disclosures that Provider is permitted to make under the HIPAA Privacy Rule. Any such request must be made in writing and sent to the Privacy Official. The Privacy Official may request that Individuals make this request on Provider's template form for requesting restrictions. **Denial of Individual's Request.** While Individuals are entitled to request that Provider restrict the Uses and Disclosures of the Individual's PHI that Provider would otherwise be permitted to make under the Privacy Rule, Provider is not required to agree to any particular restriction, with one exception set forth below. Provider will not agree to a request to restrict a Use or Disclosure that Provider is required to make under the Privacy Rule, or one that it is otherwise required by law to make.

Approval of Individual's Request. If Provider agrees to a particular restriction, Provider may not use or disclose PHI contrary to such restriction and Provider will document the restriction. Provider shall agree to an Individual's request to restrict the Disclosure of PHI to a health plan if:

1. The Disclosure is for the purpose of carrying out Payment or Health Care Operations and is not otherwise required by law; and
2. The PHI pertains solely to a health care item or service for which the Individual, or person other than the health plan on behalf of the Individual, has paid the Covered Entity out-of-pocket in full.

Provider, however, may use the restricted PHI, or may disclose such information to another health care provider to provide emergency treatment to the Individual if the Individual who requested the restriction is in need of emergency treatment and the restricted PHI is needed to provide the emergency treatment. Provider must request that such health care provider not further use or disclose the information.

Terminating the Restriction. Provider may terminate the restriction if:

- the Individual requests and agrees in writing that the restriction be terminated;
- the Individual orally requests and agrees that the restriction be terminated and the oral request and agreement is documented; or
- Provider informs the Individual that it is terminating its agreement to restrict Provider's Use or Disclosure of the individual's PHI, except that such termination is only effective with respect to PHI created or received after Provider has so informed the Individual.

If Provider decides to rescind a previously agreed to restriction, it will so inform the Individual and document its termination of the restriction.

VII. Individual's Request for Confidential Communications

Purpose of Policy

To ensure compliance with the Privacy Rule regarding confidential communications.

Policy Detail

Individuals may request that Provider communicate with them in a more confidential fashion than Provider's standard communication procedures otherwise provide. Individuals must make these requests in writing to the Privacy Official. The Privacy Official may ask Individuals to use Provider's form for these requests. Provider intends to comply with reasonable confidentiality requests, and will not require that the Individual explain the basis or reasons for the request.

Provider will try to provide reasonable accommodation for a confidentiality request by:

- limiting or modifying the information provided with respect to requests for Payment;
- sending information to the Individual at an alternative address or other method of contact;
- sending information to the Individual in a manner that conceals the information from anyone but the addressee (e.g., sending information in sealed envelopes); and
- not providing identification on the outer envelope that the content contains medical information or is from Provider.

VIII. Individual's Right of Access to PHI

Purpose of Policy

To identify how Provider will process a request from an Individual to inspect and/or obtain a copy of their own PHI that is maintained in Provider's Designated Record Set.

Policy Detail

Provider will permit an Individual to request access to inspect or to obtain a copy of the Individual's own PHI that is maintained in Provider's Designated Record Set. Individuals who wish to inspect their PHI, rather than receive a copy, will be accommodated. *[Include details regarding how Individuals will be accommodated if they wish to inspect their records, rather than receive a copy.]*

Individuals may make requests for access in writing on the forms provided by the Privacy Official, or the Individual may require the Provider to transmit a copy of PHI directly to another person designated by the Individual. The Individual's request to send PHI to a third party must be in writing, signed by the Individual, and clearly identify the designated person and where to send the copy of the PHI.

No Right to Access. An Individual's right of access does not include:

- psychotherapy notes; or
- information compiled in reasonable anticipation of, or for use in, a civil, criminal, or administrative action or proceeding.

Denial of Access. Provider may deny an Individual access *without* providing the Individual an opportunity for review, in any of the following circumstances:

- The PHI is exempt from the right of access, as noted above.
- Provider, when acting under the direction of a correctional institution, may deny, in whole or in part, an inmate's request to obtain a copy of PHI, if obtaining such information would jeopardize the health, safety, security, custody, or rehabilitation of the inmate or of other inmates, or the safety of any officer, employee, or other person at the correctional institution or responsible for the transporting of the inmate.
- An Individual's access may be denied if the PHI was obtained from someone other than Provider under a promise of confidentiality and the access requested would be reasonably likely to reveal the source of the information.
- Access may be denied to an Individual, but the Individual has the right to have the denials reviewed, in the following circumstances:
- A licensed health care professional has determined, in the exercise of professional judgment, that the access requested is reasonably likely to endanger the life or physical safety of the Individual or another person.
- The PHI makes reference to another person (unless such other person is a health care provider) and a licensed health care professional has determined, in the exercise of professional judgment, that the access requested is reasonably likely to cause substantial harm to such other person.

- The request for access is made by the Individual's personal representative and a licensed health care professional has determined, in the exercise of professional judgment, that the provision of access to such personal representative is reasonably likely to cause substantial harm to the Individual or another person.

If access is denied as outlined above, the Individual has the right to have the denial reviewed by a licensed health care professional who is designated by Provider to act as a reviewing official and who did not participate in the original decision to deny. Provider will provide or deny access in accordance with the determination of the reviewing official. Provider must promptly provide written notice to the Individual of the reviewing official's determination.

If access to PHI is ***denied***, in whole or in part, Provider:

- must, to the extent possible, give the Individual access to any PHI requested for which there is no basis for denying access; and
- must provide a timely, written denial to the Individual. The denial must be in plain language and contain the following:
    - The basis for the denial.
    - A statement that the Individual has the right to seek a review of the denial.
    - A statement that the Individual may file a complaint with Provider through Provider's Privacy Official, or with the Secretary.

If Provider determines that it does not maintain the PHI that the Individual wishes to see and Provider knows where the requested information is maintained, then Provider must inform the Individual where to direct the request.

Time Limits. Provider will act on a request for access no later than 30 days after receipt of the request as follows:

- If Provider grants the request, in whole or in part, Provider must inform the Individual of the acceptance of the request and provide the access requested.
- If Provider denies the request, in whole or in part, it must provide the Individual with a written denial.
- If Provider is unable to take action on the request within the time limits provided, then Provider may seek to extend the time for such actions by no more than 30 days, provided that:
  - Provider, within the applicable required time limit, provides the Individual with a written statement of the reasons for the delay and the date by which Provider will complete its action on the request; and
  - Provider has only one such extension of time for action on a request for access.

Approval of Access. If access to PHI is granted by Provider to an Individual, then Provider must do the following:

- Provide the access requested by the Individual by allowing the Individual to inspect and/or copy his or her PHI that is maintained in Provider's Designated Record Set. If the PHI requested is maintained at more than one location, Provider need only produce the PHI once in response to a request.
- Provide the Individual with access to the PHI in a readable hard copy form, or in another form or format to which the Individual and Provider can agree. If the information is electronic, the Individual shall have a right to obtain from the Provider a copy of such information in an electronic format and, if the Individual chooses, to direct the Provider to transmit such copy directly to an entity or person designated by the Individual, provided that any such choice is clear, conspicuous, and specific.

- Provide the Individual with a summary of the PHI requested, in lieu of providing access to the PHI, or provide the Individual with an explanation of the PHI requested, if:
  ○ the Individual agrees in advance to such a summary or explanation; and
  ○ the Individual agrees in advance to the fees imposed, if any, by Provider for such summary or explanation.

Access will be provided as requested by the Individual in a timely manner, including arranging with the Individual a convenient time and place to inspect and/or obtain a copy of the PHI, or mailing any requested copy to the Individual.

Reasonable Fees. Provider will impose a reasonable fee that aligns with state law for providing copies or summaries of PHI. Provider will notify the Individual in advance of the approximate fee, and will make available to Individuals, upon request, an approximate fee schedule for regular types of access requests, which may include a breakdown of the charges for labor, supplies, and postage. The fee will only include: (1) the cost of copying, including the cost of supplies for and labor of copying; (2) postage, when the Individual has requested that the copy, or the summary or explanation, be mailed; and (3) expenses incurred in preparing an explanation or summary of the PHI, if the Individual agrees. The costs of providing PHI in electronic form shall not be greater than the Provider's labor costs in responding to the request for the copy (or summary or explanation).

Provider may calculate its labor costs through any of the following methods:

[Note: The Provider should determine the method in accordance with state law that will be used and adjust this section accordingly.]

<u>Actual costs:</u> Provider may calculate the actual labor costs to fulfill the request, as long as the labor cost is only for copying (and/or creating a summary or explanation if the Individual chooses to receive a summary or explanation) and the labor rates used are reasonable for such activity. Provider may add to the actual

costs any applicable supply (e.g., paper, or CD or USB drive) or postage costs. Provider must be prepared to inform Individuals in advance of the approximate fee that may be charged for providing the Individual with a copy of his or her PHI.

Average costs: Provider may develop a schedule of costs for labor based on average labor costs to fulfill standard types of access requests, as long as the types of labor costs included are permissible (e.g. labor costs for copying but not for search and retrieval) and are reasonable. Provider may add to that amount any applicable supply (e.g., paper, or CD or USB drive) or postage costs. The standard rate may be calculated and charged as a per page fee only in cases where PHI requested is maintained in paper form and the Individual requests a paper copy of the PHI or asks that the paper PHI be scanned into an electronic format. Per page fees are not permitted for paper or electronic copies of PHI maintained electronically.

Flat fee: Provider may charge Individuals a flat fee for all requests for electronic copies of PHI maintained electronically, provided the fee does not exceed $6.50, inclusive of all labor, supplies, and any applicable postage.

If a higher fee is expressly permitted by state law or other law, Provider will not charge such fee in situations where the Individual is requesting access to his or her own record. Instead, Provider may charge a reasonable, cost-based fee to cover the cost to prepare and transmit the PHI. Provider may charge a higher fee otherwise expressly permitted by other law if a third party is requesting the PHI on its own behalf through a HIPAA-compliant authorization form or some other lawful process.

Retaining Documentation. Provider must document the following and retain such documentation for a period of six years:
- Documentation of the components of Provider's Designated Record Set that Individuals may access.
- The titles of the persons or offices responsible for receiving and processing requests for access.

Request for Access to Protected Health Information

Patients or their personal representatives may inspect and/or obtain copies of certain protected health information maintained by or for *[INSERT ENTITY NAME]*, in accordance with *[INSERT ENTITY NAME]* Policies and Procedures and federal regulations known as the HIPAA Privacy Rule. To assist us in responding to your request, please fill out the following information:

Patient's Name (Please print legibly):
Information Requested (Please check all that apply):

- ☐ All protected health information
- ☐ The following protected health information (please describe):

Type of Access Requested (Please check all that apply):

- ☐ I wish to inspect my protected health information.
- ☐ I wish to pick up a copy of the protected health information.
- ☐ I wish to have a copy of the protected health information mailed to the following person and location (specify name and address):

Summary of Information: At your request, we will provide you with a summary of your protected health information to which you are granted access, instead of making that information available for inspection or providing a copy. If you request a summary by checking the box in this section, we will not arrange for your inspection or provide you with a copy of the information, even if you have checked one or more boxes in the preceding section.

- ☐ I wish to receive a summary instead of inspecting or receiving a copy of the information.

Fees: If you request a copy or summary of protected health information, we may charge a reasonable, cost-based fee for the preparation of the copy or summary. You will be informed of the fee in advance.

Form of Access Requested (e.g. paper copy, electronic copy): We will provide you with access to the protected health information in the form or format you request if the protected health information is readily producible at a reasonable cost in such form or format. If not, we will provide you with a paper copy of the protected health information.

Person Requesting Access:

- ☐ Patient
- ☐ Personal representative (Print name legibly):

Please Sign:

_____

Patient Personal Representative

_____

Date   Description of personal representative's authority to act for patient

We will provide you, or a third party you have designated, with a response to your request in a timely fashion in accordance with applicable law. We have the right in certain circumstances to deny access to all or part of the information you have requested.

IX. Individual's Request to Amend PHI

Purpose of Policy

To set forth the procedures whereby an Individual may file a request to amend his or her PHI maintained in Provider's Designated Record Set.

Policy Detail

An Individual has the right to request that Provider amend his or her PHI that is in Provider's Designated Record Set for as long as Provider maintains that PHI in its Designated Record Set. Provider will require that Individuals make their requests for amendment in writing to the Privacy Official. The Privacy Official may require Individuals to make such requests on Provider's form for requesting amendments. In all cases, Individuals must provide a reason to support the requested amendment.

Denial of Request. Provider is not obligated to grant the Individual's request. Provider may deny an Individual's request to amend Provider's Designated Record Set if it determines that the PHI or record:

- was not created by Provider, unless the Individual provides a reasonable basis to believe that the originator of the PHI is no longer available to act on the requested amendment;
- is not part of Provider's Designated Record Set;
- would not be accessible by the Individual or available for inspection by the Individual under the Privacy Rule; or
- is accurate and complete.

Should Provider deny the requested amendment, in whole or in part, Provider must do the following:

- Provide the Individual with a timely, written denial. The denial must use plain language and contain the following:
- The basis for the denial.

- The Individual's right to submit a written statement disagreeing with the denial and how the Individual may file the "Statement of Disagreement."
- If the Individual does not submit a Statement of Disagreement, the Individual may request that Provider provide the Individual's request for amendment and Provider's denial with any future Disclosures of the PHI that is the subject of the amendment.
- A description of how the Individual may complain to Provider or to the Secretary pursuant to the procedures established in the HIPAA Privacy Rule. The description must include the name, or title, and telephone number of the contact person or office designated in the Privacy Rule.
- Permit the Individual to submit to Provider a written statement disagreeing with the denial of all or part of a requested amendment and the basis of such disagreement. Provider may reasonably limit the length of a Statement of Disagreement to no more than a single page, single spaced, 12-point type for each denied amendment request.
- Elect or decline to prepare a written rebuttal to the Individual's Statement of Disagreement. Whenever such a "Rebuttal Statement" is prepared, Provider must provide a copy to the Individual who submitted the Statement of Disagreement.
- As appropriate, identify the record or PHI in the Designated Record Set that is the subject of the disputed amendment and append or otherwise link the Individual's request for an amendment, Provider's denial of the request, the Individual's Statement of Disagreement, if any, and Provider's Rebuttal Statement, if any, to the Designated Record Set.
- If an Individual has submitted a written Statement of Disagreement, include the material appended in accordance with the paragraph above, or, at the election of Provider, an accurate summary of any such information, with any subsequent Disclosure of the PHI to which the disagreement relates.

- If the Individual has not submitted a written Statement of Disagreement, include the Individual's request for amendment and its denial, or an accurate summary of such information, with any subsequent Disclosure of the PHI only if the Individual has requested such action.

Time Limits. Provider must either comply with or deny the Individual's request for an amendment no later than 60 days after receipt of the request.

If Provider is unable to act on the amendment request within 60 days after the receipt of the request, Provider may seek to extend the time for its decision no more than 30 days if Provider, within the original 60day time limit, provides the Individual with a written statement of the reasons for the delay and the date by which Provider will make its decision. Provider may have only one extension of time.

Approval of Request. If Provider *accepts* the requested amendment, in whole or in part, Provider must:

- Make the appropriate amendment to the PHI or record that is the subject of the request for amendment by, at a minimum, identifying the records in the Designated Record Set that are affected by the amendment and appending or otherwise providing a link to the location of the revised information.
- Timely inform the Individual that the amendment has been accepted and obtain the Individual's help, if needed, to identify the relevant persons with which the amendment needs to be shared, and get the Individual's agreement for Provider to notify these persons.
- Make reasonable efforts to inform the following persons that certain records in the Designated Record Set have been amended and, within a reasonable period of time, to provide them with the amended information:

- persons identified by the Individual as having received PHI about the Individual and needing the amendment; and
- persons, including Business Associates, that Provider knows have in their records the PHI that is the subject of the amendment and who may have relied, or could reasonably rely, on such information to the detriment of the Individual.

When a subsequent Disclosure is made using a Standard Transaction under the Privacy Rule that does not permit the additional material to be included with the Disclosure, Provider may separately transmit the material required above, as applicable, to the recipient of the Standard Transaction.

In the event Provider is informed by another health care provider, health plan, or Business Associate of an amendment, Provider must amend the PHI in Provider's Designated Record Set that is the subject of that amendment.

The Privacy Official will be responsible for receiving and processing requests for amendments by Individuals. Provider will retain the documentation as required by the Privacy Rule for a period of six years.

Request to Amend or Correct Protected Health Information

Patients or their personal representatives may submit a request in writing to have their protected health information amended or corrected in accordance with our Policies and Procedures and federal regulations known as the HIPAA Privacy Rule. The patient or personal representative must include a reason to support a requested amendment or correction. To assist us in responding to your request, please fill out the following information:

Amendment or Correction:

I. Name of Patient (please print legibly):

II. Please specifically describe the protected health information you would like amended or corrected (including dates):

III. Please specifically describe how you would like the protected health information amended or corrected:

IV. Please give specific reasons to support your requested amendment or correction:

Person requesting Amendment or Correction (please check):

- ☐ Patient
- ☐ Personal representative (Print name legibly):

Please Sign:

_____

Patient Personal Representative

_____

Date   Description of personal representative's authority to act for patient

We will provide you with a response to your request in a timely fashion in accordance with applicable law. We have the right in certain circumstances to deny access to all or part of the amendment you have requested.

X. Individual's Request for an Accounting of Disclosures

Purpose of Policy

To ensure compliance with the Privacy Rule's requirements regarding the Individual's right to receive an accounting of certain Disclosures of his or her own PHI.

Policy Detail

An Individual has a right to receive an accounting of Disclosures of his or her own PHI made by Provider in the six years before the date on which the accounting is requested, except for Disclosures:

- to carry out Payment, Treatment, and Health Care Operations (except that Disclosures from electronic records may have to be included in an accounting if and to the extent required by the HIPAA Rules);
- to Individuals of PHI about them;
- pursuant to a proper authorization;
- to persons involved in the Individual's care or Payment for care;
- for national security or intelligence purposes;
- to correctional institutions or Law Enforcement Officials in custodial situations;
- that are part of a Limited Data Set;
- incident to a Use or Disclosure otherwise permitted or required by the Privacy Rule.

Depending on the compliance date Required by Law for a particular record or for electronic health records, Individuals have a right to an accounting of Disclosures made for Treatment, Payment, or Health Care Operations purposes for the previous three years. *[Practice note: The HITECH Act gives Individuals the right to receive an accounting of all "disclosures through an electronic health record" that occurred during the three years prior to the request for an accounting. Regulations implementing this requirement have not, as of the date of this writing, been finalized.]* An Individual may request an accounting of Disclosures for a period of time less than six years from the date of the request. All requests for an accounting must be submitted in writing on the forms available from the Privacy Official.

Content of the Accounting. Provider will provide the Individual with a written accounting that meets the following requirements:

- The accounting must include Disclosures of PHI that occurred during the six years (or such shorter time period at the request of the Individual or if the request involves electronic health records) before the date of the request, including Disclosures to or by Business Associates of Provider. The accounting will not include Disclosures made by Provider that occurred prior to the compliance date for Provider, or six years prior to the request, whichever is shorter.
- For each Disclosure, the accounting must include the following core elements:
  - The date of the Disclosure.
  - The name of the entity or person who received the PHI and, if known, the address of such entity or person.
  - A brief description of the PHI Disclosed.
  - A brief statement of the purpose of the Disclosure that reasonably informs the Individual of the basis for the Disclosure, or, in lieu of such statement, a copy of a written request for Disclosure, if any.

Multiple Disclosures to Same Person or Entity. If, during the period covered by the accounting, Provider has made multiple Disclosures of PHI to the same person or entity for a single purpose under the HIPAA Privacy Rule, the accounting may, with respect to such multiple Disclosures, provide:

- the core elements required to be in all accountings as described above for the first Disclosure during the accounting period;
- the frequency, periodicity, or number of the Disclosures made during the accounting period; and
- the date of the last such Disclosure during the accounting period.

Timing of Provider's Response. Provider must act on the Individual's request for an accounting no later than 60 days after receipt of such a request. In its response:

Provider will provide the Individual with the accounting requested; and

if Provider is unable to provide the accounting within the time required by the Privacy Rule, Provider may seek to extend the time to provide the accounting by no more than 30 days, provided that Provider, within the original 60-day time limit, gives the Individual a written statement of the reasons for the delay and the date by which Provider will provide the accounting. Provider will have only one such extension.

Imposing Fees for Accounting. Provider will provide the first accounting in any 12-month period without charge. Provider may impose a reasonable, costbased fee for each subsequent request for an accounting by the same Individual within the same 12-month period, provided that Provider informs the Individual in advance of the fee and provides the Individual with an opportunity to withdraw or modify the request for a subsequent accounting in order to avoid or reduce the fee.

Temporary Suspension of Right to an Accounting. Provider will temporarily suspend an Individual's right to receive an accounting of Disclosures to a Health Oversight Agency or Law Enforcement Official for the time specified by such agency or official, if such agency or official provides Provider with a written statement that such an accounting to the individual would be reasonably likely to impede the agency's activities and specifying the time for which such a suspension is required.

If the agency or official statement referenced in the preceding paragraph is made orally, Provider will:

- document the statement, including the identity of the agency or official making the statement;
- temporarily suspend the Individual's right to an accounting of Disclosures subject to the statement; and
- limit the temporary suspension to no longer than 30 days from the date of the oral statement, unless the agency's or official's written statement is submitted during that time.

Retaining Documentation. Provider will document the following and retain the documentation for a period of six years:

- The information required to be included in an accounting of Disclosures of PHI.
- The written accounting that is provided to the individual under this section.
- The titles of the persons or offices responsible for receiving and processing requests for an accounting by Individuals.

Form: Request for an Accounting or Disclosures of Medical Information

Patients or their personal representatives may receive a description of certain types of non-routine Disclosures of the patient's medical information made by *[INSERT PROVIDER NAME]*. This description is known as an "accounting." The right to an accounting comes from federal regulations called the HIPAA Privacy Rule. The HIPAA Privacy Rule permits you to request an accounting of certain non-routine Disclosures of medical information that may have occurred up to 6 years prior to the date on which the accounting is requested. Beginning on January 1, 2011 or January 1, 2014, depending on the compliance date required by law for a particular record, for electronic health records, individuals have a right to an accounting of Disclosures made for Treatment, Payment, or Health Care Operations purposes for the previous three years.

To assist us in responding to your request, please fill out the following information:

Patient's Name (Please print legibly):
Patient's Mailing Address
Street:
City: **State:** **Zip Code:**
Patient's Date of Birth (mm/dd/yyyy) / /
Time Period of the Accounting Request: (please check one)

- ☐ The time period between the following dates (but not greater than 6 years, or 3 years for certain routine disclosures of electronic health records).

From _____ to _____.

Person Requesting Accounting: (please check one):

- ☐ Patient
- ☐ Personal representative (Print name legibly):

Attach a copy of the documentation that establishes you as the patient's personal representative under state law.

Signature of patient OR patient's personal representative:

Patient   Patient's Personal Representative

Date   Description of personal representative's authority to make medical decisions for patient

We will provide you with a response to your request in a reasonable time period, in accordance with applicable law.

XI. Refraining from Intimidating or Retaliatory Acts

Purpose of Policy

To ensure that Individuals are free to exercise their rights under the Privacy Rule without intimidation or coercion.

Policy Detail

Provider may not intimidate, threaten, coerce, discriminate against, or take other retaliatory action against the Individual or another person for:

- filing of a complaint with the Secretary;
- testifying, assisting, or participating in an investigation, compliance review, proceeding, or hearing; or
- opposing any act or practice made unlawful by the Privacy Rule, provided the Individual or other person has a good-faith belief that the practice proposed is unlawful and the manner of opposition is reasonable and does not involve a Disclosure of PHI in violation of the Privacy Rule.

XII. Waiver of Rights

Purpose of Policy

To ensure compliance with the Privacy Rule or other applicable law regarding an Individual's waiver of his or her rights regarding his or her PHI.

Policy Detail

Provider may not seek or request that an Individual waive any right, in part or in whole, provided under the Privacy Rule, or other applicable law, regarding the confidentiality of medical information or the confidentiality of information pertaining to the payment for health care, as a condition for receiving treatment from Provider.

XIII. Documentation Requirements and Retention of Records

Purpose of Policy

To ensure compliance with the Privacy Rule regarding documentation requests and the retention of records.

Policy Detail

Policies and Procedures. Provider will maintain in written or electronic form all policies and procedures implemented with respect to PHI and all documents required to be maintained by the Privacy Rule.

Communications. If a communication document or record is required by Provider to be in writing, Provider will maintain such writing, or an electronic copy of that writing, as documentation.

Written or Electronic Record. If an action, activity, or designation is required to be documented, Provider will maintain a written or electronic record of the action, activity, or designation. If records are retained in electronic form, Provider will ensure that:

- the record-keeping system has reasonable controls designed to ensure the integrity, accuracy, authenticity, and reliability of the electronic records;
- the electronic records are maintained in reasonable order, in a safe and accessible place and are capable of being readily inspected and examined;
- the electronic records are readily convertible into legible paper copies; and
- adequate records management systems are established and implemented to ensure that documents are labeled

adequately and stored securely, backup electronic copies are made and paper copies are kept for records that cannot be clearly, accurately and completely transferred to electronic media.

Documents Provider Must Retain. Provider will retain the following documents:

- Provider's Notice of Privacy Practices that are issued to individuals.
- The following information about Disclosures that are required to be accounted for:
  - The date of the Disclosure;
  - The name of the entity or person who received the Individual's PHI and, if known, the address of such person or entity;
  - A brief description of the PHI Disclosed; and
  - A brief statement of the purpose of the Disclosure.
- Individual authorizations.
- Individuals' Designated Record Sets.
- Copies of these policies and procedures.
- The documentation of the training program for Provider's workforce members.
- Individual complaints and their outcomes.
- Records of any sanctions imposed in connection with noncompliance with HIPAA.
- Records of any PHI Used or Disclosed for research purposes, as allowed without authorization under the Privacy Rule.
- Copies of individual requests for restrictions on the Use and Disclosure of their PHI and Provider's responses.
- Copies of individual requests for confidential communications and Provider's responses.
- Copies of individual requests for a written accounting of Disclosures and Provider's responses.
- Copies of any Business Associate Agreements entered into by Provider.

How Long Provider Must Retain Documents. Provider will retain any documentation required to be retained under HIPAA for a period of six years from the date of its creation, or the date when it was last in effect, whichever is later.

Document Destruction. If Provider does not need to retain a record or document, the record or document will be disposed of in a manner that will not permit any PHI contained in the record or document to be Disclosed. Destruction of documents or records stored in electronic media must ensure that the data is wiped from electronic media so that it cannot be recovered. **Documents that are relevant to pending litigation or government investigations must not be destroyed.**

- If the document or record has been maintained in a paper format, the paper will be shredded or burned, or Provider will use some other feasible method that will prevent the reconstruction of the data.
- If the document or record has been received in an electronic format, any hardware on which the record was saved will be wiped clean before the hardware is sold, reviewed, or destroyed.
- Any electronic media containing PHI will be wiped clean to ensure that even deleted items containing PHI are eliminated and cannot be re-created before the media is re-used.

XIV. Training on HIPAA Privacy and Security Policies

Policy Statement

It is the policy of Provider to train all members of its workforce on the policies and procedures required by the HIPAA Privacy Rule and Security Rule with respect to PHI as necessary and appropriate for workforce members to carry out their functions.

Scope of This Policy

This policy applies to all Provider workforce members, including any employees whose job descriptions allow them to access Individuals' PHI.

Purpose of Policy

To set forth the training all workforce members must receive regarding the policies and procedures required by the Privacy Rule and Security Rule.

Policy Detail

Provider has provided or will provide training as follows:
- To each member of Provider's workforce by no later than the date by which Provider begins Using and Disclosing PHI.
- Thereafter, to each new member of the workforce during new hire orientation and within a reasonable period of time after the person joins Provider's Workforce.
- To each member of Provider's workforce whose functions are affected by a material change in Provider's policies or procedures within a reasonable period of time after the material change becomes effective.

Content of Training. Training sessions may include the following:
- Awareness training (live lecturing or video-based training).
- Details of applicable policies and procedures.
- Periodic reminders (via the use of methods such as e-mails, bulletin boards, pamphlets, staff meetings, etc.).
- Timely information about changes in policies and procedures.
- Information about sanctions.

Documentation. Provider will document that the training has been provided by:
- maintaining the policies and procedures in written or electronic form;
- maintaining a record of the attendance of each workforce member at any required training session on the Privacy Rule,

these privacy policies, or general training on maintaining the privacy and confidentiality of PHI;
- maintaining a record of any voluntary training undertaken by any workforce member on the Privacy Rule, these privacy policies, or general training on maintaining the privacy and confidentiality of PHI;
- maintaining a record of the test results of any workforce member following any required or voluntary training session where testing of the material presented occurred; and
- ensuring that for any action, activity, or documentation regarding training that is required by the Privacy Rule or Security Rule to be documented, a written or electronic record of such action, activity, or documentation is maintained.

Retaining Documentation. Provider will retain documentation required by this policy for six years from the date of its creation or the date it was last in effect, whichever is later.

XV. Disciplinary Sanctions for Noncompliance with Provider's Privacy and Security Policies

Purpose of Policy

To set forth the appropriate disciplinary procedures for workforce members who fail to comply with these privacy policies and procedures and to ensure compliance with the Privacy Rule and Security Rule.

Policy Detail

Provider will apply the same progressive disciplinary procedure to workforce members who fail to comply with these policies and procedures, up to and including termination for serious and/or repetitive violations, as it applies to all other instances of employee misconduct. *[Practice note: Provider should consider setting out levels of discipline here.]*

In the opinion of the Privacy Official and/or the Security Official, should the violations of a workforce member be deemed to be "serious," or the repetition of the violation be deemed evidence of a willful disregard of these policies, the Privacy Official and/or the Security Official may impose an appropriate sanction without regard to these progressive levels of discipline.

This policy does not apply to workforce members with respect to actions that are: (1) covered by and that meet the conditions of Disclosures by whistleblowers, (2) Disclosures by workforce member(s) who are crime victims, or (3) for those employees exercising any right under the Privacy Rule.

Provider will document the sanctions that are applied, if any, and retain such documentation for six years from the date of its creation or the date when it was last in effect, whichever is later.

XVI. Reporting and Mitigating Inadvertent or Improper Disclosures of PHI or Security Incidents

Purpose of Policy

(Also see Policy III) To ensure that the consequences of any impermissible or inadvertent Disclosure of PHI or Security Incidents are minimized to the extent possible and to comply with the requirements of the Privacy and Security Rules.

Policy Detail

[Describe how the organization will prevent, detect, contain, and correct security violations and Security Incidents. Also address periodic vulnerability scanning policy and procedure, periodic network penetration testing policy and procedure, and access to security violation monitoring reports. Include report templates for violation monitoring reports and follow-up action log/report templates.]

Workforce Members who are aware of or who become aware of an impermissible or inadvertent Disclosure of PHI should report the occurrence to the Privacy Official.

Workforce Members who are aware of or who become aware of a Security Incident related to or involving PHI should report the occurrence to the Security Official.

Upon receipt of such a report, the Privacy Official or Security Official will investigate the reported incident to determine the nature of the Disclosure, to whom the Disclosure was made, the circumstances under which it was made, and the reasons why it was made (to the extent possible).

The Privacy Official, Security Official, or his or her designee, will respond in a manner that will mitigate or minimize the consequences of the incident to the extent possible. This may include:

- contacting persons or entities to which the Disclosure was made to determine what further Uses or Disclosures of the PHI may have occurred;
- whenever possible, seeking to stop any further uses and/or disclosures of the PHI;
- correcting, where appropriate, any wrong or inaccurate information that was involved in the Disclosure;
- whenever possible, seeking the return of all information improperly Disclosed;
- if the situation rose to the level of a Breach, review the Breach and revise the information security program and the Provider's business practices to minimize the likelihood of a recurrence of the same, or a similar Breach;
- sanctioning any workforce member(s) responsible for the Disclosure;
- addressing the matter with any Business Associate responsible for the Disclosure and requiring the Business Associate to cure any inadequacies in its physical, technical, or administrative systems that contributed to the Disclosure or terminating Provider's agreement with the Business Associate

should the Business Associate fail to cure the defect in a reasonable period of time or should the failure not be subject to cure; and
- reporting the Disclosure to the Provider's legal counsel if, in his or her view, the Disclosure is of a nature that could give rise to litigation.
- documenting each incident involving a Breach of the privacy or security measures implemented by the Provider to protect PHI (each an "Incident Report"). Each Incident Report will include, at a minimum: (i) a post-incident review of the Breach itself, (ii) the responsive actions taken in connection with the Breach, and (iii) those revisions to the Information Security Program or the Provider's business practices that were made to minimize the likelihood of a recurrence of the same, or a similar Breach.

The initial and primary focus of all activities undertaken by the Privacy Official, the Security Official, or any workforce member in response to a Disclosure of PHI in violation of HIPAA or these policies will be to mitigate, to the extent practicable, any harmful effects of the violation that become known or which reasonably should become known through the exercise of reasonable diligence.

XVII. Administrative, Technical, and Physical Privacy and Security Safeguards

Purpose of Policy

To ensure that PHI is not intentionally or unintentionally Used or Disclosed in violation of the Privacy Rule or Security Rule.

Policy Detail

Risk Analysis, Evaluation of Security, and Ongoing Risk Management. Risk analysis is a process that may be used to identify possible threats and vulnerabilities, and to identify possible ways to reduce risk. The Security Official shall work with the Privacy Official, legal counsel, and other operational and business representatives (the "RM Group") to conduct an initial, comprehensive risk analysis of the safeguards in place to protect ePHI. The initial risk analysis will create a baseline for ongoing and future risk management and evaluation activities. The RM Group will determine how identified risks will be managed so that vulnerabilities will be brought to a reasonable and appropriate level. The RM Group will document how risks will be mitigated and managed.

The Security Official, with the assistance of the RM Group, as needed, will periodically (whenever environmental or operational changes affecting PHI occur) review and evaluate the risks to the security of PHI and these HIPAA policies to determine whether changes are needed for ongoing compliance. Risks will be evaluated based on the impact of the risk and the probability of occurrence. Risks may be documented on a chart similar to the following:

[Note: HHS has issued more detailed risk assessment tools that may assist with the risk analysis process.[2]]

---

2. *See* HealthIT.gov, Security Risk Assessment Tool, https://www.healthit.gov/topic/privacy-security-and-hipaa/security-risk-assessment.

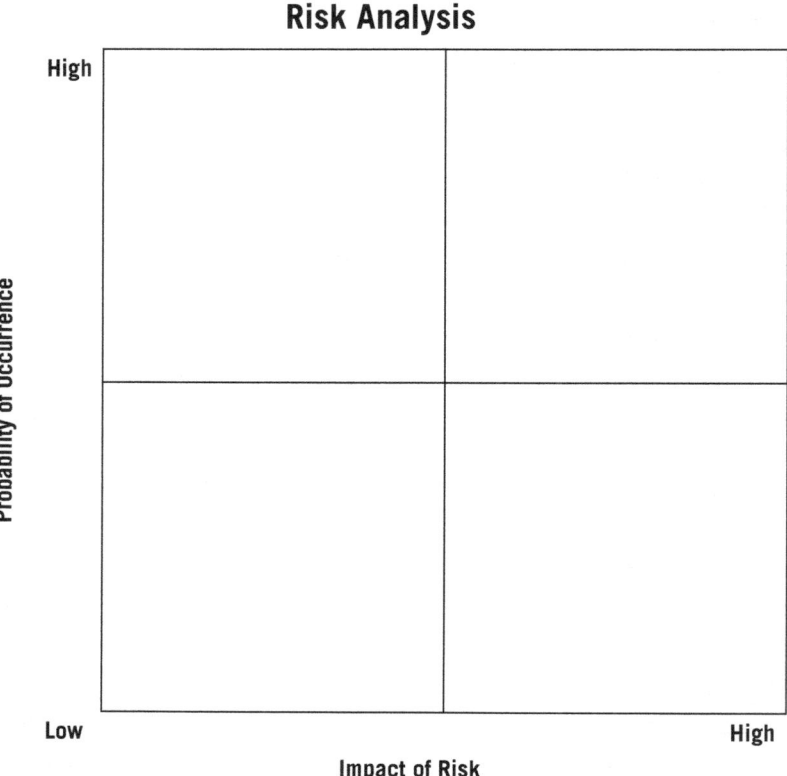

Risk Analysis

The risk analysis must contain:

- A defined scope that identifies all of its systems that create, transmit, or maintain ePHI
- Details of identified threats and vulnerabilities
- Assessment of current security measures
- Assessment of the impact of the risk and the likelihood of such risk occurring
- Risk rating.

The RM Group will be responsible for documenting and performing ongoing risk management functions as needed, including periodic review and evaluation of technical solutions, policies and procedures, workforce training, employee compliance with existing policies and procedures, Business Associate agreements, and effectiveness of audits, including the means implemented for detecting and preventing failures of the security measures put in place to protect PHI. The RM Group will determine what measures to take to address any particular risk. Depending on Provider's size, complexity, capabilities, technical infrastructure, and the probability and criticality of potential risks to Provider's PHI, the RM Group may choose to do nothing if the level of risk is acceptable; reduce or mitigate the risk; or transfer the risk to another organization by contracting with a vendor to help manage the risk. To the extent workforce members or their duties are substantially affected by a chosen action, the Privacy Official and Security Official shall be responsible to provide appropriate training.

Activity Review of ePHI System Security. Appropriate personnel in Provider's Information Technology department assigned as workforce members for Provider ("IT Group") shall audit the access privileges for each workforce member at least once every twenty-four (24) months. The IT Group must periodically run reports to review system activity, such as audit logs, access reports, or Security Incident tracking reports, to determine whether external unauthorized users are trying to penetrate Provider's systems and servers. These reports will be run *[insert frequency—every ___, hours/daily/ etc.]* using *[insert current software name]* or a similar appropriate software or product that tracks and reports suspected intrusions.

The IT Group must guard Provider's systems against malicious software and viruses using an appropriate anti-virus infrastructure, such as *[insert current software or system name and describe how it will be kept current. Also describe any other policies that may exist regarding sharing files between office and home computers, and downloading games, data, or other software. Discuss the hardware, software, and/or procedural mechanisms that record and examine activity in information systems that contain or use ePHI.]*

Any suspicious activities must be reported to the Security Official. Any reports documenting such suspicious activities shall be maintained or archived in electronic or hard copy format and shall be accessible to the Security Official.

Safeguards.

<u>Safeguards to Protect PHI.</u> Provider shall maintain four general categories of safeguards.

Administrative Safeguards: documented, formal policies and procedures that are intended to manage the selection and execution of security measures used to protect data based upon the appropriate data classification standards and manage the conduct of personnel with respect to the protection of the data.

Physical Safeguards: protection of physical computer systems and the buildings holding such systems from natural and environment hazards and inappropriate intrusion or removal.

Technical Safeguards: processes put in place to protect information, authenticate users, and control individual access to information.

Organizational requirements: provides requirements for the content of Business Associate contracts or other arrangements and the plan documents of group health plans. The Policies and Procedures and Documentation Requirements section, among other things, requires Covered Entities to implement and maintain written policies, procedures, and documentation required to comply with the Security Rule.

[Describe general safeguards that are in place, including nondisclosure acknowledgments signed by workforce members and the methods for disposing of devices and media equipment, including hardware and electronic media that stores ePHI. This should also include physical and procedural safeguards. For example, the organization may need to specify that employees should not display PHI on public bulletin boards, discuss PHI in public places in loud tones of voice, share PHI with non-authorized personnel,

review records that they do not need to see to do their jobs, visit certain Internet sites while working with ePHI, etc.]

Termination or Modification of Access to PHI: Electronic Systems. Provider must implement policies and procedures that establish access to ePHI and to modify or terminate that access as needed. *[Describe procedures for establishing who needs access to ePHI and how Provider will modify that access.]*

Access Controls. Provider must implement facility and device access controls to protect devices that hold PHI through the use of keys, locks, visitor escorts, fire protection, and access profiles that describe who may access such devices. Device and media controls are intended to assure that ePHI, as well as the device where it is stored, is destroyed in a manner that ensures that the ePHI cannot be re-created. Authentication and validation controls are used to corroborate that a person is the one claimed or the data has not been altered or destroyed in an unauthorized manner. *[Describe the physical and technical access controls Provider has in place to prevent unauthorized physical access and theft, including who is responsible for maintaining and monitoring them. How will maintenance and repairs be documented?]*

Access Restrictions for Physical and Electronic Records. Physical access restrictions to paper-based records and media containing PHI and ePHI shall be implemented. Such restrictions include, for example, limiting access by securing applicable paper-based records in locked facilities or containers, limiting the number of available keys to locked facilities or containers, and only allowing supervised access to the relevant records.

[Describe how the entity will control a person's access to facilities based on their role or function, including visitor control and control of access to software programs for testing and revision.]

Secure Storage of Physical Records. Relevant records in paper-based form will be stored in locked facilities, storage areas, or containers. In addition, the Security Official shall take steps to ensure that relevant facilities, storage areas, and containers are locked at the end of the working day, and that employees using relevant records in paper-based form return these records to their storage locations before leaving work for the day.

Access Restrictions for Electronic Records. Access to electronic versions of records containing PHI shall be restricted to only those employees who need access to such records to perform their daily job responsibilities. Such restrictions include, for example, isolating electronic records to a storage location that is only accessible by employees with appropriate administrative privileges.

Identification and Passwords. Unique user accounts and passwords shall be assigned to all employees with computer access. Such assignments shall be reasonably designed to maintain the integrity and security of all implemented access controls. Assigned passwords shall not be vendor-supplied default passwords. User passwords shall be reset at predetermined intervals and prohibitions against selecting previously used passwords shall be implemented.

Secure User Authentication Protocols. The following additional security measures shall be implemented:

- Maintaining controls on user IDs and other identifiers;
- Enforcing secure methods of assigning and selecting passwords;
- Maintaining controls for data security passwords that ensure that such passwords are kept in a location and/or format that does not compromise the security of the records they protect;
- Requiring re-login of a user should a computer remain inactive for an extended period of time;
- Restricting access to records containing ePHI to only active users and active user accounts; and
- Blocking access to records containing ePHI after multiple unsuccessful attempts to access them using a particular access method. For example, access to records containing ePHI may be prohibited if an incorrect password associated with a particular user account is provided five (5) consecutive times.

Firewall Protection. Firewall protection shall be installed on all computers in Covered Entity's control that store or are able to access records containing ePHI. The Security Official will also take reasonable steps to ensure that the installed firewall protection is up-to-date, and will regularly update firewall protections as newer versions and patches become available.

Virus Protection. The Security Official will take reasonable steps to ensure that the Covered Entity's network contains: (i) malware protection, (ii) reasonably up-to-date patches; and (iii) reasonably up-to-date virus definitions, for purposes of protecting records containing ePHI.

Encryption of PHI. The term "**encrypt**" or "**encryption**" means the transformation of data into a form in which meaning cannot be assigned without the use of a confidential process or key.

Encryption of Stored PHI. The Security Official will encrypt all PHI stored on laptops or other portable or mobile devices in Covered Entity's control that are capable of storing, receiving, or transmitting records containing ePHI.

Encryption of PHI During Transmission. The Security Official will, to the extent technically feasible, introduce encryption processes for records containing ePHI that are transmitted by electronic means over public networks (whether wireless or wire-line).

<u>Workstation Use and Location.</u> Provider will provide secure workstations and computer terminals with physical safeguards and technical access controls to minimize the possibility of unauthorized Use or Disclosure of PHI. *[Describe how this will be done for each class of workstation—on site, laptop, and home system. Describe how the inventory of laptops and other workstations is maintained and updated. Describe the authorization and/or supervision of workforce members who work with ePHI and the locations where it might be accessed.]* Computer screens at each workstation will be in secure areas or set up in a manner that permits only authorized users to read any PHI that could be on the screen. If screens cannot be positioned to prevent unauthorized viewing, the Provider may use devices, such as filters or hoods, to

protect the screen from unauthorized viewing. Computer screens will be configured to display a screen saver or go blank and log off when left unattended for longer than *[insert time period, based on risk analysis]* minutes. A password will be required to re-activate the screen. When applicable, paper documents that contain PHI must not be placed in a location where the PHI can be seen by unauthorized persons. For example, papers containing PHI should not be left face up on a counter unattended.

Passwords. The Security Official or his or her designee is responsible for password management, including password length and configuration, limiting the number of log-in attempts, monitoring expiration and discrepancies, deactivation, automatic logout, and automatic updates.

System Usage. *[Discuss how the entity will monitor system usage, including limiting the number of long-in attempts (authorized and unauthorized) and automatic logout after a predetermined time of inactivity.]*

Facsimile Machines and PHI. PHI may be sent via facsimile machine ("fax"), as long as the Provider takes reasonable precautions to protect the data. Such precautions may include measures such as:

- Including a confidentiality statement on the fax cover sheet indicating that the information is legally protected and, if the fax is received in error, the recipient should not re-disclose the information and should contact the sender immediately to arrange for the documents to be destroyed or returned.
- The sender should use caution to confirm that the number has been programmed correctly into the machine.
- If the machine has memory and storage capabilities, Provider must ensure that PHI is properly wiped from the machine when returning or discarding the machine.
- Provider should take reasonable precautions to ensure that faxes will be expected by the recipient and received by the recipient in a secure manner.

E-mail and PHI. All e-mail correspondence containing PHI should be encrypted when encryption is reasonable and appropriate. Provider should take steps to minimize the amount of PHI included in e-mail. E-mails should also include a confidentiality notice indicating that the information is legally protected and, if the e-mail is received in error, the recipient should not re-disclose the information and should contact the sender immediately to arrange for the documents to be destroyed or returned.

The sender must take reasonable precautions to reduce the chance of a misdirected e-mail. For example, the sender should confirm that the address of the recipient is accurate before using it to send PHI. Texting methods, unless they are secure (such as through encryption), may not be used to transmit ePHI. Workforce Members should use the "reply to all" feature as infrequently as possible. *[Address whether it is reasonable and appropriate to encrypt e-mails and, if not, document why it is not in accordance with 45 C.F.R. § 164.306. In light of the ready availability of encrypted e-mail solutions, it may be difficult to defend a decision not to encrypt e-mails containing PHI, particularly if the chosen alternative is less secure.]* The Security Official will assess the effectiveness of Provider's ability to balance the confidentiality of the PHI with its integrity and availability. Additional modifications may be made to this policy to improve the security of electronic communication involving PHI.

Copy Machines. The Security Official will review any storage capability of copy machines and determine whether they store ePHI that must be secured, particularly before copy machines are sold or discarded.

General Guidelines to Safeguard PHI. During business hours, a workforce member must be present whenever people who are not authorized to access PHI in that particular area are in the area where PHI is stored. After hours, if PHI will be unattended, it should be in a locked area. PHI in hard copy no longer in use must be shredded, burned, or otherwise rendered unusable, unreadable, or indecipherable, in accordance with federal guidance, when the Provider no longer needs to retain it. PHI held for a shredding service, must be kept in a locked container or a container that is not accessible by unauthorized personnel.

Transmission Security. Provider must ensure information is only transmitted to the intended individual or entity, and that there are measures in place to guard against unauthorized access to ePHI transmitted over a communications network. *[Discuss how this will be handled. Address encryption. Address wireless networks in the environment, remote access.]*

Integrity. *[Address mechanisms to ensure integrity of data during transmission—including portable media transmission (laptops, cell phones, blackberries, thumb drives). Document policies and procedures to protect ePHI from improper alteration or destruction. Document policies and procedures to ensure that electronically transmitted ePHI cannot be improperly modified without detection until disposed of properly.]*

Contingency Planning and Data Backup. Provider should establish procedures to restore any significant loss of data and to allow the continuation of the protection of ePHI while operating in a disaster situation or emergency mode. Provider, through its Business Associates and the IT Group, will implement a mechanism to protect ePHI from improper Use and Disclosure while minimizing the total impact on business operations in response to a crisis. The IT Group is responsible for restoring any loss of ePHI due to an emergency, power loss, natural disaster, vandalism, fire, movement, or replacement of equipment or other occurrences and assisting workforce members with emergency mode operations. *[Describe procedures implemented. These should address creating, approving, and monitoring emergency access IDs during an emergency situation. Policies should also address creating and maintaining retrievable exact copies of ePHI, including copies before movement of ePHI (addressable).]*

The Security Official shall work with the IT Group to assess the relative criticality of specific applications that contain ePHI to assure the appropriate level of security and planning to minimize problems for critical business functions. The IT Group shall perform periodic tests or trials of disaster recovery plans and emergency mode operations. The IT Group will back up and retain data for as long as the Security Official deems necessary to protect the availability, integrity, and confidentiality of ePHI. After the expiration of the applicable retention period, backup tapes will be overwritten or degaussed by the IT Group. *[Indicate how long backup tapes will be retained. This policy must describe the organization's data backup plan, disaster recovery plan, emergency mode operation plan, testing and revision procedures for contingency plans, and applications and data criticality analysis.]*

Audit Trails. *[Indicate how records will be maintained when electronic data is accessed or changed.]*

XVIII. Verification of Persons Requesting PHI

Purpose of Policy

To ensure that workforce members, before Disclosing PHI, have made reasonable efforts to ascertain or authenticate the identity of the persons or entities requesting a Disclosure of PHI so as to avoid violating the Privacy Rule and to minimize the likelihood of Disclosing PHI to people who are not entitled to that information.

Policy Details

Workforce Members must take steps to verify the identity of individuals who request access to PHI. They must verify the authority of any person seeking access to PHI, if the identity or authority of such person is not known to them.

Requests Made by an Individual. When an Individual requests access to his or her own PHI, workforce members will adhere to the following steps:

In Person Requests. Unless the Individual is personally known to the workforce member, Provider will request a form of identification from the Individual when the Individual requests an Individual's PHI in person. Workforce Members may rely on a valid driver's license or passport or other photo identification issued by a government agency. If the Individual does not have photo identification, the workforce member should request information that would be requested in connection with a telephone request, as set forth below. If a workforce member has any doubts as to the validity or authenticity of the identification provided or the identity of the Individual requesting access to the Individual's PHI, that person should contact the Privacy Official.

Telephone Requests. If the Individual requests PHI over the phone, the workforce member should request information that can be matched with information in the Individual's Designated Record Set, such as the last four numbers of his or her social security number or some other unique piece of information that can be used to verify the caller's identity.

Requests Made by a Parent Seeking the PHI of a Minor Child. When a parent requests access to PHI of the parent's minor child, workforce members will follow the steps below:

- Seek verification of the identity of the Individual through the steps described above.
- Seek verification of the person's relationship with the child. Such verification may take the form of confirming enrollment of the child in Provider as a dependent.
- Under laws of many States, a minor or unemancipated child may seek and agree to medical treatment in certain circumstances (e.g., pregnancy or substance abuse) without parental involvement. In such instances, Provider may not be at liberty to Disclose the child's PHI to the parent.

[Insert discussion about how records of emancipated minors will be protected. The Provider likely needs to consider applicable state laws specifically.]

Request Made by a Personal Representative. When a personal representative requests access to an Individual's PHI, workforce members will follow the steps below:

- The workforce member should require a copy of a valid power of attorney, or other appropriate document, that describes the basis for and authority of the Individual to act as the Individual's personal representative. If there are any questions about the validity of the document, the workforce member should seek review by the Privacy Official.
- The workforce member should make a copy of the documentation provided and file it with the Individual's Designated Record Set.
- The Disclosure should be documented according to Provider's documentation procedures.

Requests Made by a Public Official. If a public official requests access to PHI and the request is for one of the purposes permitted under the Privacy Rule, Workforce Members will follow the steps below:

- If the public official is making the request in person, the Workforce Member should ask the public official to show an agency badge, ID, or other official credential, or other proof of their status as a representative of the requesting agency. The workforce member should make a copy of the identification provided and file it with the Individual's Designated Record Set.
- If the request is made in writing, verify that the request is on the appropriate governmental agency letterhead.
- If the request is made by a person purporting to act on behalf of a public official, request a written statement on appropriate governmental agency letterhead that the person is acting under governmental authority or other evidence or documentation of agency, such as a contract for services, memorandum of understanding, or purchase order

that establishes that the person is properly acting on behalf of the public official.
- Request a written statement of the legal authority under which the information is requested or, if a written statement would be impracticable, an oral statement of such legal authority. If the Individual's request is made pursuant to legal process, warrant, subpoena, order, or other legal instrument issued by a grand jury, or a judicial or administrative tribunal, the workforce member should contact the Privacy Official.
- The workforce member should obtain approval for the requested Disclosure from the Privacy Official.
- The Disclosure should be documented according to Provider's documentation procedures.

XIX. Authorizations

Purpose of Policy

To ensure that all requested Disclosures, other than to the Individual whose PHI is being Disclosed, that are not either required or permitted under the Privacy Rule are made pursuant to a valid authorization.

Policy Details

Individuals may expressly authorize Disclosures of their PHI, and an authorization will be obtained for Uses and Disclosures of PHI not otherwise permitted by law. For example, PHI will not be used for marketing, as that term is defined in the HIPAA Rules, without the Individual's authorization, unless otherwise permitted by the HIPAA Rules. Before Disclosing any PHI pursuant to an authorization, workforce members should verify that the authorization form is valid. Compound authorizations (authorizations that are combined with a document that includes written permission relating to some other topic) are impermissible in many situations. Valid authorization forms must meet the following requirements:

- Be properly signed and dated by the Individual or the Individual's personal representative. If signed by a personal representative, a brief description of the personal representative's authority to make the authorization will also be required.
- Be written in plain language.
- Have a specific date or event upon which the authorization will terminate and that date or event, to the knowledge of Provider, must not have already occurred.
- Not, to the knowledge of Provider, have been revoked by the Individual.
- Contain a description of the information to be Used or Disclosed that identifies it in a meaningful and specific way.
- Contain the name or other specific identification of the person, class of persons, or entity authorized to Use or Disclose the PHI.
- Contain the name or other specific identification of the person, class of persons, or entity to whom Provider may Disclose the PHI.
- Contain a description of the purpose for each Disclosure.
- Contain a statement about the Individual's right to revoke the authorization, the procedures for revoking the authorization and a statement that the revocation is not applicable to Disclosures made by Provider in reliance on the authorization.
- Contain a statement about the possibility that the PHI that will be Disclosed pursuant to the authorization may be re-disclosed by the recipient, unless that PHI involves certain mental health information or involves information from federally funded drug or alcohol treatment programs that are subject to limits on re-disclosure under applicable state or federal law.

- Contain a statement that Provider may not condition an Individual's enrollment or eligibility for benefits on an authorization requested by Provider.

All Uses and Disclosures made pursuant to an authorization must be consistent with the terms and conditions set forth in the authorization.

All Individuals should receive a copy of any authorization that Provider requests the Individual to sign.

XX. Requests for Disclosures of an Individual's PHI from Spouses, Other Family Members, and Friends/Facility Directories

Purpose of Policy

To ensure that Provider only Discloses an Individual's PHI to family members and close friends in appropriate circumstances and does not improperly Disclose an Individual's PHI, and to enable PHI to be included in the facility directory.

Policy Details

Generally, Provider will not Disclose an Individual's PHI to third parties, except as required or permitted under the Privacy Rule or as expressly authorized by the Individual. Provider may, however, allow Disclosures to family members and close friends who are involved in the Individual's care or payment for the Individual's care, and Provider may do so only after the Individual is aware that such Disclosures may be made, has had an opportunity to object to Provider's making such Disclosures and has failed to object. If the Individual does not object, or in emergency circumstances and in a manner consistent with the Individual's best interest and any prior expressed preference, Provider may use the following PHI to maintain a directory of Individuals in the facility: name; location in the facility; general condition that does not communicate specific medical information; and religious affiliation.

If the Individual is not present, or the opportunity to agree or object to the Use or Disclosure cannot practicably be provided because of the Individual's incapacity or an emergency circumstance, the Covered Entity may, in the exercise of professional judgment, determine whether the Disclosure is in the best interests of the Individual and, if so, Disclose only the PHI that is directly relevant to the person's involvement with the Individual's care or payment related to the Individual's health care or needed for notification purposes. A Covered Entity may use professional judgment and its experience with common practice to make reasonable inferences of the Individual's best interest in allowing a person to act on behalf of the Individual to pick up filled prescriptions, medical supplies, X-rays, or other similar forms of PHI.

Provider may also Disclose PHI to a public or private entity authorized by law or by its charter to assist in disaster relief efforts, for the purpose of coordinating with such entities the Disclosures allowed by the HIPAA Rules in situations where, in the exercise of professional judgment, the Provider determines that the requirements do not interfere with the ability to respond to the emergency circumstances.

Objections to Disclosures. Provider will provide Individuals with a Notice of Privacy Practices generally describing the types of Disclosures that may be made to friends and family. If the Individual is present when Provider wishes to Disclose to friends and/or family, the Individual will be given an opportunity to object. Except in emergencies, Individuals must be given an opportunity to object to being included in the directory. *[Note: This provision must be tailored to conform to state law.]*

Verification. Except for requests for directory information from the clergy or from people who ask for an Individual by name, if a workforce member receives a request for Disclosure from an Individual claiming to be an Individuals' spouse, other family member close friend, or personal representative, the workforce member must seek to verify that person's identity as set forth in the Verification of Persons Requesting PHI Policy.

Once the identity of the person has been established, the workforce member should check the Individual's Designated Record Set to determine if this Individual is one that the Individual has objected to being the recipient of his or her PHI. If no written objection to such Disclosure is in the Designated Record Set, the workforce member may make the Disclosure.

If the workforce member is unable to verify the identity of the Individual, or the Individual objected to Disclosure of his or her PHI to that Individual, then no Disclosure will be made unless the Individual expressly authorizes it. If a workforce member is uncertain about any of these matters, he or she should contact the Privacy Official.

XXI. Disclosures to Business Associates

Purpose of Policy

To ensure that workforce members properly Disclose PHI to Business Associates of Provider.

Policy Details

All Disclosures to and Uses and Disclosures by a Business Associate of Provider must be made in accordance with a valid written Business Associate agreement. Before Disclosing PHI to a Business Associate, Provider's workforce members must determine that a valid Business Associate agreement is in place. The Business Associate agreement must comply with the Security Rule and Privacy Rule. In addition:

- all Disclosures must be consistent with the terms of the Business Associate agreement;
- Disclosures must comply with the Minimum Necessary Standard; and

- Disclosures that must be accounted for must be documented in accordance with the Documentation Requirement and Record Retention Policy.

XXII. De-identified Information, Summary Health Information, and Limited Data Sets

Purpose of Policy

To clarify when health information is de-identified and is, therefore, not subject to HIPAA and the Privacy Rule.

Policy Details

De-identified information is health information that does not identify an Individual or with respect to which there is no reasonable basis to believe that the information can be used to identify an Individual. There are two ways Provider can determine that health information is de-identified.

Remove Identifiers. The first way to de-identify health information is by removing the following 18 specific identifiers of the Individual or of relatives, employers, or household members of the Individual:

- Names.
- All geographic subdivisions smaller than a State, including street address, city, county, precinct, zip code, and their equivalent geocodes, except for the initial three digits of a zip code if, according to the current publicly available data from the Bureau of the Census:
  - the geographic unit formed by combining all zip codes with the same three initial digits contains more than 20,000 people; and
  - the initial three digits of a zip code for all such geographic units containing 20,000 or fewer people is changed to 000.

- All elements of dates (except year) for dates directly related to an Individual, including birth date, admission date, discharge date, date of death, and all ages over 89 and all elements of dates (including year) indicative of such age, except that such ages and elements may be aggregated into a single category of age 90 or older.
- Telephone numbers.
- Fax numbers.
- Electronic mail addresses.
- Social security number.
- Medical record numbers.
- Health plan beneficiary numbers.
- Account numbers.
- Certificate/license numbers.
- Vehicle identifiers and serial numbers, including license plate numbers.
- Device identifiers and serial numbers.
- Web Universal Resource Locators (URLs).
- Internet Protocol (IP) address numbers.
- Biometric identifiers, including finger and voice prints.
- Full face photographic images and any comparable images.
- Any other unique identifying number, characteristic, or code, except as permitted by this section.

Also, Provider must not have actual knowledge that the information could be used alone or in connection with other information to identify an Individual who is a subject of the information. **Retain Expert.** The second way to de-identify health information is to retain a person with appropriate knowledge of and experience with generally accepted statistical and scientific principles and methods for rendering information not individually identifiable and have that person determine that the risk is very small that the information being Disclosed could be Used, or in combination with other reasonably available information, by an anticipated recipient to identify the Individual who is the subject of the information and the expert documents the methods and results of the analysis that justified his or her conclusions.

Limited Data Sets. Information that has been stripped of many of the 18 identifying factors may still remain PHI. Nevertheless, the stripped down information may be Disclosed if the information is part of a Limited Data Set and is Disclosed only pursuant to a Limited Data Set Agreement.

Approval from Privacy Official Required. Any workforce member that is asked to Disclose de-identified information, Summary Health Information, or a Limited Data Set should first obtain approval from the Privacy Official for the Disclosure. The Privacy Official will verify that the information is de-identified, is Summary Health Information, or is part of a Limited Data Set, and that the conditions allowing for Disclosure have been met.

Once information has been verified as having been de-identified, it may be freely Used or Disclosed. Deidentified information is not PHI and is not subject to HIPAA or the Privacy Rule.

XXIII. Complaints

Purpose of Policy

To set forth Provider's procedures for receiving and responding to complaints, questions, or inquiries about Provider's privacy practices or the Use or Disclosure of PHI in the course of providing services.

Policy Details

Individuals or workforce members may file complaints about alleged violations of these policies and procedures or alleged violations of HIPAA. If someone wants to file a complaint, they will be asked to submit their complaint to the Privacy Official in writing. If the person refuses to submit the complaint in writing, the workforce member receiving the complaint should document the details in writing and forward the documentation to the Privacy Official.

Written Acknowledgment. Upon receipt of an inquiry or question, the Privacy Official will make reasonable efforts to respond in writing to the person within 15 calendar days of receipt of the inquiry. The Privacy Official may consult with the Security Official as needed during his or her evaluation of any inquiry or question. If the Privacy Official is unable to provide a reasonably accurate answer within that time period, the Privacy Official should request any information not originally provided which would be needed from the person to provide an adequate answer. If the Privacy Official is able to answer the inquiry or question, the written response should contain the appropriate answer.

Privacy Official's Investigation. If necessary following the initial response, the Privacy Official will undertake an investigation which will, if practicable, be completed within 30 calendar days of the complaint. If the Privacy Official in his/her sole discretion believes that additional time is needed, he or she may take the time needed to complete the investigation. The Privacy Official may consult with the Security Official as needed during his or her evaluation.

Upon completion of the investigation, the Privacy Official will inform the person of the results of his/her investigation and the action taken to address the subject matter of the complaint, if any.

Retaining Documents. Complaints, the Privacy Official's initial response, the Privacy Official's request for an extension and the Privacy Official's response following an investigation (if any) will be retained by the Privacy Official in accordance with Provider's Documentation Requirements and Retention of Records policy.

A copy of this complaint policy will be made available to any person upon that person's request.

XXIV. Designated Record Sets

Purpose of Policy

To set forth the scope of an individual's Designated Record Set.

Policy Details

An Individual's Designated Record Set with respect to Provider will consist of the following records containing the PHI of that Individual if kept in the Individual's paper or electronic file:

- All claims or billing records submitted to and/or maintained by Provider.
- Medical records submitted to Provider by a health care provider.
- Enrollment, payment, claims adjudication, and case or medical management records or record systems maintained by Provider.
- An Individual's written communications to Provider, written communications about the Individual or communications that were written on behalf of the Individual, and written communications from Provider, or an insurer or HMO providing benefits, concerning the Individual.
- Summaries, notes, or logs of telephonic communications to Provider by the Individual or concerning the Individual, but only if used to make decisions about the Individual.
- Requests for access, amendments, and accountings of Disclosures made by an Individual and Provider's responses.
- Complaints filed by an Individual and the Privacy Official's responses.

The Designated Record Set does not include the following:

- PHI stored in locations where the PHI is also available in other sources, or PHI included in records not focused on a specific Individual. This includes, but is not limited to, PHI stored in personal portable devices, hard drives, copy machines, fax machines, calendars, and employment files.
- Workforce Members' notes, if used only to assist the workforce member in recalling information or for other purposes and not used to make decisions about the Individual,

or notes that are incorporated into other records, such as electronic medical record.
- Correspondence or communication from the Individual if not used to make decisions about Individual, even if correspondence or communication contains PHI.
- Financial reports and accounting records.

If there is any uncertainty about whether a particular document or record is part of an Individual's Designated Record Set, the final determination will be made by the Privacy Official *[or other designated person of your choice]*.

For purposes of this policy, the term "record" means any item, collection, or grouping of information that includes PHI, and is maintained, collected, used, or disseminated by or for Provider.

XXV. Designated Personnel/Access Profiles

Purpose of Policy

To ensure that appropriate personnel or offices are designated to carry out certain functions and responsibilities.

Policy Detail

HIPAA requires documentation of the people or offices responsible for specific activities related to compliance with HIPAA.

Privacy Official. *[Insert individual's title]* is named as the Privacy Official for purposes of Provider's HIPAA policies and procedures and the federal privacy regulations. The Privacy Official may designate duties or obligations to workforce members as needed.

Security Official. *[Insert individual's title]* is designated the Security Official for purposes of Provider's policies and procedures and the federal security regulations. The Security Official may designate duties or obligations to Workforce Members as needed.

Contact Office for Questions and Complaints. The Privacy Official is the contact to receive questions and complaints, from Individuals, workforce members, and other persons regarding HIPAA or the privacy of PHI. The Privacy Official may designate others to assist with handling complaints. If a workforce member receives a complaint, the workforce member should forward the complaint to the Privacy Official, or his or her designee, for handling.

Access Profiles for Workforce. The Provider's workforce and their appropriate access profiles are described in the Minimum Necessary Standard policy. Access privileges for workforce members will be terminated or changed in conjunction with the termination of employment, contract, or change of level of access required. The IT Group will audit the access privileges *[insert frequency]* and shall report to Security Official and/or Privacy Official if any changes are needed.

XXVI. State Law Compliance

Purpose of Policy

The purpose of this policy is to provide that Provider will abide by applicable state laws relating to the privacy and security of PHI, to the extent not preempted by HIPAA.

Policy Detail

Provider will comply with both HIPAA and applicable state law not preempted by HIPAA. Provider has developed its Notice of Privacy Practices, which may be found on the Provider's website, to contain provisions to comply with state law. When it is impossible to comply with both state law and HIPAA, the HIPAA rules preempt state law except when the state law is more stringent or when the government has exempted a particular state law from preemption.

HIPAA does not preempt state laws that require using PHI to make certain reports regarding child abuse and neglect, certain infectious diseases, particular public health reporting, reporting for death certificates, and certain other mandated reports.

Provider will comply with HIPAA and related state laws and will follow state privacy and data breach laws as they relate to any potential HIPAA incident. For example, if a breach involves a social security number, drivers license number, or certain other information covered by state data breach laws, Provider will determine whether state law imposes more stringent or different requirements, such as a shorter time frame for reporting data breaches, Provider will comply with the timeframes set forth in the applicable state law. Provider is bound by the state laws referenced in its Notice of Privacy Practices.

Procedural Guidance

Particular state law questions shall be promptly referred to the appropriate legal counsel for guidance and compliance.

XXVII. Using and Disclosing Psychotherapy Notes

Background

Psychotherapy notes have a special definition under HIPAA, set forth below. They are given special protection regarding their Use and Disclosure.

> *"Psychotherapy notes"* mean notes recorded (in any medium) by a health care provider who is a mental health professional documenting or analyzing the contents of conversation during a private counseling session or a group, joint, or family counseling session and that are separated from the rest of the individual's medical record. *Psychotherapy notes* exclude

medication prescription and monitoring, counseling session start and stop times, the modalities and frequencies of treatment furnished, results of clinical tests, and any summary of the following items: Diagnosis, functional status, the treatment plan, symptoms, prognosis, and progress to date.

Policy

Provider recognizes that psychotherapy notes need to be handled separately and with additional protections regarding their Use and Disclosure. The general policy is that Provider will rarely, if ever, Use, Disclose, or possess psychotherapy notes.

If Provider does need to Use or Disclose psychotherapy notes, the Privacy Official will consult legal counsel to ensure that the Use or Disclosure is consistent with state law and HIPAA.

XXVIII. Workforce Employee Screening

[Discuss policies relating to employee background checks and confidentiality agreements. Discuss or cross reference procedures that outline hiring and termination procedures. Include templates and/or documents used to record the processing of background checks and confidentiality agreements.]

XXIX. Fundraising

Purpose of Policy

To ensure that Use and Disclosure of PHI for fundraising complies with the HIPAA Rules.

Policy Detail

Provider may Use and Disclose to a Business Associate selected PHI for purposes of raising funds for Provider's own benefit without an Individual's authorization. However, an Individual does have the right to opt out of receiving such fundraising communications.

The following PHI may be used for purposes of making fundraising communications:

- Demographic information relating to an Individual, including name, address, other contact information, age, gender, and date of birth;
- Dates of health care provided to an Individual;
- Department of service information;
- Treating physician;
- Outcome information; and
- Health insurance status.

Provider must include in any fundraising materials sent to an Individual a description of how the Individual may opt out of receiving any further fundraising communications. The opt out method must not cause the Individual to incur an undue burden or more than a nominal cost. Provider shall consider using a toll-free phone number, an e-mail address, or similar methods that will provide an Individual with a simple, quick, and inexpensive way to opt out of receiving future fundraising communications. Provider shall not require Individuals to write a letter to opt out of receiving future fundraising communications.

Provider shall include in its Notice of Privacy Practices a statement that Provider Uses certain PHI in fundraising activities.

Provider may not condition treatment or payment on the Individual's choice with respect to the recipient of fundraising communications. Further, Provider shall not send fundraising communications to any Individual who has elected not to receive such communications.

XXX. Sale of Protected Health Information

Purpose of Policy

To ensure that PHI is not sold except in strict compliance with the HIPAA Rules and other applicable law.

Policy Detail

It is the policy of Provider not to engage in the sale of PHI without first obtaining the Individual's written authorization. For purposes of this policy, the sale of PHI means a Disclosure of PHI where the Provider directly or indirectly receives remuneration from or on behalf of the recipient of the PHI in exchange for the PHI unless the Disclosure is for one of the following purposes:

- For public health purposes;
- For research where the remuneration is a reasonable cost-based fee to cover the cost to prepare and transmit the PHI;
- For treatment and payment purposes;
- For the sale, transfer, merger, or consolidation of all or part of the Provider and related due diligence;
- To or by a Business Associate or subcontractor for Business Associate activities that the Business Associate or subcontractor undertakes on behalf of the principal and the only remuneration is for the performance of such activities;
- To the Individual under the Individual rights to access and an accounting of Disclosures provisions of the HIPAA rules;
- For Disclosures required by law; or
- For any other purpose permitted by the HIPAA Rules, where the only remuneration received by the Provider is a reasonable, cost-based fee to cover the cost to prepare and transmit the PHI for such purpose or a fee otherwise expressly permitted by other law.

Appendix B

HIPAA Business Associate Agreement (Favorable to Data Source)

[Note: This template is designed to be somewhat favorable to the covered entity or data provider. It will be important to ensure the document contains, at a minimum, all of the provisions required by the HIPAA Rules, as listed in 45 C.F.R. § 164.504(e), as well as applicable state law. This template is subject to change from time to time. Other specific provisions may be desirable, or the parties may wish to remove or modify particular provisions, depending on exactly what the Business Associate is doing for the Covered Entity.]

This HIPAA Business Associate Agreement, effective as of the date indicated below, is by and between _____ and _____ (each a "party" and collectively, the "parties.") To the extent that Covered Entity Discloses Protected Health Information to Business Associate in connection with services or products provided to Covered Entity, or as otherwise required by the Administrative Simplification provisions of the Health Insurance Portability and Accountability Act of 1996, Public Law No. 104-191, codified at 42 U.S.C. § 1320d through d-9, as amended ("HIPAA"), Covered Entity and Business Associate agree to the following terms and conditions, which are intended to comply with HIPAA, the Health Information Technology for Economic and Clinical Health Act ("HITECH Act"), and their implementing regulations. Now, therefore, in consideration of the foregoing and other good and valuable consideration, the sufficiency and receipt of which are hereby acknowledged, the parties agree as follows:

1. **General Terms, Conditions, and Definitions**
   (a) "BA Agreement" shall mean this HIPAA Business Associate Agreement. *[Note: If this is an agreement between a Business Associate, as the data supplier, and its Subcontractor, it could be titled a "HIPAA Business Associate Subcontractor Agreement." Note that the Subcontractor must agree to the same restrictions and conditions that apply to the Business Associate.]*
   (b) "Breach" shall generally have the same meaning as the term "breach" in 45 C.F.R. § 164.402, except that all acquisition, access, Use, or Disclosure of Protected Health Information in a manner not permitted under Subpart E of the Privacy Rule shall be reported to Covered Entity in accordance with the terms of this BA Agreement, and Business Associate shall not be entitled to conclude, without consultation with and agreement by Covered Entity, that an acquisition, access, Use, or Disclosure of Protected Health Information is not a Breach. Covered Entity agrees to consult with Business Associate as necessary in connection with Covered Entity's determination of whether an incident is a Breach.
   (c) "Business Associate" shall generally have the same meaning as the term "business associate" at 45 C.F.R. § 160.103, and in reference to the party to this BA

Agreement, shall mean [Insert Name of Business Associate]. *[Note: If this document is being used for an arrangement between a Business Associate and a Subcontractor, the terms will need to be adjusted accordingly.]*

(d) "Covered Entity" shall generally have the same meaning as the term "covered entity" at 45 C.F.R. § 160.103, and in reference to the party to this BA Agreement, shall mean [insert name of Covered Entity]. *[Note: This term should be defined carefully if the Covered Entity is part of a hybrid entity or is a self-insured employer-sponsored health plan.]*

(e) "HIPAA Rules" shall mean the Privacy, Security, Breach Notification, Administrative, and Enforcement Rules at 45 C.F.R. Parts 160, 162, and 164, as amended from time to time.

(f) "Service Agreement" shall mean the separate agreement(s) between the parties in which Business Associate performs functions or activities on behalf of Covered Entity. *[Note: The Covered Entity may want to reference the agreement specifically here.]*

(g) Other Definitions: The following terms used in this BA Agreement shall have the same meaning as those in the HIPAA Rules: Data Aggregation, Designated Record Set, Disclosure, Health Care Operations, Individual, Limited Data Set, Minimum Necessary, Notice of Privacy Practices, Protected Health Information, Required by Law, Research, Secretary, Security Incident, Standard, Subcontractor, Transaction, Unsecured Protected Health Information, Workforce Member, and Use. Other terms shall have the definitions set forth in this BA Agreement. *[Note: Consider whether substance abuse information subject to 42 C.F.R. Part 2 is involved and, if so, whether qualified service organization agreement provisions are required.]*

(h) Notification by Covered Entity. Covered Entity agrees to notify Business Associate of any restrictions on the Use or Disclosure of Protected Health Information to which Covered Entity has agreed that may affect Business Associate's Use or Disclosure of Protected Health Information pursuant to this BA Agreement.

2. **Obligations and Activities of Business Associate**
   (a) Business Associate may not Use or Disclose Protected Health Information other than as permitted or required by this BA Agreement or as Required by Law.
   (b) Business Associate agrees to use appropriate safeguards to prevent Use or Disclosure of Protected Health Information other than as provided for by this BA Agreement, and to comply with Subpart C of 45 C.F.R. part 164 with respect to electronic Protected Health Information.
   (c) Business Associate agrees to report, in writing, to Covered Entity's Privacy Official, within three (3) calendar days, any Use or Disclosure of Protected Health Information not provided for by this BA Agreement of which it becomes aware, including Breaches of Unsecured Protected Health Information as required by 45 C.F.R. § 164.410, and any Security Incident of which it becomes aware. All reports shall include Business Associate's name and point of contact information; a description of what happened including the date of the incident and the date of discovery of the incident, if known; the types of Protected Health Information involved in the incident, if applicable; a description of what Business Associate is doing to investigate the incident and protect against further incidents; and other information reasonably requested by Covered Entity. For reports of incidents constituting a Breach, the report shall include, to the extent available, the identification of each Individual whose Unsecured Protected Health Information has been, or is reasonably believed by Business Associate

to have been, accessed, acquired, or Disclosed during a Breach of Unsecured Protected Health Information, and any other available information that a Covered Entity is required to include in a notification to the Individual under 45 C.F.R. § 164.404 and applicable state law, and any other information reasonably requested by Covered Entity. Additional information shall be reported by Business Associate immediately as it becomes available. Without limiting any other indemnification obligations of Business Associate, at Covered Entity's election, Business Associate shall reimburse Covered Entity for the cost of outside forensics investigators if Covered Entity determines an outside investigation of the Breach or Security Incident is necessary.

(d) In accordance with 45 C.F.R. §§ 164.502(e)(1)(ii) and 164.308(b)(2), if applicable, Business Associate agrees to ensure that any Subcontractors that create, receive, maintain, or transmit Protected Health Information on behalf of Business Associate agree in writing to the same restrictions, conditions, and requirements that apply to Business Associate with respect to such information.

[Note: The Covered Entity may want to add additional specificity to the provisions below if they are of particular concern.]

(e) Business Associate agrees to make available Protected Health Information to Covered Entity in the manner, time, and format reasonably requested by Covered Entity. Business Associate also agrees to make available Protected Health Information in a Designated Record Set to Covered Entity or the Individual as necessary to satisfy Covered Entity's obligations under 45 C.F.R. § 164.524.

(f) Business Associate agrees to make any amendment(s) to Protected Health Information in a Designated Record Set as agreed to by Covered Entity pursuant to 45 C.F.R.

§ 164.526, or take other measures as necessary to satisfy Covered Entity's obligations under 45 C.F.R. § 164.526.

(g) Business Associate agrees to maintain and make available the information required to provide an accounting of Disclosures to the Covered Entity as necessary to satisfy Covered Entity's obligations under 45 C.F.R. § 164.528 and applicable law. Business Associate agrees to provide to Covered Entity, within fifteen (15) days and in a secure manner, information collected in accordance with this Section 2(g) of this BA Agreement, to permit Covered Entity to respond to a request by an Individual for an accounting of Disclosures of Protected Health Information in accordance with 45 C.F.R. § 164.528 and applicable law.

(h) To the extent Business Associate is to carry out one or more of Covered Entity's obligations under Subpart E of 45 C.F.R. Part 164 of the HIPAA Rules, Business Associate agrees to comply with the requirements of Subpart E that apply to Covered Entity in the performance of such obligations.

(i) Business Associate agrees to make its internal practices, books, and records available to the Secretary for purposes of determining compliance with the HIPAA Rules. Unless otherwise prohibited by law or by the Secretary, Business Associate shall notify Covered Entity immediately upon receipt by Business Associate of any such request, and shall provide Covered Entity with copies of all materials provided to the Secretary.

[*Note: If Business Associate is an attorney, law firm, or accounting firm that may be holding records that are privileged, substitute the following:*

(i) *Business Associate agrees to make internal practices, books, and records relating to the Use and Disclosure of Protected Health Information received from, or created or received by Business Associate on behalf of Covered*

Entity, available to the Secretary, in a time and manner designated by the Secretary, for purposes of the Secretary determining Covered Entity's compliance with the HIPAA Rules, to the extent not subject to the attorney-client, accountant-client, attorney work product, or other applicable privilege. Business Associate will not disclose communications, information, legal advice, or work product with respect to Covered Entity that is subject to the attorney-client, accountant-client, or the attorney work product privilege to the Secretary or to any other government agency, person, entity, or organization (other than Covered Entity or to Business Associate's Subcontractors or agents), without first notifying Covered Entity and receiving Covered Entity's prior written approval. Business Associate will undertake all reasonable efforts to preserve, defend, and assert on Covered Entity's behalf the attorney-client, accountant-client, and the attorney work product privileges as applicable to any communication, information, legal advice, or work product with respect to Covered Entity to which access, or for which disclosure, is sought by the Secretary or by any other government agency, person, entity, or organization (except Covered Entity or Business Associate's Subcontractors or agents).]

(j) Business Associate agrees to, subject to subsection 4(c) below, return to the Covered Entity or Covered Entity's designee or, with Covered Entity's written permission destroy, within fifteen (15) days of the termination of this BA Agreement, the Protected Health Information in its possession and retain no copies. All destruction of Protected Health Information shall be done in accordance with federal Department of Health and Human Services Guidance regarding rendering Protected Health Information unusable, unreadable, or indecipherable.

(k) Business Associate agrees to mitigate, to the extent practicable, any harmful effect that is known to either party of a Use or Disclosure of Protected Health Information in violation of this BA Agreement.

(l) Notwithstanding anything in this BA Agreement or the Service Agreement to the contrary, Business Associate agrees to indemnify and hold harmless Covered Entity and Covered Entity's employees, affiliates, directors, partners, shareholders, officers, Subcontractors, agents, and sponsors *[Note: "Sponsors" could be removed if the Covered Entity is not a self-insured health plan.]*, (each of the foregoing hereinafter referred to as an "Indemnified Party") from, and at Indemnified Party's option, defend against any and all losses, liabilities, claims, fines, damages, penalties, costs, and expenses, including reasonable attorneys' fees, consultants' fees, court costs, Breach notification costs, and credit monitoring and identity theft protection fees (collectively, "Losses") to the extent that such Losses arise from, or may be in any way attributable to, any act or omission by Business Associate or Business Associate's employees, Subcontractors, agents, or representatives that constitutes or that is otherwise asserted by any regulatory agency or third party to be (i) a breach of this BA Agreement, (ii) negligence, gross negligence, bad faith, or intentional or willful misconduct, (iii) a violation of the HIPAA Rules, HIPAA, and/or the HITECH Act; and/or (iv) any Security Incident or Breach involving Protected Health Information in Business Associate's possession, custody, or control, or for which Business Associate is otherwise responsible. The provisions of this paragraph shall survive the expiration or termination of this BA Agreement for any reason. *[Note alternative language for law firms: Business Associate agrees to indemnify and hold harmless Covered Entity and its officers, agents, and*

Appendix B: *HIPAA Business Associate Agreement* **269**

employees from loss or damages occurring as a result of a breach of any duty owed by Business Associate under this BA Agreement, which is attributed to Business Associate's actual act, failure to act, error, or omission arising out of professional conduct. This indemnification does not indemnify Covered Entity, its officers, agents, or employees for consequential damages and attorney's fees. The provisions of this paragraph shall survive the expiration or termination of this BA Agreement for any reason.]

(m) Except as otherwise allowed in this BA Agreement and the HIPAA Rules, Business Associate shall not directly or indirectly receive remuneration in exchange for any Protected Health Information of an Individual unless the Individual has provided a valid authorization compliant with HIPAA and state law.

[Note: The following provision is optional. The degree of control an entity exercises over a Business Associate or Subcontractor may make the Business Associate or Subcontractor an agent and, thus, the disclosing entity could be liable for their actions.]

(n) Covered Entity, in its sole and absolute discretion, may elect to delegate to Business Associate any requirement to notify affected Individuals of a Breach of Unsecured Protected Health Information if such Breach results from, or is related to, an act or omission of Business Associate or the Subcontractors, agents, or representatives of Business Associate. If Covered Entity elects to make such delegation, Business Associate shall perform such notifications and any other reasonable remediation services (i) at Business Associate's sole cost and expense, and (ii) in compliance with all applicable laws including HIPAA and the HITECH Act. Business Associate shall also provide Covered Entity with the opportunity to review and approve of the form and content of any

Breach notification that Business Associate provides to Individuals, the government, including the Secretary, and/or the media.

(o) To the extent that Business Associate submits Standard Transactions on behalf of Covered Entity, or assists Covered Entity with submission of Standard Transactions, Business Associate shall comply with HIPAA's Transaction and code set Standards for such Transactions and shall provide documentation of such compliance upon request of Covered Entity.

(p) Unless Covered Entity agrees, in writing, that this requirement is infeasible with respect to particular data, Business Associate shall secure all Protected Health Information at rest or in transmission by a technology standard that renders Protected Health Information unusable, unreadable, or indecipherable to unauthorized individuals and is developed in accordance with Department of Health and Human Services' applicable guidance and other applicable laws and regulations.

(q) Business Associate agrees to respond to and accommodate a request for confidential communications by an Individual, including requests to communicate or correspond with an Individual by alternative means or at alternative locations, or a request for, changes in, or a revocation of, permission by an Individual to restrict Business Associate's Use or Disclosure of Protected Health Information, in a timely manner in accordance with the requirements under 45 C.F.R. § 164.522, and to make changes to Business Associate's processes to the extent that such request, if approved, may affect Business Associate's Use or Disclosure of Protected Health Information.

(r) Business Associate agrees to communicate orally and in writing with authorized employees, workforce members, agents, and business associates of Covered Entity, and shall transmit Protected Health Information to these authorized employees, Workforce Members, agents, and business associates at the request of Covered Entity, to the extent permitted by and in accordance with the HIPAA Rules.

[Note: The provisions of (s)–(v) are optional. Depending on the nature of the arrangement, the disclosing entity should consider whether other protections are beneficial, such as requiring the receiving party to undergo third-party audits. The disclosing entity should also consider removing them altogether to reduce the chance of a business associate being deemed to be an agent of the disclosing entity, which could make the disclosing entity liable for the receiving entity's breaches.]

(s) Within ten (10) business days of Covered Entity's written request, Business Associate and its agents and Subcontractors shall allow Covered Entity to conduct a reasonable inspection of the facilities, systems, books, records, agreements, policies, and procedures relating to the Use or Disclosure of Protected Health Information pursuant to this BA Agreement for the purpose of determining whether Business Associate has complied with the BA Agreement; provided, however, that Covered Entity shall protect the confidentiality of all confidential and proprietary information of Business Associate to which Covered Entity has access during the course of such inspection. The fact that Covered Entity inspects, or fails to inspect, or has the right to inspect, Business Associate's facilities, systems, books, records, agreements, policies, and procedures does not relieve Business Associate of the responsibility to comply with this BA Agreement. Covered Entity's (i) failure to detect or (ii) detection, but failure to notify Business Associate or require Business Associate's remediation of any unsatisfactory practice, does not constitute acceptance

of such practice or waiver of Covered Entity's enforcement rights under this BA Agreement.
(t) Business Associate agrees to track and monitor compliance with the provisions of this BA Agreement, and provide evidence of such monitoring to Covered Entity upon request.
(u) Business Associate must host and store Protected Health Information maintained on behalf of Covered Entity on servers and other hardware and in physical and electronic storage areas located only within the United States, and all services by Business Associate referenced in this BA Agreement will be provided in and from the United States only.
(v) Business Associate shall make itself, and any of its employees, agents, and Subcontractors assisting Business Associate in the performance of its obligations under this BA Agreement, available to Covered Entity at no cost to Covered Entity to testify as witnesses, or otherwise, in the event of litigation or administrative proceedings against Covered Entity, its directors, officers, agents, or employees based upon a claimed violation of HIPAA or other laws relating to security or privacy.
3. **Permitted Uses and Disclosures of Protected Health Information by Business Associate**
   (a) Business Associate may Use or Disclose Protected Health Information only to perform functions, activities, or services for, or on behalf of, Covered Entity as specified in this BA Agreement and the Service Agreement, provided that such Use or Disclosure complies with the HIPAA Rules. Business Associate acknowledges and agrees that it acquires no title or ownership rights to the Protected Health Information, including any de-identified information, as a result of this BA Agreement.
   (b) Business Associate may Use or Disclose Protected Health Information as Required by Law.

Appendix B: *HIPAA Business Associate Agreement*

(c) Business Associate agrees to make Uses of and Disclosures and requests for Protected Health Information consistent with HIPAA and any of Covered Entity's Minimum Necessary policies and procedures provided to Business Associate and consistent with Covered Entity's Notice of Privacy Practices. Covered Entity asserts that its Minimum Necessary policies and procedures are consistent with 45 C.F.R. § 164.514(d) and Business Associate agrees to comply with the provisions of that rule.

(d) Business Associate may not Use or Disclose Protected Health Information in a manner that would violate Subpart E of 45 C.F.R. Part 164 if done by Covered Entity, except for the specific Uses and Disclosures set forth below.

(e) Business Associate may Use Protected Health Information for the proper management and administration of Business Associate or to carry out the legal responsibilities of Business Associate.

[Note: The disclosing entity must ensure that it has obtained any patient consents or authorizations that may be required by state law to permit this re-disclosure. Also, if the disclosing entity is itself a Business Associate, the underlying business associate agreement must permit re-disclosure. Alternatively, this language could be omitted, but it may be difficult for business associates to agree to the contract unless this language is included.]

(f) Business Associate may Disclose Protected Health Information for the proper management and administration of Business Associate or to carry out the legal responsibilities of Business Associate, provided the Disclosures are Required by Law, or Business Associate obtains reasonable assurances from the person to whom the information is Disclosed that the information will remain confidential and Used or further Disclosed only as Required by Law or for the purposes for which it was Disclosed to the person, and the person notifies Business Associate of any instances of which it is aware in which the confidentiality of the information has been Breached.

[Note: The Data Aggregation language below is optional. Additionally, if the receiving entity will be allowed to create de-identified information, the BA Agreement must specify that the Business Associate is authorized to Use Protected Health Information to de-identify the information in accordance with 45 C.F.R. § 164.514(a)–(c). The parties may also wish to specify the manner in which the Business Associate will de-identify the information and the permitted Uses and Disclosures by the Business Associate of the de-identified information.]

(g) Business Associate may provide Data Aggregation services relating to the Health Care Operations of Covered Entity.

[Note: The Data Use Agreement provisions may not be necessary, depending on the nature of the arrangement.]

(h) Data Use Agreement: With respect to Limited Data Sets created or Used by Business Associate on behalf of Covered Entity, Business Associate will:

   (i) Not Use or further Disclose the Limited Data Set other than as provided for in this subsection (Data Use Agreement), which includes purposes consistent with the HIPAA Rules, including those related to Research, public health, or Health Care Operations or as otherwise Required by Law;

   (ii) Use appropriate safeguards to prevent Use or Disclosure of the Limited Data Set other than as provided for in this Data Use Agreement;

Appendix B: *HIPAA Business Associate Agreement* **275**

      (iii) Report to Covered Entity any Use or Disclosure of the Limited Data Set not provided for by this Data Use Agreement of which it becomes aware;

      (iv) Ensure that any agents to whom it provides the Limited Data Set agree in writing to the same restrictions and conditions that apply to the Limited Data Set recipient with respect to such information; and

      (v) Not identify the Individuals who are the subject of the Limited Data Set, or contact the Individuals.

4. **Survival, Term, and Termination**

    (a) Term: Except as otherwise provided herein, the term of this BA Agreement shall coincide with the Service Agreement and shall be terminable in accordance with the termination provisions of the Service Agreement, or the date Covered Entity terminates for cause as authorized in paragraph (b) of this Section, whichever is sooner.

    (b) Termination for Cause: Business Associate authorizes termination of this BA Agreement and the Service Agreement by Covered Entity, if Covered Entity determines Business Associate has violated a material term of this BA Agreement. *[Note: If the disclosing entity wishes to provide the receiving entity with an opportunity to cure a violation or breach of the contract before termination for cause, the disclosing entity could add: "and Business Associate has not cured the breach or ended the violation within the time specified by Covered Entity."]*

    [Note: For subsection (c) below, if the agreement authorizes the Business Associate to Use or Disclose Protected Health Information for its own management and administration or to carry out its legal responsibilities and the Business Associate needs to retain protected health information for such purposes after termination of the agreement, the BA Agreement can specify the following:

Upon termination of this BA Agreement for any reason, Business Associate, with respect to Protected Health Information received from Covered Entity, or created, maintained, or received by Business Associate on behalf of Covered Entity, shall:

 i. Retain only that Protected Health Information which is necessary for Business Associate to continue its proper management and administration or to carry out its legal responsibilities;

 ii. Return to Covered Entity or, if agreed to in writing by Covered Entity, destroy the remaining Protected Health Information that Business Associate still maintains in any form;

 iii. Continue to use appropriate safeguards and comply with Subpart C of 45 CFR Part 164 with respect to electronic Protected Health Information to prevent Use or Disclosure of the Protected Health Information, other than as provided for in this Section, for as long as Business Associate retains the electronic Protected Health Information;

 iv. Not Use or Disclose the Protected Health Information retained by Business Associate other than for the purposes for which such Protected Health Information was retained and subject to the same conditions set forth in this BA Agreement, related to Use and Disclosure for Business Associate's proper management and administration or to fulfill its legal responsibilities, and Subpart E of 45 C.F.R. Part 164, which applied prior to termination; and

 v. Return to Covered Entity or, if agreed to in writing by Covered Entity, destroy the Protected Health Information retained by Business Associate when it is no longer needed by Business Associate for its proper management and administration or to carry out its legal responsibilities.]

(c) Effect of Termination: Upon termination of this BA Agreement, for any reason, Business Associate shall return to Covered Entity or Covered Entity's designee or, with Covered Entity's prior written permission, destroy, all Protected Health Information received from Covered Entity, or created, maintained, or received by Business Associate on behalf of Covered Entity, that Business Associate still maintains in any form. This provision shall apply to Protected Health Information that is in the possession of Subcontractors or agents of Business Associate. Business Associate shall retain no copies of the Protected Health Information.

(d) Survival: Business Associate's obligations under this BA Agreement that are intended to survive, including Section 4 and subsections 2(c), (e)–(g), (j)–(l), (n), (r), and (v), shall survive the termination or expiration of this BA Agreement for any reason.

5. **Interpretation and Amendment of this BA Agreement**

   A regulatory reference in this BA Agreement to a section of the HIPAA Rules means such section as in effect or as amended. Any ambiguity or inconsistency in this BA Agreement shall be interpreted to permit compliance with the HIPAA Rules. This BA Agreement supersedes any and all prior representations, understandings, or agreements, written or oral, concerning the subject matter herein, including conflicting provisions in the Service Agreement. In the event of a conflict between the Service Agreement and this BA Agreement, the BA Agreement shall control. If Covered Entity determines it is necessary to amend this BA Agreement from time to time to comply with the requirements of any HIPAA Rules or applicable state law, Covered Entity shall provide Business Associate with written notice of the amendment. If Business Associate disagrees with any such amendment proposed by Covered Entity, it shall so notify Covered Entity in writing no later than fifteen (15) days after receipt of Covered Entity's notice of amendment, or the amendment will be deemed to be incorporated by reference into this BA Agreement. If the parties are unable to agree on an amendment, Covered Entity may, at its option, terminate this BA Agreement and the Service Agreement. *[Note: The preceding language is optional. The parties could negotiate in good faith instead regarding amendments.]*

6. **No Third-Party Rights/Independent Contractors**
   The parties to this BA Agreement do not intend to create any rights in any third parties, except as expressly set forth in subsection 2(l) of this BA Agreement. *[Note: The preceding phrase can be removed if there is no indemnification clause covering third parties.]* The parties agree that they are independent contractors and not agents of each other, except nothing herein affects whether Business Associate is an "agent" for purposes of compliance with 42 C.F.R. § 1001.952(d).

7. **Notices**
   Any notice required or permitted by this BA Agreement to be given or delivered shall be in writing and shall be deemed given or delivered if delivered in person, or delivered by courier or expedited delivery service, or delivered by registered or certified mail, postage prepaid, return receipt requested, to the address set forth below. Each party may change its address for purposes of this BA Agreement by written notice to the other party.

8. **Severability**
   Whenever possible, each provision of this BA Agreement shall be interpreted so as to be effective and valid under applicable law. If any provision of this BA Agreement should be prohibited or found invalid under applicable law, such provision shall be ineffective to the extent of such prohibition

or invalidity without invalidating the other of such provision or the remaining provisions of this BA Agreement.

9. **State Law**

    Business Associate acknowledges and agrees that it has implemented and will maintain appropriate privacy and security measures to protect personal information consistent with state laws and regulations, to the extent those state laws and regulations are applicable to the Protected Health Information. The confidentiality obligations hereunder are independent of and do not limit or otherwise affect the parties' other confidentiality obligations under this BA Agreement.

10. **Governing Law**

    To the extent not preempted by federal law, the BA Agreement shall be governed and construed in accordance with the state laws governing the Service Agreement, without regard to conflicts of law provisions that would require application of the law of another state.

11. **Assignment, Binding Nature, and Benefits**

    This BA Agreement binds and benefits the parties, and their respective successors, and their permitted assigns. Business Associate may not assign or subcontract rights or obligations under this BA Agreement without the express written consent of Covered Entity. Covered Entity may assign its rights and obligations under this BA Agreement to any successor or affiliated entity.

12. **Counterparts**

    This BA Agreement may be executed in multiple counterparts, which shall constitute a single agreement, and by facsimile or pdf signatures, which shall be treated as originals.

[Signature page follows]

IN WITNESS WHEREOF, the parties have executed this BA Agreement, effective _____, 20___.

Covered entity:

By: _____

Title:_____

Address:_____

_____

_____

Business Associate:

By:_____

Title: _____

Address: _____

_____

_____

Index

Abuse, victims of, 72–74, 181–182
ACA. *See* Patient Protection and Affordable Care Act (ACA)
Access control, 120, 235
Access profiles, 200, 201, 235, 254–255
Accident insurance, 19
Administrative proceedings, disclosure and, 75–78
Administrative requirement(s)
   for covered entities, 88–100
   disclosure accounting as, 95–100
   in HIPAA, text of, 163–259
   notice of privacy practices as, 89–95
Administrative safeguards, 100–105, 111–119, 234
Administrative Simplification Compliance Act, 22
American Recovery and Reinvestment Act of 2009, 5
Armed forces, 185
Assigned security responsibility, 116–117
Attorneys, 131
Audit control, Security Rule and, 120
Authentication, 121, 236
Authorization
   consent *vs.*, 33–35
   copy of, 46
   core elements of, 35–43
   cover letter for, 47
   description in, 36
   disclosures without, 55–85
   eligibility not affected by, 44–45
   employment records and, 25
   expiration date in, 38–39
   expiration event in, 38–39
   Federal Trade Commission Act and, 48–50
   in HIPAA text, 244–246
   minimum necessary requirement exemption with, 48
   no required format for, 47
   payment not affected by, 44–45
   person with, to disclose, 36–37
   person with, to receive, 36–37
   plain language for, 45–46
   purpose in, 38
   redisclosure and, 45
   required statements in, 44–45, 245–246
   right to revoke, 44
   signature in, 39–43
   state law and, 50–53
   third-party preparation of, 46–47
   treatment not affected by, 44–45
Automobile insurance, 19
Awareness, security, 117

Backup, 12, 118, 156, 240
Breaches. *See also* Security incident
   analysis of, to determine occurrence, 155–156
   defined, 153–154, 173
   HITECH Act and, 133–135, 154, 158
   individual notification in, 158–159
   law enforcement and, 157
   notification of, 154–161, 188–193
Business associate
   defined, 173
   disclosure to, 248–249
Business associate agents, 65
   notification by, in breach, 157–158
Business associate agreement, 261–280
   disclosure and, 60–64
   HITECH Act and, 124–133
   organizational requirements and, 121–122
   privacy measures and, 125–127
   sample, 137–149
   Security Rule and, 119, 121–122
Business associates, 103–104

Car insurance, 19
Children
   parent seeking protected health information of, 242
   parent signature for, 40–41
Clearinghouse, health care, 20–21

COBRA. *See* Consolidated Omnibus
    Budget Reconciliation Act
    (COBRA)
Complaints, 102, 251–252
Compliance, 15–23
Conduits, 62–63
Consent, authorization *vs.*, 33–35
Consolidated Omnibus Budget
    Reconciliation Act (COBRA), 9
Contingency plans, 118, 240
Contract termination, disclosure and, 67
Copy machines, 239
Coroner, 184
Couriers, 62–63
Court order, 182–183
Covered entities, 16–22
    administrative requirements for,
        88–100
    administrative safeguards for,
        100–105
    defined, 173
    notification of, in breach, 157–158
Cover letter, for authorization, 47
Credit-only insurance, 19
Crime victims, workforce member, 186
Cybersecurity Act of 2015, 114

Data breaches. *See* Breaches; Security
    incident
Decedents, 42–43, 188
De-identified records, 26–27, 249–251
Designated personnel, 204, 254–255
Designated record set, 173, 252–254
Destruction, of media, 155
Directories, facility, 78–82
Disability income insurance, 19
Disaster relief, 187
Disciplinary sanctions, 102, 227–228
Disclosure
    abuse victims and, 72–74, 181–182
    accounting for, 95–100, 96n29,
        217–221
    administrative proceedings and, 75–78
    business associate agents and, 65
    business associate agreement and,
        60–64
    to business associates, 248–249
    contract termination and, 67
    defined, 27–28, 173
    disaster relief and, 187
    domestic violence and, 72–74,
        181–182
    facility directories and, 78–82,
        246–248
    to family, 78–80, 186, 246–248
    to friends, 78–80, 186, 246–248
    fundraising and, 82
    general rules for, 27–29
    health care operations and, 59–68,
        179, 180–181
    in HIPAA text, 179–188
    incidental, 181
    by individual, to noncovered entity, 27
    informational disclosures and, 78–82
    judicial proceedings and, 75–78
    law enforcement and, 68–71, 183
    legally required, 183–184
    legal proceedings and, 182–183
    marketing and, 80–81
    neglect victims and, 72–74, 181–182
    oversight activities and, 74–75
    payment and, 57–59, 179, 180
    permitted, 29
    promotional, 78–82
    public health activities and, 71–72,
        98–100, 184, 185
    qualified protective order and, 77
    reasonable assurances agreement and,
        67–68
    to relatives, 78–80
    reporting, 228–230
    required, 179
    research and, 82–83, 97, 184–185
    safeguard implementation and, 64–65
    security incident reporting and, 65–67
    third-party access and, 69
    and threats to health or safety, 68–69
    treatment and, 56–57
    whistleblowers and, 186
    without authorization, 55–85
    workers' compensation and, 83–84,
        185–186
Discovery requests, 182–183
Documentation requirements, 223–225
Document storage, HITECH Act and,
    128–129
Domestic violence, 72–74, 181–182

Electronic media, 108–109
Electronic protected health information
    (ePHI), 108–109, 119, 155, 174
Eligibility, as not affected by
    authorization, 44–45
E-mail, 239

Index

Employee screening, 257
Employer welfare benefit plan, 17
Employment records, 25–26
Encryption, 121, 155, 237
Enforcement Rule, 5, 13
Enrollment, as not affected by authorization, 44–45
Entity authentication, 121

Facility directories, 78–82, 246–248
Fair Credit Reporting Act (FCRA), 59
Family, disclosure to, 78–80, 186, 246–248
Family Education Rights and Privacy Act (FERPA), 24
Fax machines, 238
FCRA. *See* Fair Credit Reporting Act (FCRA)
Federal Employees Health Benefits Program, 18
Federal Trade Commission (FTC) Act, 48–50
FERPA. *See* Family Education Rights and Privacy Act (FERPA)
Financial institutions, 130
Firewall, 237
Friends, disclosure to, 78–80, 186, 246–248
FTC Act. *See* Federal Trade Commission (FTC) Act
Fundraising, 82, 257–258

Group plan, 18

Hacking, 107–108
Health care clearinghouse, 20–21
Health care operations
 business associate agents and, 65
 business associate agreement and, 60–64
 contract termination and, 67
 defined, 28, 174
 disclosure and, 59–68, 179, 180–181
 reasonable assurances agreement and, 67–68
 safeguard implementation and, 64–65
 security incident reporting and, 65–67
Health care program for uniformed services personnel, 17
Health care provider, as covered entity, 21–22

Health Information Technology for Economic and Clinical Health (HITECH) Act, 5–6, 13, 30, 87
 and accounting for disclosure, 96
 attorneys and, 131
 breaches and, 133–135, 154, 158
 business associate agreements and, 108, 124–133
 document storage and, 128–129
 financial institutions and, 130
 history of, 123–124
 privacy measures and, 125–127
 researchers and, 129–130
 risk assessments and, 134–135
 training and, 126–127
Health insurance issuer, 16
Health Insurance Portability and Accountability Act of 1996 (HIPAA). *See also* Privacy Rule; Security Rule
 compliance requirements, 15–23
 Enforcement Rule, 5, 13
 information subject to, 23–28
 laws conflicting with, 29–30
 public perception of, 1
 state law preempted by, 50–52
 Title I, 2–3
 Title II, 3–6, 10–13
 Title III, 6–9
 Title IV, 9
 Title V, 9–10
Health maintenance organization (HMO), 16
Health oversight, 74–75, 184
Health oversight agency, 174
Health plan
 as covered entity, 16–20
 group, 16
 what is not a, 19–20
Health savings accounts (HSAs), 6, 7–8
Health threat, disclosure and, 68–69
High-risk pool, 18
HITECH Act. *See* Health Information Technology for Economic and Clinical Health (HITECH) Act
HSAs. *See* Health savings accounts (HSAs)
Hybrid entity, 175

Incidental disclosure, 181
Indian Health Service, 18

Individual
  defined, 175
  notification of, in breach, 158–159
  request for accounting of disclosure, 217–221
  request for confidential communications, 203–204
  request to amend, 212–216
  request to restrict uses and disclosures, 201–203
  right of access, 204–211
Individual plan, 18
Information, subject to HIPAA, 23–28
Information access management, 117
Informational disclosures, 78–82
Integrity, 120, 240
Internal review board (IRB), 82–83
IRB. *See* Internal review board (IRB)

Judicial proceedings, disclosure and, 75–78

Language, plain, in authorization, 45–46
Law enforcement
  disclosure and, 68–71, 183
  notification of, in breach, 157
Law enforcement official, defined, 175
Legal proceedings, disclosure and, 182–183
Liability insurance, 19
Limited data set, 63, 130, 175–176, 249–251
Long-term care, 8–9
Long-term care policy, 17

Marketing, disclosure and, 80–81
Media destruction, 155
Media notice, 161
Medicaid, 16
Medical examiner, 184
Medical savings accounts (MSAs), 6–7
Medicare Advantage, 18
Medicare Part A, 16
Medicare Part B, 16
Medicare Part C, 18
Medicare Part D, 17
Medicare supplemental policy, 17, 17n5
Military personnel, 17, 185
Minimum necessary standard, 84, 126, 181, 195–201

Minors, parent signature for, 40–41
MSAs. *See* Medical savings accounts (MSAs)

Neglect, victims of, 72–74, 181–182
Notice of privacy practices (NPP)
  as administrative requirement, 89–95
  availability of, 93–94
  defined, 176
  documentation of, 95
  elements of, 90–92
  in HIPAA text, 193–195
  joint, 94–95
  optional elements of, 92
  revisions of, 92–93
Notification
  of breach, 154–161, 188–193
  to covered entities, 157–158
  of individuals, 158–159
  of law enforcement, 157
  of media, 161
  of Office for Civil Rights, 159–160
  of security incident, 152–153
  substitute, 160–161
NPP. *See* Notice of privacy practices (NPP)

Obamacare. *See* Patient Protection and Affordable Care Act (ACA)
OCR. *See* Office for Civil Rights (OCR)
Office for Civil Rights (OCR), 13, 61, 107, 111, 128
  notification of, in breach, 159–160
  on security incidents, 152
Organ donation, 184
Organized health care arrangement, 56, 60, 94, 176, 181
Oversight activities, disclosure and, 74–75

Parent, signature of, for unemancipated minors, 40–41
Passwords, 238
Patient Protection and Affordable Care Act (ACA), 6
Payment
  defined, 28, 176–177
  disclosure and, 57–59, 179, 180
  as not affected by authorization, 44–45
PB. *See* Privacy board (PB)
Personal representative, 39–40, 243

Person authentication, 121
PHI. *See* Protected health information (PHI)
Physical safeguards, Security Rule and, 119, 234
Plain language, in authorization, 45–46
Policies and procedures
    administrative requirements and, 103–104
    applicability of, 172–173
    in HIPAA, 163–259
    scope of, 172
    Security Rule and, 122
    statement, in HIPAA, 172
    training on, 225–227
Postal Service, 62–63
Preexisting conditions, 3
Prescription Drug Benefit Program, 17
Privacy board (PB), 82–83
Privacy official, 101, 139, 164, 177
Privacy Rule, 4–5, 10–11, 18–19
    authorization of disclosure and, 34
    authorization of time period and, 38–39
    business associate agreement and, 62
    decedents and, 42–43
    defined, 177
    health care operations and, 56
    notice of privacy practices and, 89
    payment and, 58–59
    state law preemption and, 51
Procedures. *See* Policies and procedures
Promotional disclosures, 78–82
Protected health information (PHI)
    conduits for, 62–63
    defined, 23–24, 177
    de-identified records and, 26–27
    electronic, 108–109, 119
    individual request to amend, 212–216
    individual right of access to, 204–211
    inventory of, 126
    not, 24–27
    sale of, 259
Provider, defined, 178
Psychiatric records, in state law, 52–53
Psychotherapy notes, 205, 256–257
Public health, disclosure and, 71–72, 98–100, 184, 185
Public officials, 199, 243–244

Qualified protective order, 77

Reasonable assurances agreement, 67–68
Redisclosure, authorization and, 45
Relatives, disclosure to, 78–80
Reporting
    disclosure, 228–230
    security incident, 65–67, 228–230
Required by law, defined, 178
Research
    disclosure and, 82–83, 97, 184–185
    HITECH Act and, 129–130
Retaliation, 102, 104, 222
Retention of records, 153, 223–225
Revocation, of authorization, 44
Risk analysis, 112–116, 231–234
Risk assessments, HITECH Act and, 134–135
Risk mitigation, Security Rule and, 112–116

Safeguards
    administrative, 100–105, 111–119, 234
    in HIPAA text, 230–241
    Security Rule, 110–121
Safety threat, disclosure and, 68–69
Sale, of protected health information, 259
Sanctions, 102, 227–228
Screening, workforce employee, 257
Security awareness, 117
Security incident. *See also* Breaches
    defined, 151–152, 178
    notification requirements, 152–153
    procedures, 118
    reporting, 65–67, 228–230
    response requirements, 152–153
Security official, defined, 178
Security Rule, 5, 11–13
    access control and, 120
    addressable implementations in, 110
    administrative safeguards in, 111–119
    and assignment of security responsibility, 116–117
    audit controls and, 120
    authentication and, 121
    business associate agreement and, 61, 119
    compliance scope of, 110
    contingency plans and, 118
    defined, 178
    electronic media and, 108–109
    encryption and, 121

Security Rule *(continued)*
    information access management and, 117
    integrity and, 120
    organizational requirements with, 121–122
    physical safeguards and, 119
    policies and procedures in, 122
    purpose of, 107–109
    required implementations in, 110
    risk analysis and, 112–116
    risk mitigation and, 112–116
    safeguards and, 64, 110–121
    scope of, 107–109
    security awareness and, 117
    security management process and, 112–116
    technical safeguards and, 119–121
    training and, 117
    transmission security and, 121
Self-insured plans, 25, 25n34
Signature
    in authorization, 39–43
    date of, 43
    for decedents, 42–43
    parent, for unemancipated minor, 40–41
    of personal representative, 39–40
Standard transactions, 178
State law, 29–30
    authorizations and, 50–53
    compliance, 255–256
    elements of authorizations under, 52
    HIPAA preempts, 50–52
    psychiatric records in, 52–53
Storage, 64, 128–129, 129n25, 235–236
Subpoena, 182–183
Substitute notice, 160–161
Summary health information, 89, 249–251

Tax Reform Act of 1986, 10
Technical safeguards, Security Rule and, 119–121, 234

Telecommunications entities, 21
Therapy. *See* Psychotherapy notes
Third party
    access provided to, 69
    authorization prepared by, 46–47
Threats, to health or safety, disclosure and, 68–69
Training, 101
    in HIPAA text, 225–227
    HITECH Act and, 126–127
    Security Rule and, 117
Transmission encryption, 121
Transmission security, 121
Treatment
    defined, 28, 178
    disclosure and, 56–57
    as not affected by authorization, 44–45
TRICARE, 17

Unemancipated minors, parent signature for, 40–41
Uniformed services personnel, 17
U.S. Postal Service, 62–63

Verification, of persons requesting protected health information, 241–244
Veterans health care program, 17
Virus, computer, 237

Waiver of rights, 102, 222–223
Whistleblowers, 186
Workers' compensation, disclosure and, 83–84, 185–186
Workers' compensation insurance, 19
Workforce, 179
Workforce access profiles, 255
Workforce employee screening, 257
Workforce member, 179
Workforce member crime victims, 186
Workstations, 237–238

About the Authors

June M. Sullivan is an attorney and the Senior Director of Compliance and Privacy at the University of Massachusetts Medical School (UMMS). She oversees all activities related to the development, implementation, and maintenance of the Compliance and Privacy Program. She advises researchers, health care providers, employees, and students on federal and state laws in a variety of areas including privacy, compliance, risk management, conflicts of interest, contracts, and procurements. Before coming to UMMS, she was Associate General Counsel at UnitedHealthcare. Prior to that, she was a partner at the law firm of Halloran & Sage in Hartford, Connecticut, where she practiced health law for 10 years. She has a health law certificate and law degree from Quinnipiac University. She also has a master's degree in occupational therapy and a bachelor's degree in medical technology. She is certified in healthcare privacy compliance (CHPC) and healthcare compliance (CHC). She is the author of the first edition of *HIPAA: A Practical Guide to the Privacy and Security of Health Data.*

Shannon B. Hartsfield is a health lawyer with Holland & Knight LLP in Florida whose practice focuses on corporate compliance, particularly in the regulatory and data privacy areas. She is Board Certified in Health Law by the Florida Bar Board of Legal Specialization and Education. She advises clients on state and federal matters, including healthcare compliance programs, internal investigations,

HIPAA and data privacy, cybersecurity, data breaches, cyber liability and reducing risk, consumer protection relating to privacy, patient engagement, informed consent, genetic testing, long-term care, telemedicine, health technology, fraud and abuse, licensure, EMTALA, electronic medical records, and prescription drug wholesaling. Ms. Hartsfield is a past Chair of the ABA Health Law Section's eHealth, Privacy & Security Interest Group.

Ms. Hartsfield's clients include health plans and insurers, medical technology companies, assisted living facilities, continuing care retirement communities, nursing homes, hospitals, large clinics, pharmaceutical and device manufacturers and distributors, dental suppliers, veterinary supply wholesalers, pharmacies, tissue banks, medical and benefit management companies, religious institutions, and data analytics companies, among others.